3 Englisch für die Erwachsenenbildung

ON THE WAY

von
Richard Alexander, Recs Jenkins, Günter Reichwein,
Geoff Tranter und Ken Wilson

unter Leitung und Mitwirkung
der Verlagsredaktion Weiterbildung Fremdsprachen

Visuelle Gestaltung
Harald Stetzer

Ernst Klett Verlag

ON THE WAY 3

von
Dr. Richard Alexander, Lecturer in English Language, University of Birmingham;
Recs Jenkins B. A., Fachbereichsleiter Sprachen an der Volkshochschule Emden;
Günter Reichwein, Fachbereichsleiter Sprachen an der Volkshochschule Duisburg;
Geoff Tranter, Fachbereichsleiter Sprachen an der Volkshochschule Dortmund,
Landesprüfungsbeauftragter für das Volkshochschul-Zertifikat Englisch 1 in Nordrhein-Westfalen;
Ken Wilson, Hauptamtlicher Pädagogischer Mitarbeiter an der Volkshochschule Wilhelmshaven;
Gernot Häublein M. A., Englischlehrer an der Volkshochschule Landshut,
freiberuflicher Redakteur und Autor (Grammatik).

unter Leitung und Mitwirkung
der Verlagsredaktion Weiterbildung Fremdsprachen;
Leiter: Wolfgang H. Kaul M. A.;
Mitarbeit an diesem Werk:
Dr. Klaus Finger, Derrick Jenkins, Lutz Rohrmann, Verlagsredakteure;
Karin Neidmann, Redaktionsassistentin.

Visuelle Gestaltung
Prof. Harald Stetzer, Fachhochschule für Gestaltung, Schwäbisch Gmünd.

Werkübersicht

ON THE WAY 3

Lehrbuch	**Arbeitsbuch**
2 Compact-Cassetten zum Lehrbuch	**Compact-Cassette zum Arbeitsbuch**
Lehrerband	

---

1. Auflage

1 7 6 5 4 | 1993 92 91 90 89

Alle Drucke dieser Auflage können im Unterricht nebeneinander benutzt werden, sie sind untereinander unverändert. Die letzte Zahl bezeichnet das Jahr dieses Druckes.
© Ernst Klett Verlag für Wissen und Bildung GmbH & Co. KG, Stuttgart 1984. Alle Rechte vorbehalten.
Druck: KLETT DRUCK, H. S. GmbH, Korb. Printed in Germany.
ISBN 3-12-500300-8

ON THE WAY 3 ist der Abschlußband eines dreibändigen Lehrwerks für Erwachsene, die – wie Sie – an Volkshochschulen oder anderen Einrichtungen der Erwachsenenbildung Englisch lernen.

Am Ende dieses Bandes werden Sie ein Lernniveau erreicht haben, das dem des Volkshochschul-Zertifikats Englisch 1 entspricht.

Grundlage für die Auswahl der sprachlichen Inhalte und der Situationen von ON THE WAY waren die Lernzielbeschreibungen des Deutschen Volkshochschul-Verbandes und des Europarates (*VHS-Zertifikat* und *Threshold Level*). Wir haben dabei die besonderen Interessen und Lernbedürfnisse Erwachsener berücksichtigt. Bei der Gestaltung der einzelnen Lektionen war mit der Auswahl der Themen und Textsorten immer gleichzeitig die Frage nach der Natürlichkeit der Sprache und den Anwendungsmöglichkeiten des Gelernten verbunden.

Da Erwachsene zumeist nur in ihrer Freizeit – nach der Arbeit – einen Englischkurs besuchen können, muß für sie geeignetes Unterrichtsmaterial auf diese erschwerte Lernsituation zugeschnitten sein. Das Lernen damit soll leichtfallen und Spaß machen. Bereits in den ersten beiden Bänden haben wir versucht, diesen Forderungen gerecht zu werden:

● durch Konzentration auf das, was Sie auf Englisch gern sagen, schreiben und verstehen möchten; z.B. jemanden begrüßen, ihn nach seinem Namen, Beruf, Wohnort fragen; nach dem Weg oder der Uhrzeit fragen und solche Auskünfte selbst geben; etwas bestellen, beschreiben, erzählen; Freude, Zustimmung, Kritik, Bedauern ausdrücken usw.;

● durch Verteilung des neuen Lernstoffes auf mehrere kleine Lernschritte in den A-Teilen jeder Unit, der in B-Teilen in freieren Gesprächen, Lese- und Hörverständnisübungen wiederholt und gefestigt wird;

● durch Übungen, in denen Sie mit Ihrem Kursnachbarn oder in einer kleineren Gruppe spielend erarbeiten, was Sie im ‚Ernstfall‘ sagen oder schreiben könnten;

● durch eine lebendige visuelle Gestaltung, die Ihnen hilft, den Bezug zwischen Ihrem Unterricht und der Verwendung der englischen Sprache im Alltag herzustellen.

ON THE WAY 3 trägt durch einige Neuerungen gegenüber den ersten beiden Bänden Ihren Bedürfnissen als fortgeschrittenen Englischlernern Rechnung.

So finden Sie am Beginn jedes *Unit*-Blocks Wiederholungsübungen, die wir *Review* genannt haben. Wenn Sie von Anfang an mit ON THE WAY Englisch gelernt haben, werden Sie sich sicherlich erinnern, wo Sie die eine oder andere Wendung das erste Mal gehört oder gelesen haben. Wenn Sie neu dazu gekommen sind, werden die *Review*-Schritte Ihnen helfen, Vorkenntnisse aus vergangenen Schultagen zu reaktivieren und richtig in den Kurs reinzukommen.

Die *Units* 5, 10 und 15 sind in ON THE WAY 3 zu reinen Revisions-*Units* geworden. Außerdem gibt es ab *Unit* 11 noch sogenannte *Special*-Teile, die Sie auf den erfolgreichen Abschluß des Kurses vorbereiten.

Ihren Lernfortschritten gemäß nehmen die schriftlichen Textsorten in ON THE WAY 3 noch breiteren Raum ein. Ein Blick ins Inhaltsverzeichnis wird Ihnen zeigen, daß wir auch in ON THE WAY 3 versucht haben, durch große Themenvielfalt möglichst viele Anlässe zum Gedanken-und Meinungsaustausch in Ihrem Englischkurs zu schaffen.

Aktive Zusammenarbeit im Kurs bleibt auch in Band 3 die für erfolgreiches Lernen wichtigste Arbeitsform. Die Themen und Übungen im Lehrbuch fordern geradezu Ihre Aktivität. Wie gut Sie vorankommen, hängt aber auch davon ab, wieviel Zeit Sie insgesamt für das Englischlernen einsetzen können. Neben dem Kursbesuch sollten Sie in jedem Fall etwas Zeit finden, auch zu Hause zu arbeiten. Hierfür bietet sich neben dem Lehrbuch und den dazugehörigen Cassetten besonders das Arbeitsbuch mit Cassette an. Mit diesen Materialien können Sie den im Unterricht gelernten Stoff zu Hause wiederholen und festigen.

Wir wünschen Ihnen und Ihrem Kurs viel Spaß und Erfolg beim Englischlernen.

Autoren und Verlagsredaktion

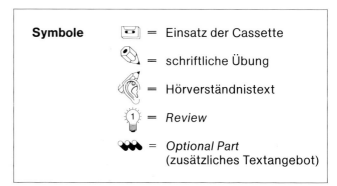

Symbole		
	🔲	= Einsatz der Cassette
	✏️	= schriftliche Übung
	👂	= Hörverständnistext
	💡	= *Review*
	🐾	= *Optional Part* (zusätzliches Textangebot)

Inhalt

Inhalt

6

Tom Hackett: Hello. I'm pleased to see that you've all come back again for another term of English. It's nice to see some new faces here, and I'd like to welcome them to the class.

But I'm afraid I have some bad news. My company are moving me to another office, so that I'm sorry to have to say that I won't be able to teach the class any more. I'm very sorry about this, but I'm afraid there's nothing I can do about it.

This is Janet Steen, your new teacher. She's been teaching English here for several years and I'm sure that you and Janet will be able to work together as well as we have in the past. I wish you all the best for the course and hope that you'll have as much fun with Book Three as we did with Books One and Two.

I'd just like to say goodbye for now and I hope to see you all again some time.

Janet Steen: Thanks, Tom. I'm sure that everybody would like to wish you all the best in your new job, and I hope you'll visit us if you're in the area again.

Perhaps I should start by telling you something about myself. My name's Janet Steen, I'm married and have got two children, a girl of 3 and a boy of 2. I used to be a full-time teacher before I got married, but now I'm a full-time housewife and mother. My husband works at the car factory and we've been living here for five years now. I've been working as a part-time teacher here at the adult education centre for about four years. Tom has told me how well you've worked together and I hope that we'll continue in the same way.

a
How does Tom Hackett introduce Janet Steen?
What does he say about the future?
How does Janet Steen introduce herself?
What does she say about the future?

b
Find a partner. Work together for about five minutes and try to find out as much as you can about each other and what your partner hopes to be able to do by the end of the course.

A 1

a Ronald Thorpe and his family have just moved into a new house and have decided to have a house-warming party. Since his neighbours, Mr and Mrs Fernman, were not in when Ronald went to their house, he sent them a written invitation.
This is the letter he wrote. Fill in the missing parts.

> 1 would be very pleased to see you   3 introduce ourselves
> 4 hope that you will be able to come   2 to invite you to
>   would like to introduce ourselves   5 have invited

July 21st

Dear Mr and Mrs Fernman,

We are your new neighbours from number 56 and we *would be very pleased to see you*. We are a family of four and have just moved here from the other side of town. We came round this afternoon to *introduce ourselves* and *to invite you to* a house-warming party we are having next Saturday evening. Mr Robertson from next door told us you were away and would not be back for a few days. That is why we are writing this letter. We *have invited* some of our friends and all of our new neighbours and we *hope that you will be able to come* to our house at about 8 o'clock. We *would like to introduce ourselves* at the party and look forward to meeting you.

Yours truly,

Ronald Thorpe

b Ronald Thorpe invites some other people to his house-warming party. Read and listen to the dialogues and then answer the questions.

– Mrs Norcott?
– Yes. Good afternoon.
– Good afternoon. May I introduce myself? I'm Ronald Thorpe. I'm your new neighbour from number 56.
– Oh, hello, Mr Thorpe. Very pleased to meet you. Would you like to come in?
– No, thank you. I'm afraid I haven't got much time. We've got the painters in and I've only come round to invite you and your husband to the house-warming party we're having on Saturday night.
– Oh, thank you very much. That's very kind of you. We'd love to come.
– That's nice. The party starts about 8 o'clock. Is that all right?
– Fine. Are you sure you wouldn't like to come in just for a glass of sherry or a cup of tea?
– No, thanks. I'm afraid I must go. But we'll see you on Saturday night then. Goodbye.

– 786901.
– Well, not too bad. And with you?

– Saturday night, you said? That suits me fine. What time did you say?
– OK. See you on Saturday...

– Hello, Geoff. This is Ron. How are things?
– Well, could be better. We're very busy at the moment. The reason I'm phoning is we're having a house-warming party on Saturday night. We'd love you to come. Can you make it?

– About 8 o'clock.
– ...

	dialogue 1	dialogue 2
Who is Ronald Thorpe talking to? Is it a neighbour/friend/colleague/...?		
How does Ronald introduce himself? How does the other person answer?		
How does Ronald invite the other person? How does the other person answer?		

c
Now listen to two more dialogues on the cassette and then answer the following questions:
Who is Mrs Thorpe talking to? How do you know?

d
You have just moved into a new house. Invite a friend, a new neighbour or a colleague – either direct, by telephone or by letter – to the house-warming party you are having.

A 2 Nice to meet you

Ronald Thorpe:	Hello, Mrs Norcott. Nice to see you.
Mrs Norcott:	Hello, Mr Thorpe. I hope we're not too early.
Ronald Thorpe:	Not at all. Come in.
Mrs Norcott:	I don't think you've met my husband, have you?
Ronald Thorpe:	No. Nice to meet you, Mr Norcott.
Mr Norcott:	Nice to meet you. But please call me Ken.
Ronald Thorpe:	OK, Ken. My name's Ron. Come into the lounge. I'll try and find my wife.

Ronald Thorpe:	Hello, Mr Brown. May I introduce my wife? Darling, this is Mr Brown, our managing director.
Cecilia Thorpe:	Hello, Mr Brown. Pleased to meet you.
Mr Brown:	Pleased to meet you, Mrs Thorpe.

Ronald:	Hello, Jim. How are things?
Jim:	Not so bad, thanks. And yourself?
Ronald:	Could be worse. By the way, have you met Peter?
Jim:	No, I don't think we've met before. Hello, Peter.
Peter:	Hello, Jim. Nice to meet you.

_____ :	Cecilia, have you got a minute? I'd like you to meet Peter Snarles. He's the colleague I told you about, who spent his holiday in Malta in that hotel we've booked.
_____ :	Oh, hello, Mr Snarles. I've heard such a lot about you from Ron.
_____ :	Hello, Mrs Thorpe. Ron has told me about your holiday plans. I'm sure you'll enjoy Malta. And the hotel's very good.

a Complete the following dialogues with sentences from the boxes.

> Pleased to meet you.   I'm glad you could come.
> How are things?   May I introduce my wife?
> I don't think you know my wife.

Ronald Thorpe: Good evening, Mr Evans. _____

Mr Evans: Good evening, Ronald. _____

Ronald Thorpe: No, we haven't met before. Good evening, Mrs Evans.

_____

Mrs Evans: Hello, Mr Thorpe.

Ronald Thorpe: _____

Darling, this is Mr and Mrs Evans.

> Hello, Jill.   No, I don't think we've met.
> How are things? (2)   May I introduce Jill?
>   have you met Jill?

Cecilia: Oh, hello Sue. Nice to see you.

Sue: Hello, Cecilia. _____

Cecilia: Could be worse. By the way, _____

Sue: _____

Jill: No, we haven't. Hello, Sue. _____

Sue: _____

b You are at a party with another person (a friend, your wife, your husband)
   and meet somebody that one of you knows. This person is then introduced.

"I give the drinks an 8, the
hors d'œuvres a 7, the dinner a 5
and the conversation a 2 to make
it a 5.5 evening."

A 3

Great party, isn't it?

– It's a great party, isn't it?
– Yes, it is. Are you from Ron's office?
– Yes, I'm his secretary. My name's Linda.
– I'm Irene. I live next door.

– They've got a nice house, haven't they?
– Yes, they really have.

– I see your glass is empty.
Can I get you a drink?
– Yes, please. I'll have another
glass of wine.
– OK. Stay where you are.
I'll be right back.

– How about a
dance?
– Yes, great!

– There are a lot of people here,
aren't there?
– Yes, it's a really nice party.

– You're one of the neighbours,
aren't you?
– Yes, that's right. I live in the
house opposite.

– You were at Ron's birthday party
last year, weren't you?
– Yes, I was.
– My name's Frank O'Connor.
I work at Ron's office.

a Make a list of the things people said to start a conversation.

_____, isn't it?

_____, aren't there?

_____, aren't you?

_____, weren't you?

_____, haven't they?

_____?

_____?

b Think of other ways to start a conversation at a party.

DON'T BE SHY!

HOW TO ENTER A CROWDED ROOM ...AND STAY IN IT!

● When you enter a crowded room, don't just stand near the door. That's what every other shy person is doing, so nobody near you will introduce themselves to start a conversation with you. Move further in, and you've more chance of meeting somebody to talk to you.

● If asked, "Do you know many people here?", don't answer, "A few", in the hope that you won't have to talk to many more. Say, "No, but I'd like to", to make sure that the person you are with will introduce you to other people.

● One thing that will not help you if you are shy is to drink a lot of alcohol. All that will happen is that you'll be unable to hold a conversation – though not because of shyness. Sip a drink slowly so that you've got something to do with your hands. This can be a great help.

● Train yourself to watch and listen carefully to other people in the room. Then you will find it easier to start or enter a conversation which will flow at least for a short while. For example, things like, "That's an interesting watch" or, "You've got a nice suntan", will often be followed with a little anecdote which people around you can listen to and then contribute some conversation themselves.

● It's not always necessary to say things which are of great importance. To start a conversation you can simply make a comment on the place where you are or even the weather. Things like, "It's quite warm in here" or, "The music's very good, isn't it?" can start a conversation. So if somebody makes a comment like that to you and you would like to have a conversation with that person, don't just simply say "Yes" or "No". Show your interest by adding your own personal comment so that the conversation can continue. And even if you can't think of very much to say, asking a question is a good way of showing your interest and invites the other person to speak to you.

● Remember a good listener is as good as a talker. There's nothing wrong with listening to others and contributing very little yourself until you find the right moment to say something worth saying.

a Which picture goes with which paragraph of the text? Number them in the right order.

b How could you start a conversation in a pub/on a train/at a disco/...?

Review

– When's Good Friday this year?
– Well, Easter Sunday's on the 20th of April, so Good Friday's on the 18th.

– What day of the week's New Year's Day next year?
– I think it's a Friday.
– Oh, good. Then it's a long weekend.

a Ask your partner on what date or day of the week the following days are/were this year:

Christmas Eve	May Day
Christmas Day	Good Friday
Boxing Day	Easter Sunday
New Year's Eve	Mother's Day
New Year's Day	Father's Day

b You get 30 days holiday a year. Which would be the best time to go on holiday this year if you wanted to include as many public holidays as possible?

Bank holidays

Have you ever been in England, short of cash and waiting for the banks to open on Monday morning so that you can cash a traveller's cheque or change some money, only to find that the doors of the bank are still shut at half past nine? And a friendly Englishman then tells you, "I'm sorry, but it's a bank holiday, you know."

Unfortunately you did not know, and the idea of bank holidays may not mean very much to you in that situation. But in Britain a bank holiday is just another way of saying a public holiday.

The name bank holiday is over a hundred years old and, as the name says, is used for days when the banks are closed. Originally, apart from the religious holidays, Easter, Whitsun and Christmas, the only bank holidays were Easter Monday, Whit Monday, the first Monday in August and Boxing Day. Today, of course, they are holidays not only for the banks but for the whole of business and industry.

Up to the 1970's these were the only public holidays in Britain, and even some of these were lost in some years, e.g. when Christmas fell on a weekend. But thanks to the trade unions the situation has improved since then.

There are now two new bank holidays in the British calendar: the 1st of January and May Day. But not only that – if any public holiday falls on a weekend, as can happen with Christmas, Boxing Day or New Year's Day, these are not lost as public holidays but are celebrated on the following Monday, which then gives all employees a long weekend. And the same thing happens with May Day, no matter on what day of the week the 1st of May may fall. May Day is always celebrated on the first Monday in May.

Two other public holidays which have been given the name bank holiday are Spring Bank Holiday and Summer Bank Holiday. Spring Bank Holiday is celebrated on the last Monday in May instead of Whit Monday which is no longer a public holiday. Summer Bank Holiday is the last Monday in August instead of the first Monday in August as it used to be.

Since different countries will probably never be able to agree on a common system of holidays, it can be very important for the traveller, as our example shows, to know the public holidays in the country he is going to.

Mark in your diary the British public holidays this year. Which of the public holidays in the text are also celebrated in your country and which are not?

a Seven holidays are hidden in this diagram. Each name ends in 'day'. Find the names of the holidays with the help of the definitions below.

Hidden holidays A 4

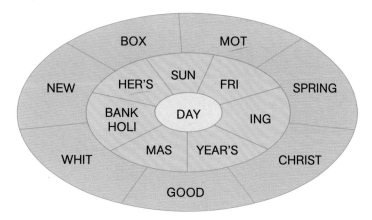

1 A day on which children give presents to the lady of the house: *Mother's Day*

2 A religious holiday to celebrate the birth of Jesus: *Christmas*

3 The day that follows number 2:

4 The day of the year when many people decide to try to give up bad habits: *Ca*

5 The day which is celebrated instead of Whit Monday in Britain:

6 The anniversary of the death of Christ: *Good Friday*

7 The day seven weeks after Easter Sunday:

b What other national or religious holidays are there in your country, e.g. Corpus Christi, All Saints' Day, Ascension Day?

"We wish you a Merry Christmas.
We wish you a Merry Christmas.
We wish you a Merry Christmas and a Happy New Year!"

A 5 Odd man out

In each of the following groups of things or people, two of them have something in common which the third does not have. This is then the 'odd man out'.

Abraham Lincoln: He was President of the USA from 1862–65 and was shot by a political enemy.

John F. Kennedy: He was President of the USA from 1960–63. His period of office was cut short when he was killed in Dallas.

Neil Armstrong: He was the first man to land and walk on the moon.

The 'odd man out' is Neil Armstrong because he's the only man not to be in politics.

a Think of definitions for each of the following and ask your partner to say which is the 'odd man out'.

football – cricket – baseball
ship – yacht – car
Margaret Thatcher – Edward Heath – Indira Gandhi
New York – Sydney – Washington D.C.

b Make your own 'odd man out' game.

The Highland Games: It's a Scottish national sports and cultural event where traditional Scottish competitions take place.

National Eisteddfod: It's a Welsh cultural festival of music and literature.

The Olympic Games: It's an international festival of sport that takes place every four years.

The 'odd man out' is the Olympic Games because it's the only event which is international.

The 'odd man out' is ... because ...

... the first	man	who ...
only	game	(not) to ...
	event	which/that ...
	city	
	...	

B 2

a Listen to the cassette and answer these questions:

1 What is Hogmanay?

The celebration of the New Year in Scotland.

The traditional Scottish Christmas.

2 How do the Scots usually spend Hogmanay?

Just with their family.

With their family and friends.

b
Read the text about Hogmanay and listen to the cassette again.

1 What are the most important aspects of Hogmanay
– according to the first speaker?
– according to the second speaker?

2 Compare the written text with what the speakers say about Hogmanay. Which parts of the old tradition are still common today?

HOGMANAY

One of the most important old pagan customs still celebrated in Scotland is 'Hogmanay' with its tradition of 'first footing'. The first person to visit a house after midnight on New Year's Eve is called the 'first footer'. According to the tradition, this 'first footer' decides whether a family will enjoy good or bad luck in the twelve months to follow. The 'first footer' should not, for example, be a woman; he should not have fair hair or be blind in one eye, and he should not carry a knife or anything sharp. A dark-haired man is usually considered the ideal 'first footer', and he should enter the house with a lump of coal in his hand, as a symbol of energy and good luck.

HOLIDAYS AND HOLY DAYS. In the calendars of all peoples certain days have been set aside for special religious or secular observance, or as possessing a special character. Among these days, some have remained primarily religious in character, some which were once of religious or superstitious significance are no longer so

c
How is this day of the year celebrated where you live?

Cumberland Reel

1

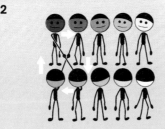

Form two rows, the men standing on the left, the ladies on the right.

2

The top two couples give each other their right hands to make a wheel and dance four steps forward.

3

They turn, give each other their left hands and dance four steps back.

4

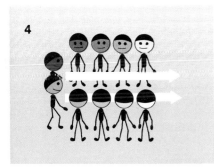

The top couple dances six steps down the middle of the two rows.

5

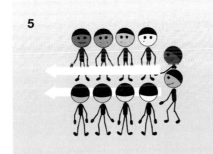

And then dances back again to the top.

6

The couple then separates, the man dances outside his row, the lady outside her row.

7

They meet at the bottom end, and dance up the middle back to the top.

8

When they reach the top, the other couples form an arch under which the couple dances down to the bottom.

9

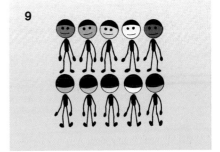

When they reach the bottom, the dancers form two rows again (as in 1) and the two couples that are now at the top start from the beginning (as in 2).

Review

1 Tom and Elsie Barnet want to go to France for a holiday.

Tom talks to his friend Len, who often drives to the Continent, about the different ferries.

- ...
- What's the food like, Len?
- On Sealink the meals are good and they serve them well.
- Is it expensive?
- You get good value for money, actually; fish and chips are £1.35, wine costs 60p a quarter bottle, lager 35p, and you can get lunch for two for about £5.50 including drinks.
- What about Brittany Ferries?
- Well, you get a lot more to choose from and it looks great! You can have eggs, all kinds of salads, fish, sausages, grapefruit — anything you can think of!

- Is it any good?
- Well, it _____ as good as it _____ ! The hot meals sometimes _____ cold and the vegetables _____ always fresh. I _____ the chicken, though and I _____ the cheeses _____ .
- What are the prices like?
- Dinner for one _____ £6.20, but that _____ the wine and you _____ as much as you _____ .

Tom then tells Elsie what Len said.

- ... about the ferries?
- Yes, he told me a lot about Sealink and Brittany ferries.
- Did you ask him what the food _was_ like?
- Yes, he said the Sealink meals _were good_ and they _served them well_ .
- What were the prices like?
- Fish and chips _____ £1.35, he said; a quarter bottle of wine _____ 60p, lager 35p and you _____ lunch for two for about £5.50 including drinks.
- What did he say about the others?
- The Brittany Ferries? Well, he said you _____ a lot more to choose from and it _____ great! You _____ eggs, all kinds of salads, fish, sausages, grapefruit – anything you _____ think of!
- What was it like?
- That was the problem. It didn't taste as good as it looked. Len said the hot meals sometimes arrived cold and the vegetables weren't always fresh. He liked the chicken, though and he thought the cheeses were nice.
- And the prices?
- More expensive than Sealink; dinner for one cost £6.20, but Len told me you could eat as much as you liked for that, and the price included the wine.

2

Sausage and chips / Breakfast / Coffee / Tea

£1.52	°£1.40	34p	34p
£1.60	£2.25	25p	15p
90p	£2.50	30p	20p
	No food served		
£1.25	•£1.25	28p	18p

○ Continental
● Bacon and egg only

GUIDE TO SNACK AND FERRY BAR PRICES

"The Prince of Brittany" (Brittany Ferries)

"The Tiger" (P & O Line)

"The Sally" (Sally the Viking Line)

(Hoverspeed)

"The Senlac" (Sealink-UK)

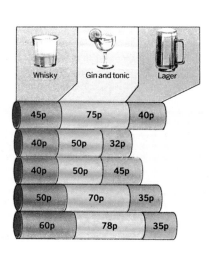

Whisky / Gin and tonic / Lager

45p	75p	40p
40p	50p	32p
40p	50p	45p
50p	70p	35p
60p	78p	35p

Listen to the cassette and say what you think about the statements.

He's/She's right.

I don't think you can say that.

That's just not true!

No, it hasn't!

That's true because...

Yes, it is!

. . .

A 1

a
Fill in the chart and then compare your schools to American schools.

b
Look at this chart and compare your schools to British schools.

Age	American schools		Your schools	Age
6	Elementary School	1st Grade		6
7		2nd Grade		7
8		3rd Grade		8
9		4th Grade		9
10		5th Grade		10
11		6th Grade		11
12	Junior High School	7th Grade		12
13		8th Grade		13
14		9th Grade		14
15	Senior High School	10th Grade		15
16		11th Grade		16
17		12th Grade		17
18				18
	High School Diploma			

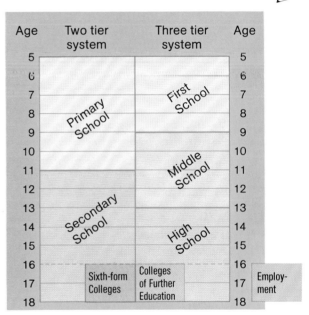

Age	Two tier system	Three tier system	Age
5	Primary School	First School	5
6			6
7			7
8			8
9		Middle School	9
10			10
11			11
12	Secondary School		12
13		High School	13
14			14
15			15
16	Sixth-form Colleges / Colleges of Further Education	Employment	16
17			17
18			18

... must be	(something) like ...
... seems to be	the same as ...
... is probably	

It's really hard to compare	the schools.
You can't really compare	the exams.
	the two.
	them.

... to ...

A 2

APPOINTMENTS

EXPORT MANAGER WANTED

For company in California, USA. Good salary and extras. For interview, contact **Steve Hodges, Tel. 01/204 7130.** Interviews will be held in London.

– You must be Mr Harrison.
– That's right.
– Well, I hope you haven't been waiting long.
– No, not at all.
– Please sit down. Now, I've looked at your application, but I still have a few questions, if you don't mind.
– Of course not.
– I see you have G. C. E. 'O' levels in seven subjects.
– That's not quite right. I've got eight actually.
– Yes, of course. I didn't see the 'O' level in German you took in 1970. Your French and German must be quite good then.
– That's true, but I think I should point out that my French is much better than my German.
– Your three years in Paris with ICI must have helped a lot.
– Yes, they did.
– And you were export manager with ICI...
– No, I wasn't. I was just an export salesman there.
– Oh, yes, of course. So I guess you went to Interchem because they offered you the job of export manager.
– No, I didn't actually. At least that wasn't the only reason. Of course, I wanted to be an export manager, but my wife and I also wanted to return home to Britain.

a Read and listen to the dialogue and note down what Adrian Harrison says to the following statements.

1 You must be Mr Harrison.
2 Your French and German must be quite good then.
3 Your three years in Paris must have helped a lot.

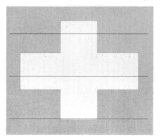

4 I see you have G. C. E. 'O' levels in seven subjects.
5 And you were export manager with ICI...
6 So I guess you went to Interchem because they offered you the job of export manager.

b Listen to the statements on the cassette and answer politely as in a job interview.

"I'm sorry, Billington, you just don't seem to fit."

a Complete the text.

ARE YOU A LIFE-LONG LEARNER?

Using a prepared questionnaire, a social science student at Sussex University spent two weeks of his summer holiday last year interviewing people in Worthing to find out what skills adults learn after they finish their full-time education – with some surprising results.

In answer to the first question – How much have you learned since you left school? – all except 16 of the 630 adults interviewed by 23-year-old Ian McGee said they _had learned_ "little" or "nothing"! But when they began to think about the questions in detail, says Ian: "They soon saw that this was not really the case."

For example, 23.3% of them then remembered that they _____ to drive a car after leaving school, 45% considered they _____ _____ to handle a bank account and 94 people (14.9%) told Ian they _____ part in at least one evening class at an adult education centre.

The interviews showed too that 52.9% were still learning: 9.7% were teaching themselves how to use a pocket calculator, 4.8% _____ to type. Another 8.1% said they _____ _____ a foreign language.

By the end of the interview, says McGee, "Most people had a much clearer idea of their own learning habits than before and thought that learning was, in fact, a life-long activity. As one old lady said, "I'm not as stupid as I thought!"

I've learned nothing since I left school, I'm afraid.

At the moment, I'm teaching myself to use a pocket calculator.

I'm learning to type.

I'm studying French.

Yes, I've learned to drive a car.

That's true, I've learned to handle an account.

Well, I've taken part in about three evening classes.

b

	Enter name, age and sex here ▶	John Smith, 26, male					Total
1 How much have you learned since you left school?	a lot						
	a little	X					
	nothing						
2 What have you learned since you left school?	to drive a car	X					
	to use a calculator	X					
	the library						
	a dictionary						
	a cheque-book	X					
	a credit card	X					
	a bank account	X					
	other skills						
3 Have you taken part in any evening classes during this time?	yes	X					
	no						
4 Are you taking part in any evening classes at the present time?	yes	X					
	no						
If so, what are you learning?		Yoga					
5 Are you thinking of taking up	a new interest?						
	activity?	X					
	hobby?						
	job?						

Mr Smith said   he **was taking** part in an evening class at the moment.
He said   he **had learned** to …

c Now interview people in your class.

d Report your results to the whole class.

Three out of five said they were …

Two out of five said they had …

B 1

a
What skills can you learn in these courses at an American adult education centre?

Look at the courses below and decide which title goes with which course.

1 CHINESE COOKING, CULTURE AND LANGUAGE 5 COOKING FOR ONE OR TWO

7 AUTO KNOW-HOW

8 DOLLARS AND SENSE FOR COUPLES 6 STUDYING SMARTER NOT HARDER

3 HOW TO MANAGE YOUR BOSS 2 BUDGETING YOUR PERSONAL CASH

4 NATURAL GARDENING

☐ Afraid of your car breaking down and not having enough money for repairs? Learn how to change a tire or do simple repairs quickly and easily. Wear "suitable" clothing for working on your car. Limited enrollment (10 students).
Instructors: Roger Jackson, M.A. and John Beam, M.A.,
Auto Repair Instructors
2 Saturdays, March 6 and 13, 9 a.m.–1 p.m.
Cerritos College Auto Tech 10; Fee: $14

☐ Have you had just a little cooking experience? Would you like to learn how to cook better meals for yourself or for yourself and that special friend? In this class you will prepare and eat a pleasing meal for one person … or two. And while you develop these cooking skills, you will meet and eat with new friends.
Instructor: Martha Lipscomb, B.S.,
Home Economist
4 Thursdays, March 11–April 1,
6.30 p.m.–9.30 p.m. Room 201;
Fee: $25 (includes all food)

☐ This course will help you to develop a personal budget. You will learn how much you can afford to spend, how to balance your personal checkbook and everything you wanted to know about managing your personal cash, but didn't know who to ask. Each participant will develop his own personal budget and will receive budget forms for future personal cash budgeting.
Instructor: Angelo Rachlin, B.B.A., M.B.A.
1 Wednesday, April 14, 5.45 p.m.–8.45 p.m. Room 217; Fee: $23

☐ This workshop is for all who want to learn more in less time. You will learn how to plan and control study time, practice a study/reading method, develop a functional note-taking system and prepare for exams. This is an excellent chance for adults to develop skills that will help them in all learning situations.
Instructor: Julia Kurkjian, M.A.,
Learning Skills Specialist
1 Saturday, March 27, 9 a.m.–4 p.m. Room 212; Fee: $10

☐ This is your chance to learn something about China's philosophical, religious, social and cultural practices and their relationship to American society. The course will concentrate particularly on food preparation, the game of Mahjong and introducing you to simple Chinese conversation.
Instructor: Joseph Chung Ching Lee, Ph.D.
8 Mondays, March 8–May 3,
7.30 p.m.–9.30 p.m. College Kitchen, Room 407; Fee: $20

☐ Would you like to have a beautiful garden of flowers, fruits and vegetables without using dangerous chemicals or poisons? Increase your production with natural methods of gardening and planting. Learn safe methods to control harmful insects. There will be demonstration slides and many helpful tips.
Instructor: Betty Asolas,
Horticulturist
7 Tuesdays, March 2–April 20,
7 p.m.–9.30 p.m. Room 401; Fee: $19

☐ This course is for couples who find managing money a source of trouble in their relationship. You will look at what money means in a relationship and what you can do as a team to make money work for you—and not against you.
Couples only!
Instructor: Dr George Ara, Ph.D.,
Psychologist
1 Tuesday, March 9, 7 p.m.–10 p.m. Room 206; Fee: $10 per couple

☐ One of the most important persons in anyone's life is their boss. This course will give helpful information on how to improve your relationship with your boss. For a fun evening come to this course and learn something helpful while you're at it!
Instructor: Dr Daniel Albert, Ph.D.,
Psychologist
1 Tuesday, March 30, 7 p.m.–10 p.m. Room 216; Fee: $10

---

b
Listen to the dialogues on the cassette and then answer the following questions.

Dialogue 1	Dialogue 2
Which course at the adult education centre does John recommend?	Which course did Frank take at the adult education centre?
How do you know?	How do you know?

3 **Review** Interview your partner about his/her home and fill in the check-list below.

> *Do you have to cut the grass?*

> *Are you allowed to . . . ?*

☐ house ☐ rented

☐ flat ☐ owned

Duties

Yes	No	
☐	☐	cutting grass
☐	☐	cleaning steps/stairs
☐	☐	decorating
☐	☐	paying rent/other costs
☐	☐	keeping quiet after 10 p.m.
☐	☐	doing the garden
☐	☐	cleaning the road in front of the house/flat

Rights

Yes	No	
☐	☐	keeping pets
☐	☐	having visitors/guests
☐	☐	adding extra rooms/buildings
☐	☐	using the garden/back yard
☐	☐	having parties
☐	☐	repairing the house/flat
☐	☐	parking the car in front of the house/flat

> *I/We don't have to . . .*

> *I/We aren't allowed to . . .*

> *I/We can . . .*

"Wait until you see how we've done the living-room!"

A 4

– Could we have a word with you before you go, Mrs Jones?
– Yes, of course. What's the trouble?
– Well, it's my brother. He wants to come down from Newcastle with his family. He's written us a letter and he wants to know if it would be all right for them to live here with us until they can find a flat somewhere. Now, Mrs Jones, you've always been a good landlady to us – I mean, you've always been fair to us and the other tenants. So, I thought I should ask you first before we did anything. Would it be OK for them to stay here with us?
– Well, Mr Scott, that depends. How long would they be here, if you invited them?
– Probably about six months.
– Well, I'm terribly sorry, but I'm afraid that's out of the question, Mr Scott. I hate to turn you down, but I'm not allowed to have so many people in a flat. Perhaps we can find another answer to your brother's problem somehow. I wonder if we could talk about this again in a day or two, say the day after tomorrow?
– Yes, certainly. Thank you.

Work in pairs. One of you is the landlord/landlady and the other is the new tenant. The landlord/landlady must decide what to allow and what not to allow.

The new tenant wants to

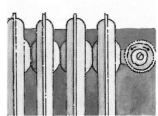

– pay the rent by cheque
– put new glass in the front door
– leave his bicycle in the hall
– build a garage

– have a bar in the cellar
– grow vegetables on the balcony
– play football in the garden
– paint the front of the house

Could I/we ...?
Would it be OK for me/him/her to ...?
Would it be all right for me/him/her to ...?
I wonder if I/we could ...?

Yes, by all means.
Certainly.

That depends.

I hate to turn you down, but ...
I'm terribly sorry, but ...
I'm afraid that's out of the question.
I'm/You're not allowed to ...

That would cost too much.
We've got to think of the other tenants/...
I'd prefer ...
...

A 5 Moving house needn't be so much trouble. Pickfords' helpful guides tell you what you need to do yourself, what you have to get done and what Pickfords will do for you.

Pickfords

WHAT YOU SHOULD DO

Washing. Arrange a day to wash clothes. Then you won't need to worry about dirty clothes in your new home.

Painting and decorating. It is hardly necessary to say that it is best to get the decorating in the new house done before you move.

Furniture planning. You need to decide where you want your furniture in the new house.

Clothes and personal articles. Pack these before you move.

Dirty dishes. Wash up.

Beds. Take the sheets and blankets off the beds.

Keys. Put the keys to cupboards, etc. in the bags Pickfords give you and keep them yourself.

Garden tools. These should be cleaned and put together.

Money, documents and things of value. Take them with you personally.

Electrical appliances, e.g. cooker, fridge. Call someone to fix them in your new home.

Water, gas, electricity. Get the meters read.

Medicines, etc. Check that all bottles and tubes are closed tight.

WHAT PICKFORDS WILL DO

Take down pictures, mirrors, shelves, etc.

Pack (and unpack) small articles — glass, plates, dishes, and so on.

Take up loose carpets.

a What should you get done and what should you do yourselves?

You should You needn't	pack your clothes. take up loose carpets. get the decorating done.

b What other things do you need to remember when you move house?

Fakenham, just outside town. 3 bedrooms, bathroom, large living-room, dining-room, spacious kitchen, garden, single garage. Offers around £21,500. Phone 270648.

① Outside

TV aerial broken

screws missing

small hole in roof!

garage damaged

no doors

too small

needs painting

this pipe blocked

② Inside

Hall: dark; electric wires loose on stairs

Living-room: wooden floor; wood/coal fire; no central heating!!

Dining-room: no door to kitchen

Bedroom 1: large enough for our furniture

Bedroom 2: wall-paper coming off; walls in terrible condition; needs a lot of work!

Bedroom 3: OK as spare room; space for shelves

Kitchen: no hot-water system (something wrong with gas pipes??)

Bathroom: no toilet (toilet outside!); no hot water; big but cold – could be nice (washing-machine)

Cellar: steps damaged

Garage: in very bad condition, but OK for bicycles for the time being

A young couple has decided to buy this house.
Make a list of the things which will need doing
– before they can move in.
– after they have moved in.
Will they be able to do all the jobs themselves? If not, which will they have to get done by workmen and why? Discuss with a partner which jobs you could do your-selves and which jobs you'd prefer to get done. Which would you like to do yourselves?

HOME SWEET HOME

a

home (həum) *n.* **1.** the place or a place where one lives: *have you no home to go to?* **2.** a house or other dwelling. **3.** a family or other group living in a house or other place. **4.** a person's country, city, etc., esp. viewed as a birthplace, a residence during one's early years, or a place dear to one. **5.** the environment or habitat of a person or animal. **6.** the place where something is invented, founded, or developed: *the U.S. is the home of baseball.* **7. a.** a building or organization set up to care for orphans, the aged, etc **b.** an informal name for a mental home.

Which examples go with which dictionary definitions?

○ Asia is the home of the tiger.

○ Young children should have a good home.

○ Wherever my wife and children are is home to me.

○ Several thousand homes have been built in the area already.

○ There's no place like home.

○ I shall be at home on Saturday.

○ The Children's Home was damaged by fire.

○ Robert works in London all week and goes home at the weekend.

○ Angela Brown's home was Edinburgh.

○ England is the home of football.

b
Statistics on the homeless:
England:
in 1981 there were over 68,000 homeless families. This was 16.7 per cent more than a year before.
West Germany:
in 1982 there were more than 100,000 registered homeless people.
New York:
in 1981 there were about 36,000 homeless people.

HOME SWEET HOME IN NEW YORK

This box is against the wall of a bank on Park Avenue, New York. The man who lives in the box in the richest country in the world is one of many thousands of homeless people in New York. Boxes may not be much, but they are home for the box people.

c

The Queen of England and her family own or sometimes live in the following places:
The Palace of Holyrood House
Kensington Palace
Buckingham Palace
St James's Palace
Balmoral
Sandringham
…

How many homes does a person need?

Why do some people have more than one home?

What do you think of this situation?

Compare it with the situation of the homeless.

29

① **Review**

jazz
classical music
reggae
rock
opera
country and
　　western music

horror film
western
comedy
thriller
musical
science fiction film
sex film

My favourite film/piece of music is...

A film/piece of music I really like is...

I enjoy watching.../listening to...

I don't like...I prefer...

I'm not really interested in...

I hate...

a　What kind of films do you think the above are?
　　What sort of music is on the above records?
　　What kind of films do you enjoy watching?
　　What kind of music do you enjoy listening to?

It wasn't bad.

b Tell your partner about a film you have seen recently, either in the cinema or on TV. Say what kind of film it was, who was in it, whether you liked it or not and why.

It was excellent/ very good.

It wasn't very good.

It was terrible/boring.

A 1

LIFE AND DEATH OF A SUPERSTAR

In August 1962, the greatest sex-symbol Hollywood has ever known died from an overdose of sleeping pills. She was 36.

Norma Jean Martenson was born on June 1, 1926 in Los Angeles. As a child she led a very unhappy life, brought up as she was in twelve different foster families and then sent to a children's home. As Marilyn Monroe, she later became one of the most famous film stars of all time.

Her first role was in *Scudda-Hoo, Scudda Hay* in 1946, where she had to say just one word: "Hello!". But the 20th Century-Fox bosses who saw the film before it reached the cinemas didn't like her at all, and she was cut out of the film altogether.

Two years later she was given a small role in *The Asphalt Jungle*. Other small roles followed from time to time, and then between 1953 and 1955 she acted in several films, including *Gentlemen Prefer Blondes* and *The Seven-Year Itch*, which made her the number one Hollywood star.

Her career was threatened when a newspaper wrote that Marilyn had appeared nude in a calendar several years earlier because she needed the money. However, her fans still thought the world of her, and they bought six million copies of the calendar. One reporter asked her, "Didn't you have *anything* on?", to which she replied, "Oh, yes. I had the radio on."

In real life she wasn't like the 'dumb blonde' she played in many of her films, even if she is probably best remembered for these roles. In fact she hated this image, and in 1955

she left Hollywood to study at the Actors Studio in New York.

In 1956 she returned to Hollywood to make *Bus Stop*, and the critics loved it. She was now recognized as a fine and skilful actress.

In 1957 she made *The Prince and the Showgirl* with Sir Laurence Olivier in London, and although the critics didn't think much of the film, they liked her performance in it.

One of her best films was *Some Like It Hot*, in which she appeared with Jack Lemmon and Tony Curtis in 1958. Critics described it as "the funniest film of the last ten years". Billy Wilder, the director, said, "Marilyn not only has sex-appeal – she moves beautifully, has a lovely voice and a strong personality.

She's a clever actress who keeps improving all the time." Marilyn Monroe was also named by Italian critics as "the best foreign actress of 1958".

In spite of her success, Marilyn Monroe was a very unhappy person. After the film *Misfits*, her marriage to her third husband, Arthur Miller, broke up, and she became more and more depressed. Now directors and actors hated working with her, because they never knew whether she would turn up at the studio or not. For this reason, she was fired by 20th Century-Fox while working on the film *Something's Got to Give* in 1962. A few months later she was found dead at her home in Los Angeles. On hearing of her death, Sir Laurence Olivier said, "It was Hollywood that destroyed her."

Which expressions in the text show a positive opinion and which of them a negative opinion of Marilyn Monroe or her films?

b Think of a film star, perhaps from a film you have seen recently on television or at the cinema. In groups, write at least three statements about him/her to show what your group thinks about him/her. With the help of these statements, the other groups have to try and guess who it is. Read the statements aloud one by one.

A 2 a Listen to the statements on the cassette and find out what the people think about video games.

VIDEO GAMES

FOR AND AGAINST

Many towns today seem to have at least one video-game centre, and machines with names like 'Space Invaders', 'Space Monster' and 'Pac-Man' have taken over most pubs. Our roving reporter went out to interview people and find out their opinions of these games.

"I'm not particularly keen on video games and don't play myself. But I don't think they do any great harm. If adults want to go into video-game centres, why not? I think people should be free to choose whether they want to do certain things or not. It's not for the Government to decide for them."

D. Murphy, clerk

"I must say I find them very enjoyable. We've got a couple of video games at home, and for us it's an interesting way of spending our free time. My children love playing as well, and I'm sure it doesn't do them any harm. In fact I think it's a good way for people to let off steam. And after all, you go mad if you don't get away from your everyday worries now and then."

B. Russel, housewife

"In my opinion they shouldn't be allowed. I think they're a terrible waste of time and money. They've just opened one of these video centres near our home, and it attracts the wrong kind of people. They also have a bad influence on children who play them over and over again. A lot of these video games are just a kind of war-game and are not good for children at all. I know some parents who don't seem to mind if their children spend all their money on these stupid machines. Just as long as it keeps them quiet."

M. Pringle, teacher

b
Now read the statements. How do the people interviewed express their opinions of video games?

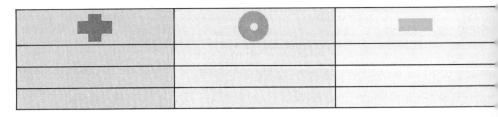

In the last few years there has been an increasing amount of sex and violence in films. In particular there has been an increase in the number of films showing violence against women.
In the following article, a film critic describes some of the scenes from one of these films and gives his opinion of this kind of film.

a What is the critic's opinion of such films, and which parts of the text show his opinion?

Gewalt

Violence as Entertainment?

By
NORMAN
BARRY

An early scene in the film *Avenger* shows a group of muggers break into Ron Charleston's house, tear the clothes off the housekeeper, rape her one by one and finally kill her. A short time later the same thing happens to the hero's handicapped daughter, who then jumps from a high window and lands on an iron fence, killing herself.

This is the start of what is supposed to be 100 minutes of cinema entertainment, although some people may consider it a strange kind of entertainment which treats women as nothing more than objects, to be attacked, raped and brutally murdered.

Of course, the director of the film does not wish us to feel sympathy for the criminals. Indeed, he wants to make us so angry that when the hero takes the law into his own hands and kills the muggers one by one, he has our full support. And in many cinemas some people actually stand up and cheer each of these murders.

This kind of film can be seen almost any week in any town. They seem to be saying: look at these awful men, see how brutal they are. Yet there also seems to be something much worse in these films – a kind of hatred of women, the pleasure of seeing them treated in this way. Why, for example, is the victim in films like these always a woman? Why not the hero's brother or his best friend? The answer is quite simple. Violence of man against man is not so good for ticket sales, while violence against women is.

The question is whether such films actually do any harm. I fully believe that they do. Experiments at the University of Michigan have shown that watching violence makes people violent. I experienced this myself when the hero killed the men who had raped and murdered his housekeeper and daughter. I felt that it served them right!

I dislike myself for that and I dislike the film for making me feel that way. I dislike it even more for

leaving me with the nasty picture of a group of muggers stripping a woman in order to rape her. I'm not a violent person, but if this film can have this influence on me, what might it do to someone who finds violence attractive? Is there really no connection between films like this and the increase in sexual violence on the streets? The directors will no doubt say that their films do not cause violence but simply show life as it is. Yet at first sight it is impossible to say which is cause and which is effect.

I am not saying that the censor should have greater powers, because there is no reason to believe that a censor is any wiser than the rest of us. But I would like to see greater self-censorship. If a film director wishes to be accepted as a responsible film-maker, he must himself accept a responsibility to the rest of society. And to show rape as cinema entertainment is not a sign of social responsibility.

critic	director
People will be influenced by the violence in such films	that's the real life, he makes films for normal people.

b What film scenes are described in the article?
What two different kinds of violence are shown in these scenes?
Underline in the text the reasons the critic gives for his opinion and list them in the box.

c In the following radio interview, the film critic puts his arguments to the director of the film.
Listen to the interview and list in the box what the film director says in reply to the critic's arguments.

d What is your opinion of the various arguments?

Review

– Good afternoon, sir.
– Good afternoon. My name's Graham Hughes. I've booked a room for six nights.
– Yes, I see, Mr Hughes. I have your booking here. — I'm very sorry, but there's a problem.
– Oh, really? Nothing serious, I hope.
– Well, you wanted a room with a bath, but unfortunately all our rooms with baths are taken. All I've got is a room with a shower, if you'd be prepared to take that.
– Oh, that'll be all right. I don't mind.

– ...
– I'm terribly sorry, sir. But we're fully booked.
– But you confirmed our reservation.
– That's right. But there's a group of Australians who were going to leave today. Now their flight has been cancelled, and they're not leaving until tomorrow. Your room will be free tomorrow morning.
– That's no use to us. We need a room tonight.
– I'm very sorry. But there's nothing I can do, I'm afraid.
– But where are we going to stay tonight?
– Well, the only thing I could do is to put you up in a single room for one night, and we could put an extra bed in the room for you.
– Well, I don't think much of that, of course. But it looks as though we'll have to take that for one night then. I suppose it's better than nothing.
– I'm really very sorry, but that's the best I can do.
– Well, OK. It can't be helped, I suppose.

You check in at a hotel and talk to the hotel clerk.

What do you say or ask if ...

... you have reserved a double room with bath ...		... he has no double room with bath and he can only give you separate rooms with showers?
... you are on business and are expecting a number of phone-calls in your hotel room ...		... there is no telephone in the room he has given you?
... you have a late appointment so that you expect to get back to the hotel late at night ...	... but the hotel clerk tells you ...	... the front door will be locked at midnight and there is no night porter on duty?
... you have a stiff knee and the doctor has told you that you shouldn't walk up too many stairs ...		... your room is on the fifth floor and there is no lift?
... you have some very important documents with you and you are not sure whether you should leave them in your room ...		... there is no safe in the hotel?
... you have to leave at seven o'clock the next morning and you want an early breakfast ...		... breakfast is not served before 7.30?

That'll be all right.

That's all right.

I don't think much of that.

That's no good.

It can't be helped, I suppose.

That's no use to me.

That's not what I ordered. A 3

Form similar dialogues.

– Here you are, sir.
– Oh, that's not what I ordered.
– Really, sir?
– No, I ordered fish, not steak.
– Oh, I'm terribly sorry. My mistake. I'll bring your fish right away.

you ordered	you get
red wine	white wine
fruit juice	beer
cake	pears & cream

– Excuse me, Miss. This knife's dirty.
– Oh, I'm sorry, madam. I'll get you a clean one right away.

dirty glass
no fork

– Is everything all right, sir? *Haf*
– Well, the pork's a bit tough.
– Is it? I'm terribly sorry. I'll have a word with the cook.

coffee/cold
milk/sour
cream/gone off

soup	too warm
bread	cold
chips	burnt
boiled potatoes	all fat
coffee	salty
tea	not done
wine	tasteless
steak	tough
lamb chops	bitter
meat	hard
knife	smells bad
spoon	dirty

I've got a complaint about ... A 4

– Good morning, can I help you?
– Yes, I hope so. I've come to complain about this radio I bought here yesterday.
– What's wrong with it?
– There's something wrong with the short wave. I can get stations on medium wave and long wave all right, but not on short wave.
– Let me have a look at it.—
Well, you're quite right. It doesn't work. Have you got your receipt?
– Yes, here you are.
– Thank you. Well, we'll send it back and have it repaired for you.
– No, I'd rather exchange it for a new one right away or have my money back, please.

– I've got a complaint about this shirt I bought yesterday.
– Oh, I'm sorry to hear that. What's wrong with it?
– When I got home I found a spot on the front.
– Could I have a look?
– Yes, of course. Here you are.
– Oh yes. You're right. Shall I get you a new one?
– Yes, please...

I've got a complaint/I've come to complain about ...
It doesn't work properly.
There's a spot ...
That's not what I wanted.
It's too ...

a

you have bought	at home you find
a typewriter	It doesn't work.
a pair of socks/ woollen stockings	They're different sizes.
an electric shaver	It gets hot when you use it.
a pocket calculator	It doesn't work properly.
a steam iron	It's broken.
a pair of tights	They don't fit.
a cotton shirt	It's not pure cotton.
a blouse	There are two buttons missing.
a silver ball pen	It doesn't write properly.

COMPLAINTS

"See what I mean?"

b
Fill in the missing parts of
the following letter.

have it repaired	complaint
it didn't work properly	receipt
have my money back	exchange it
something wrong with	damaged
	doesn't work

Nietzschestraße 10
6800 Mannheim
West Germany

August 29th

M.M. Hikers, Ltd.
Department Store
27 Peachtree Street
Oxford

Dear Sirs,

While I was on holiday in England last week, I bought a
teasmade type 46782/X from your shop as a present for my
parents. Unfortunately, when my parents tried it out for
the first time *it didn't work properly*. There must
be *something wrong with* the heating element. I've
tried several times but it still *doesn't work*.
Also when we opened the box, we found that it was
damaged on the outside.

That is why I am writing this letter of *complaint*
I'm returning the teasmade to you by separate post,
together with a copy of the *receipt*.
As I am very disappointed with the teasmade, I neither wish
to *have it repaired* nor to *exchange it*.
I would therefore like to *have my money back*

I look forward to hearing from you and receiving the
money as soon as possible.

Yours faithfully,

Wolfgang Zeller

c Write a letter of complaint about one of the items
in a, including the following points:

– what product you bought and when
– your complaint
– what you want done about it

B 2

Good evening. In today's programme in the series "Customers' Rights," we're looking into the question of shopping by post...

a Listen to the interview and say what two aspects of shopping by post Richard Green talks about.

b Richard Green gives three pieces of advice in the first part of the interview. What exactly does he say? The following pictures will help you.

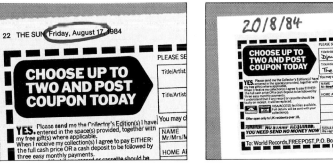
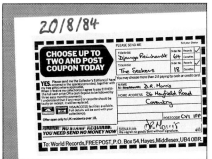

c In the second part of the interview Richard Green mentions four things that the customer should do if he has a complaint. Number the pictures in the right order and say what advice he gives.

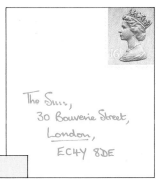

d Is there a Consumer Advice Centre in your area? Have you ever needed their help? How can they help?

a Work in pairs. Choose four cartoons and write one sentence about each, saying what negative aspects of television or video it criticizes.

b Which of these aspects is most important in your opinion?

"It makes you wonder what kind of people stay at home just to watch this rubbish!"

"What a load of bloody rubbish!"

"Good morning, my little window on the world of murder, rape and robberies! What's new?"

"That is the end of today's programmes. Check all fires and electrical appliances. Switch everything off. Go to bed. Go straight to sleep!"

"You're lucky – this was a bookshop when I was a kid."

"Roger had to go out on business, but earlier this evening he recorded himself eating."

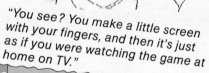

"You see? You make a little screen with your fingers, and then it's just as if you were watching the game at home on TV."

"Dad—the computer was right. It is spring."

Review

If your headache is really bad, call the doctor.

I think it would be a good idea...

If... you should...

If I were you, I'd ...

Why don't you..?

You'd better...

Tell the following people what you think they should do.

pissed (betrunken)

tyre (Rad)

Survival Quiz

Decide in groups what you would do in the following situations.

1 You are walking along a mountain stream when suddenly you begin to sink in the soft sand on the bottom! Would you:
- [ ] move as quickly as possible to the side of the stream?
- [ ] kick with your legs and feet?
- [ ] lie on your back in the water?

2 You are lost in the woods. At last you find a path and follow it until you come to a fork. Would you:
- [ ] follow the narrower of the two paths?
- [ ] follow the broader of the two paths?
- [ ] turn around and follow the first path in the other direction?

3 You have been lost in the woods for several days – and you feel very hungry! Would you:
- [ ] cook and eat insects?
- [ ] eat only the fruits, nuts etc that the birds eat?
- [ ] eat only plants?

4 You fall into your camp fire and burn your face and arms badly. Would you:
- [ ] put oil or butter on the burned areas?
- [x] put cold water on them?
- [ ] pull all burned clothes from the burned skin?

Report your decisions to the rest of the class. Give reasons.

> *In that situation, we'd ... because ...*

> *If we began to sink in the soft sand, we'd ... because ...*

Explain what would happen if you did the other things.

> *If you tried to move quickly in a situation like that, you'd probably ...*

Jagd

A 1

SEAL HUNT PROTEST

On the eve of today's meeting of EEC environment ministers in Brussels, 2000 animal lovers from all over Britain protested outside the Department of the Environment in London against the Canadian hunt for baby seals which takes place off Newfoundland each spring. This year a total of 195,000 animals were killed.

The demonstrators want Canada to stop killing the seals, at least until more exact counts of the animals have been made.

They feel that the EEC should stop the fur trade with Canada until the Canadians agree to end the hunt.

a Which of the following slogans are about things mentioned above?

Fell handel

CANCEL EXPORTS TO CANADA

STOP THE SEAL HUNT

NO MORE FURS FROM CANADA

END SEAL HOLOCAUST NOW!

NO! TO IMPORTS OF FUR COATS

SEAL HORROR MUST STOP

EEC MUST HALT IMPORTS FROM CANADA

KILL THE SEAL TRADE

b Look at the slogans again. What do the demonstrators want?

They want the government to	stop ...ing ...
Canada	
the EEC	stop the ...
	end the ...

c Form groups and make protest slogans about problems like these:
   – Your town is planning to cut down another area of the local forest to build a new road.
   – Heavy lorries going through your town at night keep on waking up children and older people. And there have been a lot of accidents recently.
   – ...

in leTeter Zeit

d Look at the other groups' slogans and say what you think they would like to stop.

A 2

WHAT CAN I DO FOR THE ENVIRONMENT?

Here are nine pieces of advice from a book called 'Alternatives'. It's interesting to give each of them a mark, like this:

3 Yes, good advice. I already do that.
2 Yes, good advice. I'll do that.
1 Fairly good. I ought to try that.
0 That's just nonsense.

IN SHOPS

2 (✗) Buy beer, milk and soft drinks in glass bottles which are re-usable. Refuse to accept bottles and cans which are non-returnable.

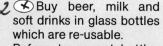
ablehnen

◯ Whenever possible, don't buy things wrapped in plastic.

◯ Refuse paper bags. If anyone says you must have a bag, explain that it used to be part of a tree.

TRANSPORT

3 (✗) Ride a bike or walk, or travel by public transport. Do without the car whenever possible.

◯ Join a pressure-group to keep heavy lorries out of your town.

WATER

(1) Use less water — for example, when washing up or having a shower.

RE-USE

◯ Never throw anything away without asking whether someone else could use it — for example, boxes or old tyres for an adventure playground.

ENERGY

(1) Use less electricity, gas, oil — for example, if you feel cold, put on a pullover instead of turning the heating up.

RECYCLING

(1) Collect re-usable materials such as newspapers, old clothes, glass, waste metal etc.

24 – 27 Very good. Continue the good work.
20 – 23 Good. But you can improve.
15 – 19 OK. But you should try to do better.
10 – 14 Are you really thinking enough about the environment?
0 – 9 Oh, dear! You'd better try harder.

a Now look at your partner's answers. Tell him/her how he/she could improve.

You ought to … You shouldn't really … It's not a good idea to … It would be better if you didn't … I wouldn't … (if I were you).	Yes, good advice. I'll do that. Yes, good advice. I ought to try that. You're right. I never thought of that. Why?/Why not? I disagree. I think …

b Advise your partner how he/she can help to protect the environment in other ways.

lösen

Farmers all over the world must look for ways to solve environmental problems.
Here is the story of a West Indian sugar plantation manager's plan
to control rats in his fields.

A 3

When the rats started to cause damage to his sugar plants

the plantation manager brought in a number of mongooses. They started to kill and eat the rats

Ernte

and as a result, the sugar crop improved again.

At the same time, there were also a lot of insects in the sugar fields.

   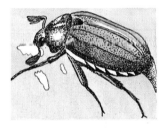

They, however, did not cause very much damage, because of the lizards, which ate most of them.

Eidechsen

Unfortunately, the number of mongooses increased so quickly that very soon there were no more rats.

When they couldn't find rats to eat, they began to kill the lizards! Soon there were not enough lizards to control the number of insects,

which then also rapidly increased and completely ruined the whole sugar crop. The damage was now much greater than before.

a Whose fault was the ruined sugar crop? The rats', the insects', the mongooses', the manager's, or was it just bad luck?

b Perhaps it was bad luck that the rats became a problem for the manager.

If they hadn't (become a problem), he ___wouldn't have___ brought in the mongooses.

Or was it a bad decision to bring in the mongooses?

If he hadn't (brought in the mongooses), the sugar crop ___would have___ been better.

Maybe the manager didn't look far enough ahead.

If he had (looked far enough ahead), he ___would have___ seen the danger.

vermehrt

It was a shame that the mongooses increased so fast.

If they hadn't, they _wouldn't have_ killed all the rats.

they _would have_ had enough to eat.

It was a real pity that the mongooses ate all the rats.

If they hadn't, they _wouldn't have_ begun to kill the lizards.

they _would have_ been no danger to the lizards.

It was most unfortunate that the mongooses ate the lizards.

If they hadn't, everything _would have_ been all right.

the insects _wouldn't have_ been able to increase.

It was a shame that the insects increased so much.

If they hadn't, they _wouldn't have_ caused so much damage.

they _would have_ been no problem.

It was a pity that the manager didn't know more about ecology.

If he had, he _would have_ been much more careful.

he _wouldn't have_ made such a big mistake.

c Here are some other ideas for solving the problem.

I'd/We'd have brought in the Pied Piper of Hamelin.

solch

– shoot the rats
– spray poison on the sugar plants
– poison the water
– cut down all the sugar plants
– kill the rats with gas
– bring in dogs to kill the rats/ mongooses
– let nature solve the problem

What would you have done? Decide which idea would have worked best.

B 1

A WINTER'S TALE

COLD, FLOODS AND HEAVY SNOWSTORMS LEAVE A CONTINENT IN CHAOS

In January 1982, Europe was hit by some of the worst weather it has ever known. It was so cold that clocks stopped in Bremerhaven. Country postmen in Sweden were ordered to stay at home; the authorities were afraid that they would die of cold if their cars broke down.

In Britain the record cold – with temperatures far below zero (–16 F/–27 C in Scotland) – came after more than a month of heavy rain, floods and snowstorms. Many thousands of people had no heat or light because of damaged power lines. Travel by rail, air and especially road became dangerous or impossible. In Perth, Scotland, one driver was found, alive but helpless, with his mouth stuck to his car door after he tried to breathe warm air into the frozen lock.

atmen

In northern France, ten centimetres of snow fell as a result of the arctic air, blocking trains, causing traffic chaos and leaving 150,000 Normandy homes without electricity. In Rouen, they had to use salt on the ice-covered streets after over 100 people slipped and broke arms or legs.

In Munich it snowed for 15 hours, and more people went shopping on skis than by car. On the Munich–Salzburg autobahn, drivers were caught in a 12-hour, 30-mile traffic jam. At the same time, there was a 24-mile wide cloud of industrial smog over Berlin, and hundreds of people went to hospital with chest pains and breathing difficulties.

In Poland, the already high waters of the Vistula were filled with blocks of ice, leaving the centre of Plock under water. The police and army had to evacuate more than 10,000 people from their homes. All over the Continent, both in the East and the West, people were fighting against a common enemy that knew no borders, the hard winter weather!

a What happened where?

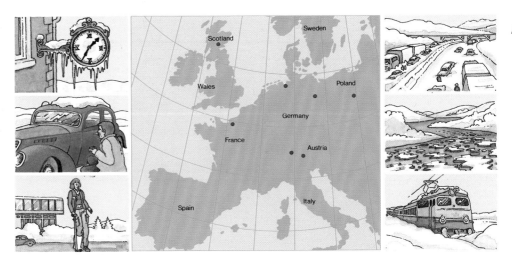

'drawn
erläutern

b Say what would have happened if they
  – hadn't ordered the postmen in Sweden to stay at home.
  – hadn't found the driver stuck to his car door.
  – had gone shopping by car in Munich.
  – hadn't evacuated the people in Plock.
  – had left the people without electricity.
  – had put salt on the streets in Rouen sooner.

c When was the hardest winter you can remember? What happened? What did you have to do? Why? Was there anything you liked about the situation?

d What advice can you give other people in the class if there is another bad winter? What should/shouldn't they do, e.g. put salt on the roads/pavements?

---

a Plan an evening/a day out with members of your English class.

  – Has anybody got any suggestions?
  – Yes. Why don't we visit the zoo?

Shall we go out for a meal together?

Any other ideas?

Let's all go for a picnic.

I know! What about a beach party?

We could organize a barbecue somewhere.

How about...?

b When you have decided what you would like to do, find a date when everybody can come.

What about the rest of you?

I could come on...

  – Can we arrange a date?
  – Would the 9th or 10th of next month be possible?
  – I'm not sure I can come on the 9th.

...is impossible for me, I'm afraid.

I can't come on...either.

Perhaps. I don't know.

A 4

by 4 o'clock

– Hello. Could I speak to Helen Jones, please?
– Good evening, Helen. This is Grace Holwood of the Glastonbury W. I.

– Well, is there any chance of setting the date for our bowls match? I think it ought to be fairly soon.
– Could we possibly arrange something for next month?

– The 29th? Hold the line a second while I check... Yes, we're free then. What time would suit you?
– Yes, that'll be all right.

– Right! Bye! See you then.

– Speaking.

– Hello, Grace. How nice to hear from you! What can I do for you?

vorschlagen

– Yes, fine. When would you suggest?

– I'm very sorry, Grace, but there's no chance next month, I'm afraid. Half the team won't be at home, including our captain, Joyce. They'll still be on holiday. It might be possible, though, to fit you in at the end of this month. Could you make it on the 29th?

– Can you get here for 4 o'clock?
– Lovely. That's settled, then. See you all here in Watchet at 4 o'clock on Wednesday the 29th.
– Bye!

Make a note of your activities for the coming week.
(Don't forget to make a note of the times!)
If you have a job, don't forget to fill in your working hours.

Possible activities for your week (choose six)	Things to do with your partner (choose one)
appointment at the dentist's	go to a disco
supper with the parents-in-law	go to the sauna
cinema/concert/football match	go swimming
union meeting/birthday party	go out for a meal
meet ... at pub	go for a game of tennis
weekly shopping	go for a run in the woods.
take kids to the zoo	come round for a game of cards
English class	come round to look at slides
grandmother coming to dinner	meet for coffee somewhere

Medow (Niece)
Lawn (Raven)

Now make arrangements to meet other people in your class.

Is there any chance of ...?
Could we possibly arrange ...?
Could you make it on ...?
Can you get here for ...?
When would you suggest?
What time would suit you?

There's no chance ...
It might be possible ...
That's settled, then.
See you ...
Right!

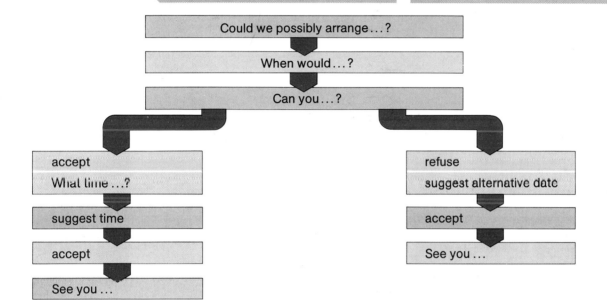

Could we possibly arrange ...?

When would ...?

Can you ...?

accept	refuse
What time ...?	suggest alternative date
suggest time	accept
accept	See you ...
See you ...	

– What made you join the Constitutional Club?
– Oh, I've been a member ever since they got a
 bowling green of their own. *Besitzen*
– So you don't just come down here for the beer?
– Oh, no! If I want a drink, I go along to the Labour Club.
 The beer's cheaper there. Besides, there's always a
 good chance of a game of billiards at the Labour Club.

A 5

warum bist du

What made you join ...?
What made you become a member of ...?
Why did you join ...?
Why did you become a member of ...?

health club
folk club
sports club
walking club
English club
...

play tennis
fresh air/exercise
speak English
sing along
keep fit
...

Do you belong to any clubs? What are they like? Why did you join?

B 2

Mrs Farthing, you've been playing the piano here at the Radmoor Social Club...

Listen to the two interviews with people who work in a social club in England.

a
Which of these activities are possible at the social club?

b
Say where the other activities are possible.

member
(Mitglied)

c
Listen to the interviews again. Then use the words in the boxes to complete the following.

Mrs Farthing

would like _____.

thinks _____.

enjoys _____.

knows _____.

stolz sein
hochmütig

is proud of _the ladies' darts team_

says _____.

Saturday evenings
the ladies are active
all the members
the ladies' darts team
more lady members
people want company

Mr Hubbard

thinks _____ .

would like _____ .

explains _____ .

believes _____ .

is happy because _____ .

| more ladies are coming |
| the club tradition |
| people want entertainment |
| more lady members |
| the club is popular |

Complete the following sentences using the words 'card', 'map', 'menu', 'ticket'. The dictionary definitions should help you.

a Where's the Yukon River? I can't find it on the _map_.

b I always study the _menu_ very carefully before I decide what to order.

c There are two _cards_ missing from this pack!

d She drew me a ~~ticket~~ _map_ of how to get to the station.

e He couldn't get a _ticket_ for the show.

f I never send Christmas _card.s_

g It's only a small restaurant, but it's got a marvellous _menu_

h I got a _postcard_ from them last week. They're on holiday in the Alps.

i – Well, here we are at the airport at last, but I wish we'd brought the piano.
   – The piano?! Why?
   – Because the plane _tickets_ are on top of it.

card [kɑːd] **1.** *n.* (*a*) small rectangle of stiff paper for writing on; **I'll send you a card from Paris** = I will send you a postcard; **birthday card/ Christmas card** = decorative card sent to someone on their birthday/at Christmas. (*b*) rectangle of stiff paper with a design on it, used for playing games; **pack of cards**; **playing cards** = ordinary cards, marked in four designs (diamonds, hearts, clubs, spades); **card games** = games using packs of special cards; **they were playing cards** = they were playing games of cards (for money). (*c*) (**visiting**) **card** = small piece of stiff paper with your name and address printed on it; **identity card** = card with photograph, (and sometimes fingerprints) and biographical details; **embarkation card** = card filled in when leaving a country; **banker's card/cheque card** = plastic card given by a bank which guarantees payment of a cheque.

map [mæp] **1.** *n.* diagram of a town/country as if seen from above; **a map of the moon; street map** = diagram showing streets with their names; **physical map** = diagram showing mountains/ rivers, etc.; **political map** = diagram showing the borders of countries/administrative districts,

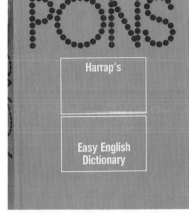

menu ['menjuː] *n.* list of food available in a restaurant; **fish isn't on the menu.**

ticket ['tikit] **1.** *n.* (*a*) piece of paper/card allowing you to travel; piece of paper which allows you to go into a theatre/cinema, etc.; piece of paper showing a price/information; piece of paper which you are given when you leave a coat in a cloakroom; **theatre ticket; cloakroom ticket;**

Now try the following sentences using the words on the right.

j I like to come back from my holidays with a real _Suntan_

k We can't decide whether to buy him a set of artists' water ~~colour paint~~ or whether he would prefer to try oil ~~colour~~ _oil skin paint_

l I see you were in Spain. I wish I had a _suntan_ like that.

m Blue is such a wonderful _colour_

n There's not enough _paint_ to do the bedroom as well.

colour, *Am.* **color** ['kʌlə] **1.** *n.* (*a*) shade/tint which an object has in light; **the primary colours are red, yellow and blue; her dress was a dark green colour; colour film/colour photograph/ colour TV** = not black and white; **colour scheme** = arrangement of colours (as in the furnishing of a room); **she is off colour today** = she is feeling unwell. (*b*) shade (of a person's skin); **colour bar** = bar to someone because of the colour of his skin. (*c*) paint; **water colours** = paint which has to be mixed with water. (*d*)

paint [peint] **1.** *n.* liquid in various colours used to colour something; **I gave the ceiling two coats of paint; don't sit down—the paint is still wet; box of paints** = box with blocks of colour which are mixed with water to make pictures. **2.** *v.* (*a*) to cover with colour; **he painted the front door blue.** (*b*) to make a picture (of someone/ something); **he painted the portrait of his mother; she painted the village church.**

suntan, *n.* brown colour of the skin caused by the sun; **suntan oil/cream** = oil/ cream used to protect the skin from the effects

R 1 THE BALLOON GAME

If I died, nobody would be able to...

I'm the only person who...

Without... everybody would...

A...is much more important than... because...

Without me nobody would...

The world needs...because

I disagree, I think...

That's just not true.

I don't think you can say that

A...is (far) less important than a...

factory-worker
teacher
engineer
politician

farmer
doctor
priest
musician

Imagine you are one of eight people flying in a hot-air balloon over the ocean. Suddenly the balloon gets out of control, starts to lose air and slowly falls down out of the sky towards the water. If it lands in the sea, all eight of you will die. If one of you jumped into the water on purpose, the other seven would be saved. What you all do for a living is shown above. Choose one of the professions and find excuses for not jumping and reasons why one of the others should jump.

R 2 How do you spend your evenings?

A survey published a short time ago in an American magazine showed how people spend their evenings. Here are the results:

a Make a similar survey for your class. Write your own questionnaire in groups. Remember that it is important to find out the following details:
   – what activities   – how often
   – what he/she likes best   – member of clubs, etc
   – what he/she doesn't like   – who with

b What are the differences compared with the American survey?

What do you do? Every day, or almost every day, the percentage of people who:

WATCH TV	72%
READ A NEWSPAPER	70%
LISTEN TO MUSIC AT HOME	46%
TALK TO OR PHONE FRIENDS OR RELATIVES	45%
EXERCISE OR JOG	35%

SPEND THE EVENING JUST TALKING TO SOMEONE	30%
READ A BOOK	24%
PURSUE A HOBBY	23%
WORK IN THE GARDEN	22%
HAVE SEX	11%

Prozentsatz (handwritten note above WATCH TV)

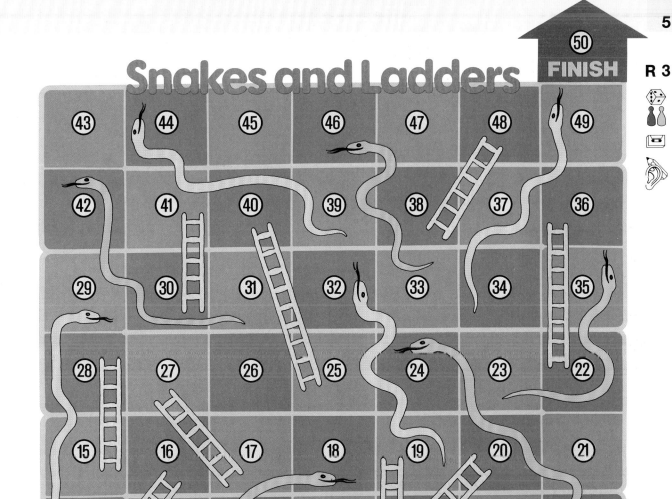

Snakes and Ladders

FINISH

START

Rules of the game

1 This is a game for two or more players. Each player needs a dice and a counter.
2 The players throw their dice in turn. When you land on a square which is the head of a snake or the bottom of a ladder, you must listen to the cassette and give a suitable answer.

You land on the bottom of a ladder: If you can't find a suitable answer, you stay where you are. If you can, you move up to the top of the ladder.
You land on the head of a snake: If you can find a suitable answer, you stay where you are. If you can't, you go down the snake.

3 The first player to arrive at the FINISH wins. You must throw the right number to reach the FINISH.

R 4 You saw a leaflet in a travel agency and booked a weekend holiday in the country. However, you were very disappointed because there were a number of differences between what was promised in the leaflet and what you actually got. You have written your comments on the leaflet and decide to write a letter of complaint to the travel agency.
Write the letter, using the notes you have made.

YOUR WEEKEND IN WARWICKSHIRE

Friday: After your journey (relax) in our comfortable hotel before enjoying a delicious four-course meal.

room next to main road

Saturday: Drive through the beautiful local countryside and visit Warwick Castle nearby. Entrance price is included.!! Then lunch at your hotel or take a (packed lunch) followed by a pleasant drive to the attractive Park Gardens with English tea in the Park Restaurant. Return to your hotel to relax after a full day and then enjoy dinner from a first-class menu.

They charged us £2 for the family!

2 dry sandwiches!

closed!

disco next to restaurant

Sunday: After breakfast take a walk down to the river where the local band gives a morning concert of Gilbert & Sullivan music from the stage of the charming open-air theatre. Lunch at your hotel is the perfect end to an unforget-table weekend. We wish you a safe journey home and hope to see you again soon.

terrible smell from the river!

We certainly won't forget it!

not at those prices!

R 5 a The anagram game

An anagram is a word made by changing the order of the letters in another word.
Look at the definitions and find the anagrams from the words in the box.

1 a kind of beer
2 not right
3 a place with lots of trees
4 to come back
5 part of the body
6 a religious/public holiday
7 a high building
8 where plants and flowers grow
9 a man may have one
10 not day

lager
wrong
forest
return
heart
easter
tower

garden
beard
night

softer   thing
large   earth
danger   wrote
grown   eaters
turner   bread

b **Two words in one**

What word goes with both definitions?

1	a place with trees and grass	*park*	to put a car somewhere
2	something you read	*book*	to order (e.g. a hotel room)
3	you give this to the waiter		advice *beraten*
4	not heavy	*light*	you get it from a lamp
5	to write your name (e.g. on a cheque)	*sign*	this tells you what to do or what not to do
6	something that tells you the time	*watch*	to look at something (e.g. TV)

Read the following texts. Where do you think they come from?

R 6

1 The author, Kurt Vonnegut, was born in Indianapolis in 1922 and studied for a degree in biochemistry at Cornell University. During the Second World War he was a soldier in Europe. He was a prisoner-of-war in Dresden, at the time when the city was destroyed by Allied bombers in 1945. Graham Greene has called him 'one of the best living American writers'.

Is it from
a ☐ a novel/short story?
b ☐ the back of a book?
c ☐ a dictionary?
d ☐ a magazine article?

2 A pleasant day. Romance at work may take a promising step forward. If you're going on holiday you'll have a marvellous time in the sunshine. This week you may have to take care of other people's children as well as your own. Don't buy more than you really need and don't borrow money.

a ☐ an advice page in a woman's magazine?
b ☐ regulations for company employees?
c ☐ a horoscope?
d ☐ a brochure for young couples?

3 YES, I'LL JOIN CND.
PLEASE SEND ME MY NEW MEMBER'S PACK.
RATES Adult £6, 2 people at same address £9,
Student £3, Youth CND (under 21) £1.50

a ☐ a postcard?
b ☐ an advertisement in a magazine?
c ☐ a brochure?
d ☐ a magazine report?

4 Too many pubs these days have records playing so loudly that it's impossible to have a quiet talk. My husband and I can't stand the noise. We don't enjoy going out any more. We visited a pub recently and they even had loud music playing in the toilets.

a ☐ a tourist's guide?
b ☐ a newspaper report?
c ☐ a letter to the editor of a newspaper?
d ☐ a personal letter?

5 8.30 a.m. meeting with Ron Fisher
10 a.m. must ring Plexi Plastics
12.00 lunch with export manager
2.30 p.m. must see the doctor

a ☐ an invitation?
b ☐ a programme?
c ☐ a timetable?
d ☐ a personal notebook/diary?

6 As soon as they discover you are a stranger, most Americans are very friendly and will put themselves to great trouble to help you. Many of them first came to the city as strangers themselves, and they remember how threatening a strange city can be. If you need help or want to ask a question, choose a nice-looking person and say: "I'm a stranger here. Can you help me?"

a ☐ a holiday brochure about the USA?
b ☐ a guide to living in the USA or for visitors to the USA?
c ☐ an advertisement for the USA?
d ☐ regulations for visitors to the USA?

Now listen to the cassette. Is what you hear the same as what it says in the texts? If it's not the same, say what you think the differences are.

R 7

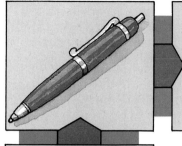
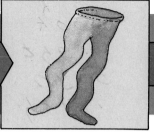

THROW AGAIN BUT GO BACK

Free parking if the object you have just come from is useful for learning English.
If not, go back 4 squares from there.

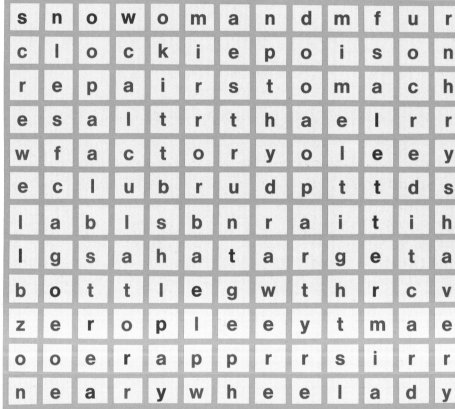

s	n	o	w	o	m	a	n	d	m	f	u	r
c	l	o	c	k	i	e	p	o	i	s	o	n
r	e	p	a	i	r	s	t	o	m	a	c	h
e	s	a	l	t	r	t	h	a	e	l	r	r
w	f	a	c	t	o	r	y	o	l	e	e	y
e	c	l	u	b	r	u	d	p	t	t	d	s
l	a	b	l	s	b	n	r	a	i	t	i	h
l	g	s	a	h	a	t	a	r	g	e	t	a
b	o	t	t	l	e	g	w	t	h	r	c	v
z	e	r	o	p	l	e	e	y	t	m	a	e
o	o	e	r	a	p	p	r	r	s	i	r	r
n	e	a	r	y	w	h	e	e	l	a	d	y
e	c	m	t	p	i	p	e	n	c	i	l	e

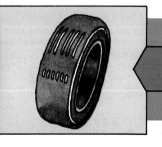

THROW AGAIN AND GO ON

Game

THROW AGAIN AND GO ON

a There are 16 objects in the pictures. Mark the names of these objects in the word-box.
b Make a list of other words you find in the box.
c Compare your list with your partner's. How many did you discover?
   (65 words is good; 85 words is very good; over 100 words is excellent!)
d In groups of 3 or 4, play the Picture-link Game with a dice and a counter for each player.

Rules of the game

– To begin, you each chose a picture and place your counter on it. This picture is your 'home' picture.
– Now throw the dice in turn to move forward but, before you can move, with each throw of the dice you have to explain to the other players what there is in common between the object you are standing on and the one you would land on if you moved forward. If you can't think of anything that the two pictures have got in common, do not move forward!
– The first player to reach his/her 'home' picture for the third time wins.
– To finish, you must throw the exact number needed to land on your 'home' picture and explain what the two objects have got in common.

Free parking if the object you have just come from is useful for learning English. If not, go back 4 squares from there.

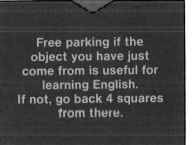

THROW AGAIN BUT GO BACK

Review

The Refresher

Try this gentle exercise in the classroom — you'll feel much better after it. It's easy to do: you just close your eyes, relax your head, arms and hands forward and let your body hang down as far as it will go comfortably.

Hold still for ten seconds and then straighten up again slowly. This relaxes head, neck, shoulders, arms and back and gently stretches the legs. The fresh blood in your head has a wonderfully refreshing effect. Remember to do everything slowly and gently.

a   Underline the correct words in the following:

1   Stand **straight/ slowly/ gently**, with your feet and legs eighteen to twenty inches apart, and your arms at your sides.

2   Allow the body to relax forward **straight/still/ gently**, by letting your head, hands and arms just hang.

3   After a while, the body will come over a little further until, without forcing, it will come right over ...

4   ... like this. Hold **slowly/ still/gently** in this position for ten seconds.

5   Straighten up **straight/ slowly/still**, letting your head, hands and arms stay relaxed.

6   Straighten your back, lifting your head up last.

b   Do the 'Refresher' exercise together in pairs. While one reads the directions aloud, the other does the exercise. Make sure the exercise is done the way the text says you should do it!

See who can think of the most original family in the class. Have fun!

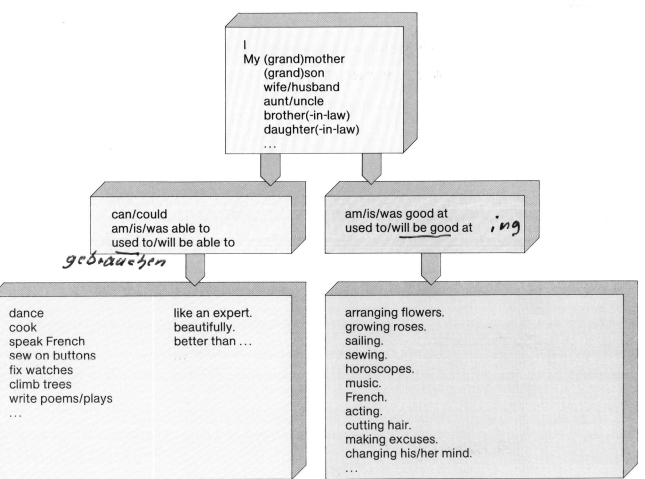

I
My (grand)mother
(grand)son
wife/husband
aunt/uncle
brother(-in-law)
daughter(-in-law)
…

can/could
am/is/was able to
used to/will be able to

gebrauchen

am/is/was good at
used to/will be good at *ing*

dance
cook
speak French
sew on buttons
fix watches
climb trees
write poems/plays
…

like an expert.
beautifully.
better than …
…

arranging flowers.
growing roses.
sailing.
sewing.
horoscopes.
music.
French.
acting.
cutting hair.
making excuses.
changing his/her mind.
…

"You have beautiful eyes, Veronica."

A 1 a Read the brochure and underline in the text the promises the Language Centre makes.

BIG BEN
LANGUAGE
CENTRE

We have been specialists in the organization of host-family accommodation for groups of adult language learners since 1966. Our centre, offices and families are all in a pleasant area within easy reach of the centre of London (20—30 minutes by tube).

Our host-families are allowed only one or two visitors at one time in single or double rooms. In this way, learners are given the best possible opportunity to improve their English by talking to their host-family.

OUR AIM *Ziel*

is to make it possible for groups of people to come to England to learn the language without any of the worries which often spoil such an adventure. To this end we offer the following assurances: *Zusicherung*

- The prices are guaranteed
- Specially chosen host-families
- Trained teachers
- Professional guides
- Our offices can be contacted round the clock
- No persons under 16 years of age will be admitted to courses

Zugelassen

GROUP PRICES INCLUDE:

1 A copy of our programme will be sent to each member of the group at least 4 weeks before the start of the visit.

2 The group will be met on arrival by the director or one of his assistants and brought straight to our centre.

3 All members of the group will be given an information sheet with the name and address of their host-family, the address of our centre and other useful information, and a map of our district.

4 On arrival at our centre, each member of the group will be introduced to his/her host-family, who will then take him/her home by car. A light meal will be provided.

5 A talk will be given on things of general interest, including explanations about travel, food, telephones, postage, money etc. A wallet with bus and underground maps and information sheets will be given to each member of the group.

6 We can arrange cheap tickets for many theatres, concerts, the Tower of London etc., and organize cheap group travel for any trips you may wish to make on public transport while in England.

7 Our assistants will be available at all times to give advice.

8 Bed, breakfast and evening meal will be provided by the host-families. (Full-board accommodation may be arranged at a small extra charge.)

Gebühr

b Now say what the Language Centre promises.

The Language Centre promises	to	send ... meet ... ...
	groups	guaranteed prices. specially chosen host-families. trained teachers. ...
	that someone that they that people in the groups	will bring ... will be able to ... will be brought ... ...

c What promises do these advertisements make?

BE A SUCCESSFUL WRITER

Make money writing and earn while you learn

The Writing School, founded in 1949, shows you how to write articles, short stories, novels, romances, radio and TV scripts that sell and keep on selling. Top professional writers, through the medium of the School's comprehensive home-study courses, give you individual tuition, showing you how to produce manuscripts that are fresh and readable. You get personal advice on selling your articles/stories to publishers—who are always on the lookout for exciting new talent.

All you supply is the ambition to succeed, and then spend just a few hours each week in a pleasurable occupation that will bring you great personal satisfaction, and useful extra income. Study at leisure in the comfort of your own home, or on boring rail, sea or air journeys. Sounds interesting? It is. And you can't lose! If you have not recovered the cost of your tuition by the time you have completed your course, your fees will be refunded.

Please write for our booklet HOW TO BE A SUCCESSFUL WRITER and unique FREE 15-day trial offer. No stamp needed.

FIND YOUR IDEAL PARTNER
and avoid embarrassing, wasteful introductions

Psychosocial Matching

a **superior** technique which will find just your kind of person

Psychosocial Matching is scientifically-based yet highly personal. **We don't** let a computer make the decisions — we don't think they can. **We don't** just introduce you to people with the same interests. **We don't** just rely on intuition. **We do** give personal attention to everyone finding ideal partners by matching social and psychological profiles.

Send now for confidential details or phone 01-680 8659

LEARN ENGLISH FAST
English for foreigners, by experienced British teachers.
960 0657

RADLETT SCHOOL OF MOTORING
Sympathetic, friendly instruction in new Escorts. DoT, ADI qualified. Free door-to-door service. Full hour's tuition. All areas covered. Radlett 7931. 17—WH—139

Hypnosis...
builds a better you.

Got a problem? A bad habit? Need to lose weight, stop smoking, relax more? Bothered by headaches or stomach problems? Need to improve your powers of concentration or memory, or become more creative or successful? Wondering how to get more joy out of your sex life? Or improve your E.S.P? Or simply cope with the stress and anxiety in your life? You can find the key to these and other problems through hypnosis.

Wake-up your unlimited potential with Barrie Konicov's brilliant SELF-HYPNOSIS programs on cassette tapes. So successful they're COMPLETELY GUARANTEED. Your money back if not satisfied.

Available at:

A 2

– Sandra, you've always been good at languages. Maybe you can help me.
– What's the problem?
– Well, I've been trying to learn German for some time now, but I don't seem to be making any progress. What's the best way to go about learning a foreign language?
– The thing is, everyone learns in a different way, so the best way for you depends on how urgently you need to learn and how much time you can spend learning.

– I really do want to learn German, and time's not a problem, but I just can't seem to remember all those words in each lesson.
– I think I can help you there. One way to learn new words is to read each one aloud and then write it down on a sheet of paper.
– Just the one word?
– No, generally I find it very useful to write down whole sentences. Later you can test yourself to see if you can remember what the sentences mean.
– That sounds like a good idea. I think I'll try it.

The best way for you depends on	how quickly urgently seriously hard	you want to ... need to ... can ...

dringend

what you need it for.
what you want it for.

One way to learn Another way to learn	a foreign language new words spelling grammar ...	would be to is to	practise with a native speaker. visit the country. find someone to help you. join an evening class. start with something simple. ...

Now ask your partner: "What's the best way to go about learning to ...?"

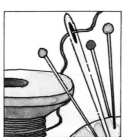

knit

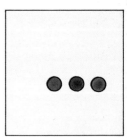

THE FAST WAY TO LEARN A FOREIGN LANGUAGE

All you need to get started is a lot of enthusiasm, about 28 hours' spare time, a cassette-recorder or record-player and the absolutely fantastic SHAM course. Yes, in a surprisingly short time, you too will be able to speak the language of your choice like a native. Easily and naturally.

Wahl   Eingeborener

Why waste time going to evening classes when SHAM can help you to learn the grammar and most important words of the language of your choice in your own home. You'll learn a foreign language in much the same way as you learned your own language — simply by listening, understanding and speaking — whenever you like and most important of all, at your own speed.
No language is too difficult for you thanks to the SHAM self-study method. People who have failed time and time again with other methods have learned easily and quickly with SHAM.
Join the thousands of people (businessmen, tourists and students) who have used SHAM so successfully. Don't hesitate; write today. Fill in our no risk form. Money back if not completely satisfied. You won't regret it.

zufrieden   Bedauern

zögern   erfolgreich

Choose among 20 languages

☐ American English	☐ Hindi
☐ Arabic	☐ Irish
☐ Chinese	☐ Italian
☐ Dutch	☐ Japanese
☐ English (for foreign students)	☐ Portuguese
☐ Finnish	☐ Russian
☐ French	☐ Spanish
☐ German	☐ Swahili
☐ Greek	☐ Welsh
☐ Hebrew	☐ Zulu

Sam Harvey's Autodidactic Method
P. O. Box 657, London SW 16

I have ticked the language I want to speak.
Mr/Mrs/Miss/Ms _____
Address _____
_____
_____
Tel.: _____ Age (if under 18) _____

a Underline the promises the advertisement makes.
b According to the advertisement, how will you learn with the SHAM method? How will you be able to speak the language?
c What does the advertisement say are the advantages of a self-study course?
d Compare a self-study course to learning a foreign language in a group with other students.

Review

a You are worried that the person you are with has not seen the following signs. What do you say?

I wouldn't go near that if I were you!

Watch out! You have to... because...

If you want to overtake, you should allow plenty of time. ore

You shouldn't...because...

Be careful! ...

b Lots of people get very nervous when they travel. Why? What about you and your family?

Many people are afraid of accidents
             to get into a car
             (that) they'll be sick
        ...
	because ...
	That's why ...

Some people are (very/quite/a bit) worried about ... that ...	
My/Our biggest/greatest worry/problem is ...	

My biggest problem is driving in strange cities. That's why I never go by car.

My father-in-law is worried about flying because he feels helpless. So he never gets on a plane.

a Which goes with which?

1 If you go on smoking, you'll regret it.
2 Look out! Mind your head!
3 Be careful. Don't eat that without washing it.
4 Watch out, this is very strong. Three glasses are enough to make you drunk.

A 3

 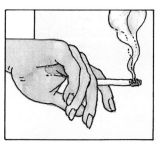  

I wouldn't … if I were you.
If you …, you'll regret it.
Don't/You shouldn't … without …

b What would you say in the following situations?

Don't slam the door

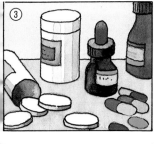 

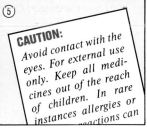 

LETTERS

MOTHER CARES
Sorgen

I may perhaps have failed as a parent, but I must admit that the problems I have with my children are slowly but surely turning me grey. I am really very unhappy about some of the things they do, and do not know how to deal with them. *Fluchen*

They smoke pot, they swear, they do not go to church, they do not go to youth clubs, they do not bring their friends home. Instead, they go out to pubs and discotheques. And I am worried to death about them getting into trouble there. For example, at the age of 15 my children were introduced to pot and sexual experience by their schoolfriends.

Sex we came to an agreement on. I told them it bothered me and asked them not to be careless and not to do anything they might regret. On drugs my children argued that 'soft' drugs were harmless. They did not seem to be at all worried by the dangers of pot. They said that the effects of beer and whisky were much more harmful.

Well, I simply said that if they took drugs, they would worry me sick. I always try to be reasonable with them like this because I love them and do not want to lose them. What bothers me most of all, however, is that they never seem to take any notice when I try to talk to them about these things. The more I talk, the less they listen to my point of view. I just do not know what to do next in a situation which seems beyond my control.
Mrs Loretta Nicholls, Barrhead

a What things are turning this mother's hair grey?

She's worried (to death/sick) about them (very) unhappy

(not) ... ing ...

What worries/bothers her is that ...

b Which of these things (would/used to) worry you?

c What other things (would/used to) bother you as parents?

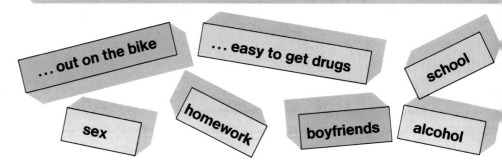

... out on the bike

... easy to get drugs

school

sex

homework

boyfriends

alcohol

A 5 a In the cartoon opposite, four young people give their reasons for taking drugs and drinking. Who says what?

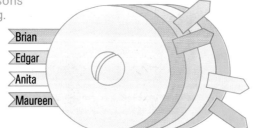

Brian
Edgar
Anita
Maureen

The reason Brian takes drugs is...

enjoys drugs and alcohol.

thinks young people can't do what they want to.

thinks life has no meaning because of the bomb.

feels society doesn't think enough about the individual.

b On what occasions do adults drink? Why? Collect other reasons adults give for drinking.

c Compare the reasons for drinking given by adults with the reasons these young people give for drinking and taking drugs.

BRETÉCHER — where there's life

event (Ereignis)

B 2   a Look at the pictures and then listen to the cassette. Where do you think the talk is taking place?

b Which title would you give the talk? Why?

c Listen to the cassette a second time and say if the following statements are true or false.

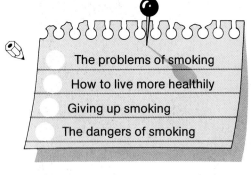

- The problems of smoking
- How to live more healthily
- Giving up smoking
- The dangers of smoking

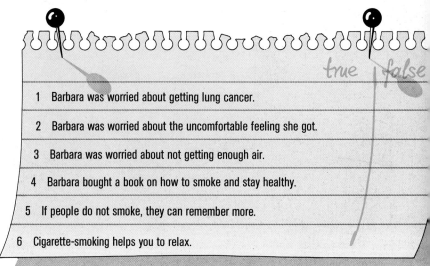

true false

1 Barbara was worried about getting lung cancer.

2 Barbara was worried about the uncomfortable feeling she got.

3 Barbara was worried about not getting enough air.

4 Barbara bought a book on how to smoke and stay healthy.

5 If people do not smoke, they can remember more.

6 Cigarette-smoking helps you to relax.

d Listen to the cassette a third time. What reasons does Barbara give for the following things?
1 Why she decided to give up smoking.
2 Why she didn't manage to stop smoking at first.
3 Why people think they enjoy smoking.
4 Why people get fat.

e What ways do you know of giving up smoking?
If you have given up smoking yourself, explain why you did it and how.

Read the following descriptions of events and customs in Britain. Find those:

a which only take place in Scotland   *2*
b which only take place in Wales
c with sports events
d with musical events
e with dancing
f with singing
g with other competitions
h concerning food
i which take place in the spring

j which take place in the summer
k which take place in the autumn
l which take place on the same day every year
m which are of interest to children
n which take place in the evening
o which take place in the streets
p which have a religious connection
q with a political connection

1 Guy Fawkes Day

In the evening of this day (5th November) people in Britain celebrate with fireworks and large fires (bonfires) the failure of the Gunpowder Plot. In 1605 a group of men, including Guy Fawkes, tried to blow up the Houses of Parliament in London, but were caught in the cellar before they could do so. This is a day which British children look forward to, as it is the only day in the year on which fireworks are let off. In addition to lighting and watching fireworks, the children make 'Guys' out of old clothes stuffed with paper and straw, which are then burnt on the bonfires. Afterwards, people roast chestnuts and potatoes in the ashes of the bonfire.

2 The Highland Games

A national sports and cultural event held in the summer, at which traditional Scottish competitions take place. One of the oldest and best known is the Braemar Gathering, near Balmoral. Most games have a programme of piping and dancing competitions, as well as performances by bands playing the bagpipes, and athletic events. Strong athletes wearing the traditional Scottish kilt 'toss the caber' (a very large piece of wood like a treetrunk) and throw many other strange objects as far as they can.

3 Pancake Day

A popular name for the last Tuesday before Lent − the time when people give up something, especially food, and fast for 40 days till Easter. The feastday gets its special name because this is when British people make pancakes out of eggs and flour

and flavour them with orange and lemon juice. In some towns there is a tradition in which housewives run through the streets with their pancakes in a frying pan, 'tossing' them, or throwing them into the air to turn them, at every corner. The winner is the one to get to the finish first − with the pancake still in the pan!

4 May Day

This is a very old feastday on which people celebrate the coming of summer. The May Queen is crowned with flowers, and in some villages in Britain people dance around the Maypole which is put up in the centre of the village on the 'green' − an open square covered with grass. This is the day on which an old English folk dance called the Morris Dance is performed by men dressed in white costumes decorated with ribbons and bells. Today the first Monday in May is a bank holiday, and the trade unions organize mass rallies and demonstrations in many cities.

5 Llangollen International Musical Eisteddfod

A cultural festival of music and literature usually held in July. For a week Llangollen, a little town in Wales, becomes the most cosmopolitan place in Britain, full of colour, energy, national costumes and the sound of music. There are singing, music and folk dancing competitions in which choirs and groups come together from all over the world. About 200 choirs from 20 to 30 countries perform. In the evenings concerts are given by specially invited orchestras and singers.

6 Hallowe'en

On this day − 31st October − children receive, among other things, apples as gifts − but they have to 'duck' for them; that is, they have to catch them in their mouths from a barrel of water! At Hallowe'en people also make lanterns out of turnips and candles, and in the evenings processions are held through the streets in some towns. The name is the most common term for All Hallows' Eve and refers to the day before All Saints' Day or All Hallows' Day. It used to be an important day in the Church calendar.

Review

1 a

Merry Christmas!

Best wishes on your wedding day.

All the best to the three of you.

Many happy returns!

We hope you'll be very happy.

Congratulations on passing your exam.

We wish you all the best in your new home.

What do you say in the following situations?
- A colleague of yours tells you she has got the new job she applied for.
- A friend tells you that it is his birthday today.
- A colleague of yours is getting married.
- Your next-door neighbours have just had a baby.
- On Christmas Day you meet friends in the street.
- You phone your parents/children just after midnight on January 1st.

- A friend of yours tells you she has passed her English examination.
- It's a colleague's silver wedding anniversary.
- Your neighbour is just leaving for a holiday in Portugal.
- A friend of yours has just moved into a new house.
- A colleague of yours has just won a prize in a crossword competition.

b

What a shame! — Poor Linda! — Oh, dear! — What a pity!

I'm sorry to hear that. — That's a real shame.

Which of the things above could you say when you hear the following news?

"Have you heard that Linda's had an accident?"
"I'm afraid our weekend in Paris is off."
"I tried to get tickets for the concert, but it was sold out."
"My brother's just got divorced."
"My son's broken a leg and has had to go into hospital."

"I've lost my wallet with all my papers."
"I've just been given my notice."
"I'm afraid I didn't do very well in the exam."
"I've just had a terrible argument with my brother."
"My son's just been arrested at a demonstration."

c Now listen to the cassette and give suitable replies.

a How does Claudia express her feelings and good wishes?

A 1

ENGAGEMENTS

MR K. OLBISON
MISS J. BACKHOUSE
Mr and Mrs R. Backhouse have great pleasure in announcing the engagement of their daughter Janine to Kevin, the youngest son of Mr and Mrs T. Olbison. Love and congratulations from Mum, Dad and Deryle.

– Hello, Janine. This is Claudia.

– Oh, hello, Claudia.

– I've just read in the paper that you and Kevin have got engaged. That's wonderful news. Congratulations!

– I'm so happy for you, and I'm sure you'll be very happy together.

– Thank you, Claudia.

– That's very nice of you, thank you. Actually, we're having a little party on Friday. I hope you'll be able to come.

– Oh, yes. I wouldn't miss it for the world. Thank you for the invitation. I'll look forward to it. Give my regards to Kevin, and see you on Friday.

– Yes, see you then. Bye.

In the small ads of local newspapers you find 'Personal Announcements' for various events such as birthdays, engagements etc. Decide which events the following announcements are for:

births
coming of age (18)   5,
21st birthdays

engagements
marriages
wedding anniversaries

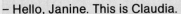

PERSONAL ANNOUNCEMENTS

THOMPSON. — To a very dear daughter, Jackie, congratulations on your 21st. Birthday. "May health and happiness be with you always." "Our love." — Mam and Dad.

RODGERS.— — All the best, mum and dad. "May your silver turn to gold." "Health and happiness always." "Love." — Roberta. Congratulations, Gran and Grandad. "Lots of love." — Samantha Jane.

COOK—SHERWOOD. — Mr. and Mrs. Cook are pleased to announce the Engagement of their youngest son, Iain, to Elaine, eldest daughter of Mr. and Mrs. Sherwood. "Best wishes to you both." — May, Jeff and Family.
COOK—SHERWOOD. — Congratulations, Iain and Elaine, on your Engagement. "Best wishes." — Andy and Lyn.

BATTERS. — On July 18th, to Jennifer (nee Gilling) and Andrew, a daughter, Suzanne.

5 **ROBINSON.** — Congratulations, Cheeky Charlie (Wayne), on your 18th Birthday. "Health, wealth and happiness always." — From Marie, Dave, Julie and Paul.

6 **PICKERING.** — Congratulations, Janet, on your 21st Birthday. "Love and best wishes." — Liz, Brian, Wayne and Keeley.

7 **SUTTLE.** — Congratulations, Lynn, on your 18th Birthday. "Lots of love." — Mam, John, Joanna and Jonathan.

8 **O'CONNELL.** — Congratulations, mum and dad, on your Silver Wedding Anniversary, many happy years together. "Love" — Karen, Steve and Andrew. Congratulations to Mum and Dad on your Silver Wedding Anniversary. Sorry I can't be with you. "Love" — Anthony.

9 **BRUIN.** — Congratulations, grandma and grandad. "Hope you have a nice day." — From All Your Grandchildren.

10 **SPEARMAN GIBBS—COATES.** — On July 26th, at St. Laurence Church, Kirby Misperton, by Rev N Jones, Dennis, youngest son of Mr. and Mrs. H. R. Spearman Gibbs, to Glennis Ann, only daughter of Mr. and Mrs. A. R. Coates.

11 **DE SAULLES.** — Congratulations, Mark, on your 21st Birthday. Wishing you all the best for the future. — From Mam, Dad, Susan, Steven and Linda.

12 **SUTTLE.** — Congratulations on your 18th Birthday, Lynn. "Hope you have a smashing day." "See you when I get back." "Lots of love." — From Kaz.

13 **THOMPSON.** — Congratulations, Jackie, on your 21st Birthday. "Health and happiness always." — Aunty Connie, Aunty Irene, Michael, Sally and Stephanie.

c What expressions are used in the advertisements to express good wishes?

d Listen to the cassette. Which of the ads goes with the dialogue you hear?

e Choose one of the advertisements and make a phone-call to express your good wishes.

February 23rd

A 2 Sarah Gordon lives in the United States and has received an express letter with some important news from her mother, who lives in England.

a
Read what Sarah writes in answer to her mother's letter.
What news did Sarah get?

b
What is Sarah's and the other people's reaction to the news, and what do they say?

c
What does Sarah think is important for Pamela in this situation, and what suggestions does she make?
Underline what Sarah says.

d
Six months ago Harry Haslam, an English colleague of yours who lived next-door to you for several years with his wife Elizabeth and their two children, Brenda (13) and Anthony (9), moved back to England. Their children used to go to school with your children and you were good friends. You often visited each other and you were sorry to see them leave when they had to return to England.
Now you receive a letter from Harry Haslam with this news:

Write a letter back to Harry Haslam to express your feelings, to express sympathy and to ask if you can help in any way.

Dear Mother,

I'm sorry I haven't written earlier, but I only found your letter today when I got back from a business trip to Seattle. I was deeply shocked to hear about Roger and Pamela. That's really awful. We all know what a careful driver Roger was. He never took any risks. It's really hard to understand how such a terrible thing could happen. How are Uncle Eric and Aunt Mildred? I can imagine that it must have been a terrible shock for them.

But above all, how's Pamela? Is she still in hospital? I'm so sorry for her. I only hope she'll be all right soon. It's sure to take time for her to get over it. It's most important that she shouldn't feel alone. She should know that in this situation we'll help her in any way we can. It might be a good idea for her to get away from it all when she gets out of hospital. Couldn't you go and visit her to see if she'd like one of us to stay with her for a while? I could arrange to come over for a couple of weeks, or if she likes, she's always welcome to come over here and stay with me for a while. I'd be glad to have her here. There's room enough to put her up, and I could easily take a few days off. It would be no trouble at all for me. Please talk to her about it.

Jim and Kate from next door, who Pamela and Roger met on their visit here last year, were both very upset to hear of the accident and send their condolences.

The most important thing for Pamela now, I think, is to remember that life goes on. She must try to leave the past behind and think of the future.
Give my love to everybody,

Sarah

I'm afraid I've got some terrible news. Elizabeth was killed in a road accident last Thursday while she was taking the children to school. It wasn't her fault. A motorbike suddenly came round a sharp bend at high speed on the wrong side of the road. In trying to avoid it, Elizabeth lost control of her car and ran into the front of a lorry. She died in the ambulance on the way to the hospital. The doctors said it was a wonder the children weren't killed as well. They are still in hospital but they ought to be home soon. I can only hope they'll

With patients who are seriously ill, relatives and doctors sometimes have the diffi- **B 1**
cult decision as to whether it is better to try to delay death by using very expensive
and sometimes very unpleasant methods of treatment or whether the patient should
be allowed to die a natural death.
After a talk on this subject by the Archbishop of Canterbury, an English newspaper
published the following article.

a In which paragraphs of the text are these questions discussed?
   – What a doctor should do if the patient is too ill to make a decision. _____
   – Whether patients should be told they will not recover. _____
   – Whether patients should be allowed to decide for themselves. _____

THE LAST TABOO

öbwohl   *wenige*

Although there are very few taboos left in our society, we still seem to find it embarrassing to talk about death. This point was made last night in an after-dinner speech by the Archbishop of Canterbury, to the doctors and students of the Royal College of Nursing in London. He spoke of the problem facing the relatives and doctors of dying patients: whether to tell them they will never recover or whether to remain silent. *ob*

There is, however, no good reason for this silence, nor for the lonely way of death in the western world. Few people actually die in pain. It is this silence on the subject of death that causes the greatest problems for the patients. If

people were no longer afraid of death, and doctors could tell them the truth, patients would suffer less; so it is most important that this silence should be broken.

But in order to break this silence, there is a change needed in the way we think of death in our society. In other words, it is important that the subject of death should no longer be considered a taboo. We need to become more honest about it and we need to train our doctors and nurses to deal with it in a different way.

For if the care of the dying is to be improved, then the patient himself must control decisions about his own treatment. He has the right, for example, to refuse treat-

ment – but if he is not told the facts, no patient can make any sort of decision about this. Only if he is aware that he is dying can he possibly know whether to accept or refuse extraordinary (and possibly unpleasant) methods of keeping him alive.

There remains the problem of what to do when the patient is not in a condition to decide for himself – when he is unconscious or too weak to take part in these decisions. The opinion of most doctors on this – and the Archbishop agrees with them – is that where medical help only serves to put off the time of death, treatment can be stopped.

Is this encouraging euthanasia? We think not: there is

a clear difference between stopping useless treatment and giving drugs to bring about the death of the patient more quickly. There is no great problem for doctors here.

Of course, as long as there is a chance that his patient will recover, the doctor's duty is clear: he must continue to treat him. What happens, however, when the health service cannot afford to give all its patients the necessary treatment? The Archbishop thinks that doctors should not be faced with this question. The most important decision for the doctor is how best to care for his patient, to help him back to health. Or, if this is no longer possible, how best to help him face death more easily. These decisions, said the Archbishop, should never have anything to do with money or who the patient is.

Grund
Fall

b What other questions are discussed in the article?

c What answers are given in the text to the various questions?

d Who do you think should decide whether a patient should be
   allowed to die?

e If you were dying, would you prefer to be told?

decesions
Entscheidung

Review

2 Have you made any definite plans for the future, e.g. after the lesson, the weekend, next week, the summer?

> I'm going for a drink after the lesson.

> I'm taking my motorboat up to Holland next week.

> I'm going climbing at the weekend.

a
Say what these plans are and when you have made them for.

b
Take notes of what the other people in your class say.

when \ who	Frank			
after the lesson				
at the weekend	Climbing			
next week	Holland			
in the summer				

c
Now say what other people are doing and when.

> At the weekend Frank's going climbing, and next week he's taking his motorboat to Holland.

d
What are your plans for the weekend?

stay at home/go home	hire a car
go for a walk	invite friends over
go for a ride on the bike	take the car in for a service
get my hair cut	play with the children
take things easy	decorate the spare bedroom
tidy up the cellar/garage	…

> I'm staying at home on Saturday morning.

I'm not sure.	I may stay at home on Saturday	morning.
I'm not certain.	I might stay at home on Sunday	afternoon.
I don't know yet.		evening.

e
– You said you were going for a swim on Saturday. Wouldn't you like to play tennis instead?
– OK. Let's play tennis on Saturday, and I'll go swimming on Sunday morning.

– You said you might go climbing at the weekend. We're going on a bicycle tour. Wouldn't you like to join us?
– That's a good idea. I'll go climbing next weekend instead.

Form similar dialogues.

Can you pick me up? A 3

– Hello, Chris. This is Julie.

– Chris, I wonder if you could do me a favour and pick me up at the station on Friday?

– Well, that depends. What time can you pick me up? Are you working late on Friday?

– Fine. Then I'll take the 11.58. It gets in at one o'clock. Will that be all right?

– Don't worry, that's all right. I'll get a weekend return ticket. It's not much more expensive than a single anyway. So that's no problem.

– Yes, thanks. Bye.

– Hello, Julie.

– Yes, of course. That's no trouble at all. What train are you taking?

– No, I finish work at lunchtime. So I'll be free all afternoon.

– Yes, fine. But I'm afraid I won't be able to take you home in the car on Sunday after all. Ethel needs the car on Sunday.

– Fine. See you on Friday then at the station. Give my regards to Carol.
– Bye.

You are in London and want to visit a friend in Shrewsbury.
Phone him/her and ask if he/she can pick you up at the station. Look at the timetable and your diary and make the necessary arrangements.

London Shrewsbury
Train Services

Mondays to Saturdays

Euston	Shrewsbury
07.40	**10.26**
08.40	11.37
09.33	12.36
10.10	**12.54** SO A
10.40	13.38
11.40	14.26
12.40	15.38
13.40	16.31
14.40	17.38
15.40	18.42
17.10	19.54
17.40	**20.22**
18.10	21.16
19.10	22.21 C
19.40	**22.29**
20.40	23.36 SX
20.40	23.43 SO
22.35	02.22 SX D
23.15	03.03 SX D

Sundays

Euston	Shrewsbury
09.40	13.10
11.40	15.15
12.40	16.15
13.40	**16.58**
16.40	19.22
18.40	21.18
19.40	**22.34**
22.15	02.22 D

A   26 May to 22 September
C   On Saturdays depart Euston
    18.40
D   Via Crewe
SX Mondays to Fridays
SO Saturdays only

Heavy type denotes through trains. On other trains change at Wolverhampton
Connections cannot be guaranteed
Refreshment facilities on most services London to Wolverhampton

...tion without notice

A 4

HOW WILL YOU BE SPENDING THE 36 HOUR DRIVE TO SPAIN?

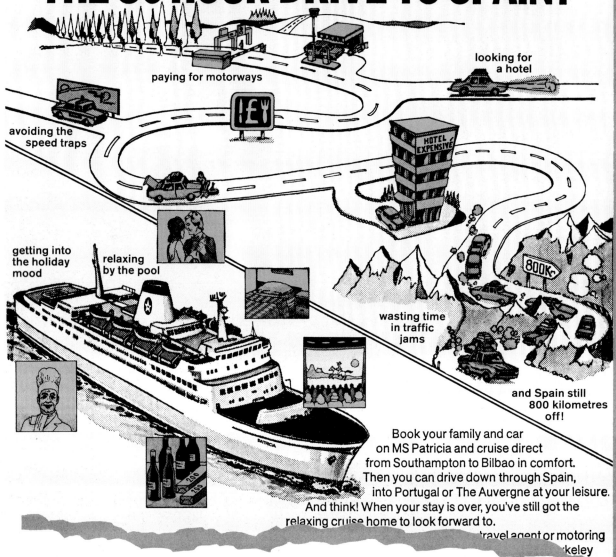

paying for motorways

looking for a hotel

avoiding the speed traps

HOTEL EXPENSIVE

getting into the holiday mood

relaxing by the pool

800K

wasting time in traffic jams

and Spain still 800 kilometres off!

Book your family and car on MS Patricia and cruise direct from Southampton to Bilbao in comfort. Then you can drive down through Spain, into Portugal or The Auvergne at your leisure. And think! When your stay is over, you've still got the relaxing cruise home to look forward to.

travel agent or motoring
keley

a

While you're paying for motorways,
I'll be buying duty-free goods.
While you're avoiding the speed traps,
I'll be relaxing by the pool.
While you're ...

AUSTRALIA

STATE EMBLEMS

VICTORIA – The Garden State.
FLORAL – Pink Heath.
FAUNA – Leadbeaters Possum.

QUEENSLAND – The Sunshine State.
FLORAL – Cooktown Orchid.
FAUNA – Koala.

NEW SOUTH WALES – The Premier State.
FLORAL – Waratah.
FAUNA – Platypus.

SOUTH AUSTRALIA – The Festival State.
FLORAL – Sturt's Desert Pea.
FAUNA – Hairy-Nosed Wombat.

WESTERN AUSTRALIA – State of Excitement.
FLORAL – Red and Green Kangaroo Paw.
FAUNA – Numbat.

TASMANIA – The Holiday Isle.
FLORAL – Tasmanian (Southern) Blue Gum.

NORTHERN TERRITORY – Outback Australia.
FLORAL – Sturt's Desert Rose.
FAUNA – Red Kangaroo.

Page
6

es.

Sciences,

RUARY

C CALENDAR 1990

MARCH

Sun.	Mon.	Tue.	Wed.	Thu.	Fri.	Sat.
				1	2	3
4	5	6	7	8	9	10
11	12	13	14	15	16	17
18	19	20	21	22	23	24
25	26	27	28	29	30	31

ONESDAY	THURSDAY	FRIDAY	SATURDAY
OOL VACATIONS en are as supplied by e State Education nts. Some schools may starting day of pupils. after Xmas break. It is st to check with your	P **1**	SYDNEY SUNRISE SUNSET **5.17** 7.00 MELB'NE SUNRISE SUNSET **5.35** 7.33 **2**	**3**
7	V **8** F	5.24 6.54 5.43 7.26 **9**	**10**
ALENTINE'S DAY **14** :imal Currency :roduced 1966	P **15**	5.31 6.48 5.50 7.18 **16** Lithuanian Independence Day	**17**
21	V **22** F	5.37 6.40 5.58 7.09 **23**	**24** National Day, Estonia
28	"E's-E-2-C" Calendar EASY TO SEE – Easy (E's-E) to (-2) See (-C) (the cryptic use of words by substituting letters for words) best describes what this calendar sets out to achieve – dates, holidays, events and information, presented in the plainest possible manner, and easy to see. If you have found this calendar useful why not recommend it to your friends, or better still, it makes an acceptable Christmas gift.	The material in this calendar is mostly copyrighted to Easy to See Publications or its contributors. Please do not reproduce any of the contents without prior consent being obtained.	

Page 5

H WEDNESDAY

ALLEN CALENDARS – P.O. BOX 326, KINGSGROVE 2208 (02) 50-0321

JANUARY

Sun.	Mon.	Tue.	Wed.	Thu.	Fri.	Sat.
	1	2	3	4	5	6
7	8	9	10	11	12	13
14	15	16	17	18	19	20
21	22	23	24	25	26	27
28	29	30	31			

FEB

1990 E

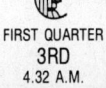

FIRST QUARTER
3RD
4.32 A.M.

SUNDAY	MONDAY	TUESDAY

SUMMER TIME
Note that times-of-day in this calendar are normal Eastern Standard times and must be corrected whenever Daylight Saving operates.
(Add 1 Hour)

School Vacations
ALL PRIMARY & SECONDARY STATE DEPARTMENTAL SCHOOLS

		Break-up				Resume		
N.S.W.	–	Fri.,	Dec. 15th	1989	Mon.,	Jan.	29th	1990
VIC.	–	Fri.,	Dec. 22nd	1989	Thu.,	Feb.	1st	1990
QLD.	–	Fri.,	Dec. 15th	1989	Mon.,	Jan.	29th	1990
TAS.	–	Wed.,	Dec. 20th	1989	Tue.,	Feb.	20th	1990
S.A.	–	Fri.,	Dec. 15th	1989	Tue.,	Jan.	30th	1990
W.A.	–	Wed.,	Dec. 20th	1989	Tue.,	Jan.	30th	1990
A.C.T.	–	Fri.,	Dec. 15th	1989	Mon.,	Jan.	29th	1990
N.T.	–	Fri.,	Dec. 15th	1989	Mon.,	Jan.	29th	1990

WESTERN DIVISION N.S.W. RESUME MONDAY, FEBRUARY 5TH, 1990

DAY No. 35 | **4** | WK. No. 6

Independence Day, Sri Lanka

5

6

New Zealand National Day
Waitangi Treaty 1840

42 | **11** | 7

12

13

PEOPLE'S DAY (Sth. Tas.)
Royal Hobart Regatta

49 | **18** | 8

19

20

56 | **25** | 9

26

27

PANCAKE DAY

INDEX TO INFORMATION (See Top of Back Cover)

TIDE CHART — FEBRUARY 1990

NOTE:—These tides always indicated at Standard Time.—Tide heights are in metres to two (2) •

Tidal predictions for States are supplied by the Tidal Laboratory of the Flinders Institute for Atmospheric
copyright reserved.

TIMES AND HEIGHTS OF HIGH AND LOW WATERS

Columns grouped by: **QLD. — BRISBANE** | **N.S.W. — SYDNEY (Fort Denison)** | **VIC. — POINT LONSDALE (Port Phillip Heads)** | **S.A. — PORT ADELAIDE (Outer Harbor)**

Day	a.m.	m	p.m.	m	a.m.	m	p.m.	m	a.m.	m	p.m.	m	a.m.	m	p.m.	m
THU 1st	1.00	2.02	1.07	2.13	6.01	0.42	12.09	1.48	3.36	1.50	3.57	1.43	1.20	0.73	1.16	0.5
	7.02	0.49	7.37	0.41			6.25	0.35	9.25	0.21	9.37	0.32	7.08	2.34	7.38	2.5
FRI 2nd	1.53	2.00	1.53	1.91	12.51	1.52	1.05	1.33	4.07	1.48	4.41	1.43	1.48	0.80	1.23	0.5
	7.59	0.63	8.22	0.46	7.04	0.48	7.13	0.45	10.05	0.15	10.18	0.41	7.26	2.16	8.00	2.5
SAT 3rd	2.58	1.99	2.56	1.70	1.48	1.53	2.11	1.20	4.38	1.46	5.30	1.42	2.17	0.92	1.33	0.6
	9.13	0.75	9.23	0.51	8.18	0.53	8.09	0.54	10.47	0.12	11.01	0.51	7.44	1.97	8.27	2.5
SUN 4th	4.19	2.02	4.19	1.56	2.53	1.56	3.36	1.12	5.13	1.43	6.26	1.38	2.53	1.10	1.40	0.7
	10.45	0.80	10.42	0.53	9.41	0.54	9.18	0.59	11.32	0.11	11.46	0.61	7.49	1.73	8.56	2.3
MON 5th	5.42	2.12	12.21	0.75	4.05	1.61	5.03	1.13	5.53	1.39	12.19	0.13	3.45	1.38	1.10	0.8
			5.50	1.54	11.03	0.49	10.28	0.58			7.36	1.34	7.04	1.51	9.16	2.1
TUE 6th	12.00	0.49	1.38	0.64	5.14	1.69	12.12	0.41	12.34	0.70	1.10	0.17			12.03	0.8
	6.53	2.25	7.07	1.61			6.07	1.19	6.40	1.33	8.48	1.31	7.31	1.8		
					11.31	0.53							10.31	1.7		
WED 7th	1.10	0.41	2.36	0.55	6.13	1.77	1.07	0.33	1.30	0.77	2.10	0.23	3.48	2.10	6.13	1.8
	7.50	2.38	8.06	1.72			6.58	1.27	7.41	1.26	9.56	1.30	11.27	0.64	10.40	1.4
THU 8th	2.08	0.34	3.23	0.49	12.27	0.46	1.53	0.27	2.40	0.82	3.24	0.28	4.30	2.37	5.59	1.9
	8.39	2.46	8.53	1.82	7.06	1.83	7.45	1.33	9.15	1.20	11.06	1.31	11.35	0.49	10.57	1.1
FRI 9th	2.57	0.30	4.04	0.48	1.20	0.40	2.35	0.24	4.08	0.80	4.47	0.30	4.56	2.54	5.55	2.0
	9.22	2.49	9.36	1.90	7.53	1.84	8.29	1.39	10.38	1.18			11.46	0.45	11.08	0.9
SAT 10th	3.39	0.30	4.38	0.48	2.08	0.37	3.14	0.23	12.12	1.35	6.00	0.29	5.16	2.61	5.53	2.1
	10.00	2.47	10.13	1.96	8.38	1.81	9.11	1.41	5.35	0.72			11.53	0.47	11.23	0.8
									11.52	1.21						
SUN 11th	4.17	0.34	5.09	0.48	2.54	0.37	3.49	0.26	1.09	1.40	12.59	1.26	5.31	2.64	5.55	2.2
	10.35	2.43	10.50	2.01	9.19	1.74	9.50	1.42	6.46	0.60	7.00	0.28	11.57	0.47	11.40	0.6
MON 12th	4.52	0.40	5.36	0.48	3.38	0.39	4.19	0.30	1.56	1.45	1.57	1.32	5.45	2.64	12.05	0.4
	11.06	2.35	11.23	2.04	9.55	1.64	10.26	1.42	7.41	0.47	7.51	0.29			6.06	2.4
TUE 13th	5.25	0.47	6.00	0.46	4.18	0.43	4.46	0.35	2.34	1.47	2.46	1.37	12.02	0.59	12.17	0.4
	11.35	2.25	11.58	2.04	10.29	1.52	11.01	1.42	8.25	0.35	8.32	0.31	6.03	2.62	6.25	2.5
WED 14th	6.01	0.57	12.04	2.12	4.59	0.47	5.13	0.40	3.04	1.46	3.28	1.40	12.27	0.55	12.34	0.3
			6.26	0.47	11.03	1.41	11.37	1.42	9.03	0.26	9.07	0.34	6.25	2.55	6.51	2.6
THU 15th	12.35	2.02	12.35	1.97	5.43	0.52	5.43	0.46	3.29	1.44	4.05	1.40	12.56	0.57	12.52	0.4
	6.39	0.67	6.56	0.50	11.39	1.31			9.36	0.21	9.38	0.39	6.49	2.44	7.15	2.6
FRI 16th	1.16	1.97	1.10	1.80	12.17	1.41	12.23	1.21	3.53	1.42	4.37	1.37	1.24	0.63	1.08	0.4
	7.24	0.79	7.33	0.56	6.32	0.58	6.20	0.53	10.08	0.18	10.08	0.44	7.09	2.30	7.36	2.6
SAT 17th	2.05	1.90	1.55	1.62	1.03	1.38	1.16	1.12	4.18	1.39	5.08	1.34	1.50	0.73	1.21	0.5
	8.22	0.90	8.19	0.64	7.31	0.63	7.06	0.61	10.39	0.18	10.42	0.49	7.26	2.14	7.55	2.5
SUN 18th	3.08	1.85	3.00	1.49	1.58	1.36	2.23	1.05	4.47	1.35	5.42	1.29	2.15	0.87	1.33	0.6
	9.40	0.96	9.23	0.71	8.46	0.66	8.05	0.67	11.13	0.19	11.17	0.55	7.41	1.95	8.15	2.4
MON 19th	4.30	1.85	4.23	1.44	3.02	1.36	3.43	1.03	5.19	1.30	6.22	1.24	2.43	1.08	1.36	0.8
	11.09	0.94	10.44	0.71	10.08	0.64	9.20	0.69	11.48	0.21	11.53	0.61	7.49	1.72	8.37	2.2
TUE 20th	5.50	1.93	12.27	0.85	4.10	1.40	5.04	1.06	5.54	1.26	12.24	0.24	3.23	1.37	12.46	1.0
			5.48	1.49	11.17	0.58	10.30	0.66			7.13	1.19	6.54	1.49	8.36	1.9
	11.53	0.64														
WED 21st	6.49	2.06	1.25	0.74	5.10	1.48	12.08	0.49	12.33	0.67	1.07	0.27	11.13	0.91	6.12	1.7
			6.52	1.60			5.58	1.13	6.38	1.20	8.20	1.16			10.23	1.8
					11.24	0.59										
THU 22nd	12.53	0.53	2.12	0.63	6.00	1.57	12.49	0.40	1.23	0.73	1.57	0.31	3.53	2.09	5.28	1.9
	7.36	2.20	7.41	1.73			6.40	1.21	7.32	1.14	9.29	1.16	10.57	0.66	10.25	1.2
FRI 23rd	1.43	0.42	2.53	0.54	12.10	0.50	1.23	0.30	2.25	0.78	3.02	0.34	4.23	2.38	5.27	2.0
	8.18	2.33	8.24	1.86	6.42	1.67	7.18	1.30	8.42	1.09	10.36	1.19	11.07	0.48	10.43	1.0
SAT 24th	2.29	0.32	3.32	0.45	12.53	0.40	1.58	0.22	3.41	0.77	4.13	0.35	4.47	2.58	5.32	2.2
	8.56	2.43	9.07	1.98	7.23	1.75	7.56	1.39	10.05	1.09	11.35	1.25	11.20	0.40	11.02	0.8
SUN 25th	3.12	0.25	4.08	0.37	1.38	0.32	2.34	0.16	4.56	0.70	5.23	0.33	5.07	2.68	5.38	2.3
	9.34	2.50	9.49	2.09	8.06	1.80	8.36	1.48	11.19	1.15			11.33	0.39	11.22	0.8
MON 26th	3.55	0.21	4.44	0.31	2.23	0.26	3.11	0.14	12.26	1.32	12.23	1.26	5.25	2.71	5.48	2.4
	10.11	2.51	10.30	2.19	8.48	1.80	9.17	1.56	6.00	0.58	6.22	0.32	11.45	0.41	11.44	0.5
TUE 27th	4.38	0.21	5.17	0.28	3.12	0.23	3.49	0.16	1.11	1.40	1.22	1.38	5.47	2.67	6.06	2.5
	10.48	2.46	11.12	2.25	9.33	1.75	10.00	1.63	6.50	0.44	7.12	0.31	11.58	0.44		
WED 28th	5.22	0.27	5.50	0.28	4.03	0.24	4.28	0.23	1.53	1.46	2.14	1.49	12.11	0.54	12.13	0.4
	11.24	2.33	11.54	2.27	10.19	1.66	10.45	1.67	7.35	0.30	7.57	0.32	6.09	2.54	6.25	2.6

b What do you think life will be like in 30 years' time?

I think people will all be living in large apartment blocks.

In my opinion, people will be retiring at the age of 45.

I imagine that nobody will be working more than 30 hours a week.

I expect there will be fewer cars on the roads.

I think the average family will have at least two cars.

I'm afraid the air and the oceans will be polluted.

I think women will have equal rights.

In my opinion, people will be queueing for petrol.

B 2

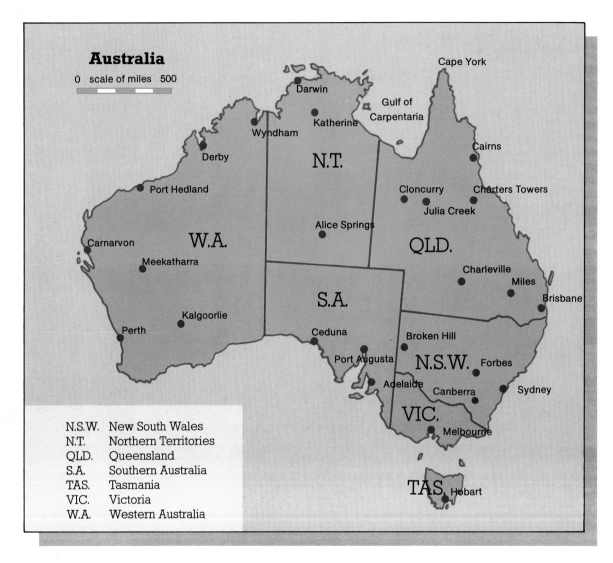

Australia

0 scale of miles 500

Cape York
Darwin
Gulf of Carpentaria
Katherine
Wyndham
N.T.
Cairns
Derby
Cloncurry Charters Towers
Port Hedland
Julia Creek
Alice Springs
Carnarvon
W.A.
QLD.
Meekatharra
Charleville
Miles
Brisbane
S.A.
Kalgoorlie
Ceduna
Broken Hill
Perth
Port Augusta
N.S.W. Forbes
Adelaide
Canberra Sydney
VIC.
Melbourne
TAS. Hobart

N.S.W.	New South Wales
N.T.	Northern Territories
QLD.	Queensland
S.A.	Southern Australia
TAS.	Tasmania
VIC.	Victoria
W.A.	Western Australia

In the wide open spaces of Australia – known to Australians as the 'outback' – medical services are provided by doctors who visit their patients in small planes. They keep in touch with the needs of their districts – which may cover many thousands of square miles – by means of a system of radio bases and local transmitters operated by the settlers of the outback themselves. The flying doctors provide a service for people who otherwise would have no chance of getting medical treatment.

In the interview you will hear on the cassette, Ron Marsh, an Australian journalist who is writing a series of articles about the Flying Doctor Service, will be dealing with the history and development of the service.

The Australian flying doctor service is probably the only institution of its kind in the world, isn't it?

a
Listen to the cassette and mark with a cross the things in the pictures which are talked about in the interview.

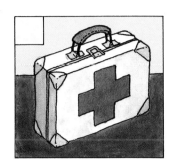

b
Listen to the cassette a second time. Underline on the map the places Ron Marsh talks about and write down the dates he mentions.

c
Listen to the cassette a third time and take notes on what he says about these places and dates.

"Oh, yes, I forgot! He only lands for private patients."

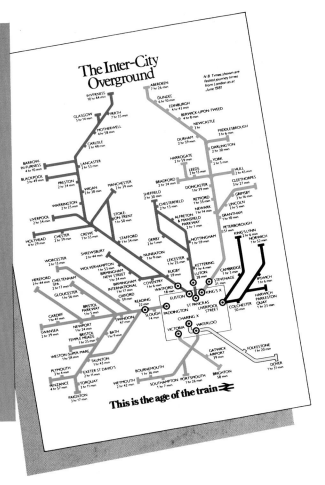

24 London edition

HOW TO CHOOSE YOUR RAIL TICKET and save money.

This is the age of the train ⇌

This British Rail leaflet describes various return tickets which are available from London.
The 'Inter-City Overground' map shows the train connections from each station in London to different parts of Britain, as well as how long a particular journey takes.
With the help of the leaflet, decide which is the best ticket to buy in the following cases. Also find out which station you will have to leave from and how long the journey will take.

1 You are going to Edinburgh for about three weeks.
ticket? _____ station? _____
how long? _____

2 You are going to Liverpool and want to return in about six weeks' time.
ticket? _____ station? _____
how long? _____

3 You are going to Brighton and want to return the same day.
ticket? _____ station? _____
how long? _____

4 You are going to Cardiff on Friday and want to return on Monday.
ticket? _____ station? _____
how long? _____

5 You are going to live and work in England for a year and will have to travel regularly between London and Colchester.
ticket? _____ station? _____
how long? _____

ORDINARY RETURN

Ordinary Tickets

If you want to be free to travel on any train at any time, or if none of the other Fare Deals suit your journey plans, you should ask for an Ordinary Single or Return.

An Ordinary Single is valid for 3 days and an Ordinary Return for 3 months, except for travel within a radius of about 35 miles from London (see pages 10/11) and locally in some other areas, where both are valid on the day of issue only.

Some examples of Second Class Ordinary Returns from London are shown on page 17.

Season Tickets

Season tickets can save you time and money if you make the same journey regularly. They are available for a week (Suns to Sats) or any period from a month to a year.

AWAYDAY RETURN

Awayday Return – the cheap day ticket

Seeing the sights, visiting friends and relations, shopping, or just enjoying a day out, they all make sense with an Awayday Return. It can often work out cheaper than going by car, and it saves you the bother of driving and parking into the bargain.

An Awayday Return is valid for one day only. On Saturdays, Sundays and Bank Holidays, Awayday Returns can be used on any train. On Mondays to Fridays Awayday Returns cannot be used on some morning and evening rush hour trains (see pages 10 and 11).

Some examples of 2nd Class Awayday Returns from London are shown on pages 18 and 19. Some 1st Class Awayday Returns are available too; please ask at your local station.

WEEKEND RETURN

Ask for a Weekend Return, and enjoy a long weekend away.

Visit someone you don't often see, or get away from it all for a couple of days. With a Weekend Return you can leave on Friday, Saturday or Sunday, and return the same weekend on Saturday, Sunday or Monday. You can travel on most trains — there are some Friday and Monday restrictions to the East, North East and West of England (See pages 14-16).

1st and 2nd Class Weekend Returns are available for most journeys over 75 miles, and certain shorter journeys.

Some 2nd Class examples from London are shown on page 20.

MONTHLY RETURN

A Monthly Return is just the ticket if you're going on a long holiday or trip.

Staying with friends or relatives, or taking a holiday? With a Monthly Return you can go any day (your ticket must be dated for that day even if you buy it in advance) and return within one month. If you make your outward journey between Monday and Friday inclusive you cannot return before Saturday. On most days you can use any train; on Fridays there are a few restrictions (see pages 14 and 15).

1st and 2nd Class Monthly Returns are available for most journeys over 75 miles, and certain shorter journeys. Some 2nd Class examples from London are shown on page 21.

Your English-speaking friend does not know what these things are for. Explain them to him/her.

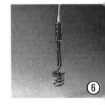

A riddle

I'm never tired and I never complain.
I can work quickly all day and all night.
I'm never ill and I don't need a holiday.
I work more accurately than most men and women.
I'm never hungry and I never take a coffee-break.
What am I?

Now write a riddle with your partner and ask the rest of the class to guess the answer.

A 1

BEC INTRODUCED their fully automatic System B robots at their Liverpool factory yesterday. To look at, the system reminds you less of a factory than of a TV studio with several rows of machines, electric wires lying on the ground everywhere and strange objects all around. Certainly the place does not look like a normal factory.

The production manager, Bob Smiley, had this to say about the system: "I know they don't look like the kinds of robots people have seen in films. They have a different shape. And they don't look human. But these robots are computer-controlled and so can work by themselves. This will mean that BEC can make its products much more easily and more cheaply." The company say the system is the biggest of its kind in the world. They think the robots will do the work more efficiently than employees, and so a large amount of money will be saved.

Mike Cooley, a trade-union official, was not happy with the employers' explanations: "We don't doubt that it's the most modern computer-controlled robot system in the world, and that it can do the job more quickly than a hundred human workers. But in our opinion it can't do the work better than workers can. And we doubt whether it will actually save as much as the employers say it will. What the employers do not say is that technical progress is destroying jobs much faster than it can create new ones. What are the men and women without work going to do now?"

a What will be different with the robot system?

BEC can make their products	more easily.
The System B robots work	cheaply.
The new system does the job	quickly.
	efficiently.

It can't do the work	better than workers can.
Technical progress is destroying jobs	faster than it can create new ones.

b What is the new system like?

The robots/system	are/is like	a TV studio.
	remind(s) you of	...
	look(s) like	

c What do the following remind you of?

d Do you think a machine/robot could do your job
better than you?
Do machines work more quickly than you?
What can they do more efficiently?

e What sort of machines do you have in your home?
What would life be like without them?
What was life like before people had them?

A 2

THE WORLD OF PERSONAL COMPUTERS

The purpose of this article is to introduce the reader to the world of personal computers. A well-known computer magazine has suggested that the idea behind the personal computer is to bring computer technology within the reach of the ordinary man in the street. If this is true, people should know more about computers, so that they can decide for themselves whether they want or need one in their home. But in order to know how a computer works, you need to know something about the various parts of the computer and what they are for.

Hardware

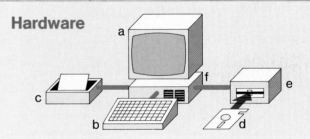

a MONITOR – shows the computer's calculations and what you type
b KEYBOARD – sends your information to the computer
c PRINTER – produces paper copies of what is shown on the monitor
d DISC – stores computer programs and large amounts of information
e DISC DRIVE – reads information from a disc in the same way a record-player plays a record
f MICROPROCESSOR – the most important part of the computer; it controls everything the computer does

a What are the various parts of the computer for?

The idea behind the personal computer is to …
The monitor is used to …
In order to … you need a printer.
The purpose of the disc is to …
…

b Which description goes with which program?

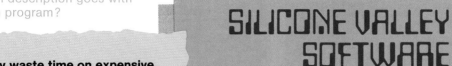

1 Why waste time on expensive typing lessons? Your computer can teach you in only ten lessons!
2 Are you sick and tired of writing all those Christmas and birthday letters? This program makes all writing easy and fun to do.
3 A good way to improve your English.
4 Improve your game. You have to be good to beat the master.
5 Your child can learn to read before he/she gets to school.

Have a look at our new range of quality software – it's a dream come true!

● technical perfection

● super prices

● generous terms

● smooth service

Trust the specialists in this field, and kiss the usual dull and dry programs goodbye!

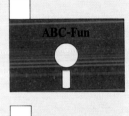
Better English by Computer

ABC-Fun

Letter Writer

Typing Teacher

Chess Master

c What are these software programs for?
d Do you think any of these programs could be useful to you?
e Do you think a personal computer could help you in your job or at home?

a What do you think are the advantages and disadvantages of computers?

b Listen to the conversation on the cassette about computers and modern technology. Which of the speakers is against computers?

c Listen to the cassette again and list 3 advantages and 3 disadvantages or dangers the speakers see with the introduction of modern technology.

B 1

d Which of the following things do the speakers say a personal computer can do?

e Which of these things does one of the speakers say people will be able to do at home with a computer?

help a small businessman
add up wages
solve the problem of unemployment
help you with your garden
anything you like

do the housework
type letters
do work for a bank
look after the children
organize the office

f Who do you think profits most from computers?

– None of us could remember the way to that restaurant you recommended.
– Couldn't you? But I drew Peter a map.
– Really? He probably lost it.

– I loved that restaurant John took us to.
– Did you? I didn't like it at all.

I didn't like	the chocolate	you/... sent me.
liked	that book	told me about.
can't find	hotel	recommended.
couldn't find	shoe-cream	suggested.
tried out	pub	gave me.
didn't care for	handkerchief	lent me.
loved	wine	...
was very pleased with	photograph	
	...	

Did you?	But I ...
Didn't you?	Well, I ...
Can't you?	
Couldn't you?	
Really?	
...	

If you're	not thirsty at the moment	we could take the bus instead.
	not hungry just now	change places.
If you	don't feel like walking	go for a drink later.
	don't want to stand in a queue	go to the early performance instead.
	don't want to drive	eat after the show.
	want to take a bath first	go in my car.
	want to sit by the window	go out later.
	...	...

That's a good idea.

I don't think that's a very good idea, I'm afraid.

Well, it doesn't really bother me one way or the other.

Dear Mary,

I promised to tell you about our trip to the eastern part of the USA.

And then we visited Lancaster County in Pennsylvania. This is where the Protestant sect called the Old Amish Order live. I had heard about them before, but I never realized that they had come from Germany in 1710. I was surprised to find that they still speak German after 270 years in the USA (although it's actually called Pennsylvania Dutch!). Oh yes, and their name is said to go back to Jakob Amman, who was their leader.

Well, Lancaster County really is an interesting place to visit because you can see the Amish people living and working on farms much as their people have been doing for the past two hundred years. I would never have dreamt that anyone in America would choose to live so far behind the times, without cars and electricity. But the Amish people do! You see them driving their carriages pulled by horses along the roads. Look at the pictures I have sent you.

And I wouldn't have expected to see men and women today wearing clothes in the style of two centuries ago either. And not just on special occasions or for festivals, but all the time. The men have all got beards and the women wear long dresses and white caps. Even the children dress the same as the adults. Well, except for the beards, that is!

Obviously, religion plays an important part in the lives of these people. But I was surprised to find out that they don't have any churches. They meet instead at each other's homes every two weeks.

Best wishes,

Joan

a What was the writer's reaction to what she saw in Lancaster County?
She hadn't expected to ...
She would never have ...
She was ...
She ...

b Say what you found surprising when you were on holiday in another country or another town.

A 4

I'm standing in the market place of the small town of Dolgellau in County Gwynedd in North Wales. From here I can see a total of five public houses. All of them are closed because it's Sunday and because the latest attempt to introduce Sunday opening to this part of Wales has once again failed. I'm here to find out just what the local people here think about this decision. I asked a few of the people I met on the street.

I think it's a pity. I was in favour of them opening the pubs. As you can see, this place is absolutely bloody dead on Sundays otherwise.

I don't agree with the decision. Anybody would think we were living in the Middle Ages!

I think it's wrong to get drunk on a Sunday. So I'm all in favour of the pubs staying shut.

To tell the truth, I don't think it makes any difference; those who want to drink on Sunday have always found ways and means anyway.

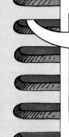

Sunday opening! No! I'm absolutely against it.

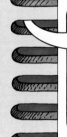

Personally, I don't care when the pubs are allowed to open and when they're not. I never go in them anyway, so it makes no difference to me.

a Say how you feel about the following.

It makes no difference to me.

I don't think it makes any difference.
    care what/how ...
    mind if they are/aren't ...

I don't agree with that. I think ...
I'm (absolutely) against that. I think ...

I'm all in favour of that. I think ...

- In many British towns there is a by-law which says you may not sell fish and chips on Sunday.
- Theatres in London are not allowed to open on Sunday.
- Many English people wash their cars and/or cut the grass on Sunday.
- Some groups of people in Britain are against Sunday sport.

b How would you feel if the pubs/theatres/snack-bars in your area were made to close on Sunday?
c What aspect(s) of Sunday in your country would you like to change? What do the others in the class think of your ideas?

B 2 **a** What are the feelings of the young and old towards Sunday and religion where you live? Do they go to church? What do they do at the weekends and on Sunday?

b Now read the following article which is about religion and the young and old in Walés. After the article there are five sentences which give the meaning of five of the seven paragraphs. Which sentence goes with which paragraph?
NB: In Britain a chapel is a church used by people who do not belong to the established Protestant or Roman Catholic Church.

THE CHAPELS WITHOUT THE PEOPLE

Once the people of Wales used to be a very religious nation. The large number of chapels to be found reminds the visitor of the tradition. In most Welsh towns you find several large and elegant chapel buildings. In the original buildings there was room for five or six hundred people. Some of them are now in ruins. But others are being carefully looked after by their elderly congregations.

Things have changed. Fewer and fewer people are now going to chapel or church. You hear many reasons why this is so. "People didn't go to chapel because they believed in God. They went because the neighbours did. It was just a habit," one person tells you. Another explains, "You were not allowed to do this and not allowed to do that. Dancing and drinking, all the things the poor enjoyed – none of these things were allowed." A young woman gave an example, "If a single girl was expecting a baby, she had to leave the chapel."

And one old lady who still goes to chapel told me what it was like in her youth: "Sunday was a special day for the family – different from weekdays. We went to chapel, came home and changed out of our best clothes; then we put

them on again for Sunday school, came home and changed out of them again; then back into them for evening service. On Sunday you were not allowed to sew on a button or clean the floor."

But modern times have brought changes. In recent years the two generations have lost touch with one another. "There are two different groups living in the Welsh valleys now," said a member of the church in Aberdare, "the young and the old." And it is true. They seem to lead separate lives, walking silently past each other in the streets of the old industrial villages.

On Saturday night, the town centre is full of young people, many of them out of work. They move noisily from pub to pub, looking for something to do, eating food out of paper and plastic boxes as they go, throwing coke cans into the road. A restless energy fills the streets on Saturday nights; and the old people stay at home.

But then, on Sunday morning, a smaller and very different group fills the streets. Old ladies in hats carry thick bibles in one hand, while in the other they hold walking-sticks to help them down the steep hills. They walk slowly to freezing chapels which they have visited every Sunday for 70 or 80 years.

By contrast, the young generation has lost the sense of a religious community. An old miner explained to me what it meant for him to be a member of a chapel. When his wife died nine years earlier, the chapel had been his support. "I don't know what I would have done without the chapel. It had given us so much comfort and hope in life. Where else would I have gone in those long and lonely hours and weeks?"

The older generation still goes to chapel on Sundays.
Young and old people live differently.
Young people don't know what to do.
Many people have stopped going to chapel.
Sunday used to be a very religious day.

c Read the article once more. To what events, things or people do these numbers or amounts refer?

the large number _____

most _____

_____ five or six hundred _____

some _____

fewer and fewer _____

many _____

all _____

two _____

two _____

many _____

_____ seventy or eighty _____

_____ nine _____

so much _____

d What persons or things are described as follows?

different _____   restless _____

elderly _____   separate _____

freezing _____   steep _____

industrial _____   thick _____

religious _____   Welsh _____

_____   _____

e Who does what in the following ways?

_____ noisily _____

_____ carefully _____

_____ silently _____

_____ slowly _____

f Say what you think about the situation described in the article.
   Do you find it normal or not? Why?/Why not?

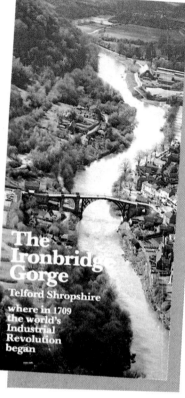

The Ironbridge Gorge

Telford Shropshire

where in 1709 the world's Industrial Revolution began

The Ironbridge Gorge was the scene of the remarkable breakthrough which led Britain to become the first industrial nation and the workshop of the world. The area still retains much of the atmosphere of those times.

   The Ironbridge Gorge Museum consists of a number of industrial monuments spread over about six square miles. It was named 'The European Museum of the Year' in 1978.

a   Look at the photos and the map. Find where the places illustrated are on the map.

b   Make notes on what products you think used to be made or what used to happen there. Say what you can see there today.

c   Now listen to the cassette. A man describes a visit he made to the museum. Mark the parts he visited on the map.

d   Now listen to the cassette again and note the following:

– the years in which the things he mentions were first built or used

_____   _____

_____   _____

_____   _____

– the years in which the places were closed and why

_____

_____

_____

Blists Hill Open Air Museum. The site of a coal mine, a steelworks and a blast furnace where iron was manufactured. Many houses and buildings have been moved to the museum and rebuilt here.

Coalport China Works Museum. Fine bone china was made here from the end of the eighteenth century until 1926. The works has been restored as a museum of its products and people.

Ironbridge. The most important monument to the iron-workers of the eighteenth century spans the River Severn here. The bridge tollhouse contains an exhibition on the history of the structure, and also a Tourist Information Centre.

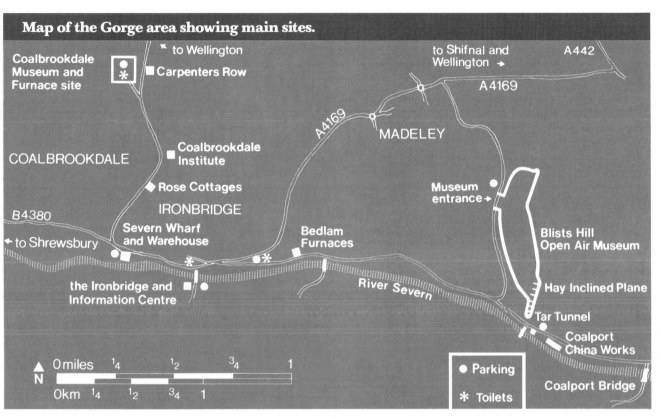

Map of the Gorge area showing main sites.

to Wellington

Coalbrookdale Museum and Furnace site

Carpenters Row

to Shifnal and Wellington →

A442

A4169

A4169

MADELEY

Coalbrookdale Institute

COALBROOKDALE

Rose Cottages

IRONBRIDGE

Museum entrance →

Blists Hill Open Air Museum

B4380

Severn Wharf and Warehouse

← to Shrewsbury

Bedlam Furnaces

the Ironbridge and Information Centre

River Severn

Hay Inclined Plane

Tar Tunnel

Coalport China Works

Coalport Bridge

0 miles ¼ ½ ¾ 1
N
0 km ¼ ½ ¾ 1

● Parking

✳ Toilets

The Severn Warehouse. Iron products from the Coalbrookdale Company were stored in this early nineteenth century building before being loaded onto boats and transported on the River Severn. It contains an audio-visual exhibition telling the history of the company.

Coalbrookdale Museum. This contains the iron-founding collection, Abraham Darby's furnace, and illustrations of iron-making processes.

Review

1
- you have money on arrival
- you can spend money on the boat

- rate of exchange not so good
- danger of loss/theft

- safer
- lower bank charges
- better rate of exchange

- you must go to a bank on arrival

- better rate of exchange
- safer than cash

  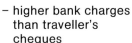

- higher bank charges than traveller's cheques
- only available in Europe and not fully accepted in all European countries

- safe
- you can pay in hotels, shops, etc
- you pay the bill later

- you may spend too much
- you can't use it everywhere

> *If you take cash, you don't have to go to a bank as soon as you arrive.*

> *It depends on whether you . . .*

> *You can only use... at a bank/ in certain hotels.*

> *If you take traveller's cheques, it's not that much of a problem if they are stolen.*

> *Some credit cards can be used anywhere in the world.*

When was it stolen? **A 1**

– Good evening. Can I help you?
– Yes. My wallet's been stolen.
– I see. Just a moment, sir. I'll get a form.
  Now, can you give me your name and address, please?
– My name's Hans Schmidt and I live in Frankfurt.
– And your address in the UK?
– I'm staying at the Hotel Esplanade.
– Right. Now, when was the wallet stolen?
– I'm not quite sure. It was sometime this afternoon. I had it when I left
  the hotel at lunch time, and I bought a ticket on the bus when I came
  to the city centre. Then I walked round the market area and when I
  decided to buy some apples I suddenly noticed that it had gone.
– I see. What was in it?
– All my money and papers.
– How much money did you have?
– About £50 in notes and small change, some German Marks and £250
  in traveller's cheques.
– That's quite a lot of money to lose.
– Yes, and the problem is I'm going back to Germany the day after
  tomorrow. What can I do?
– You should be able to get new traveller's cheques from the bank.
– Well, that would help, but I also had my identity card and my car papers
  in the wallet.
– In that case you should get in touch with your consulate as soon as
  possible. They'll be able to give you new papers.
– OK.
– Could you describe the wallet for me, please?
– It's an ordinary wallet, about this big, dark brown and made of leather.
– Right. Would you just sign here, please?
– Certainly. Is there anything else I should do?
– As I said, get in touch with the consulate without delay, and report the
  loss of the traveller's cheques to your bank as soon as possible – the
  sooner the better, in fact. I don't think there's much hope that you'll get
  your money back, but the thief might throw the wallet away and some-
  body may bring the wallet with your papers either to us here or to the
  Lost Property Office. Give us a ring or come round tomorrow. Perhaps
  we'll have some good news for you.
– OK. Thanks for your help.

Play the scene in the police station with your partner.
One of you is the police officer who fills in the theft report.

You arrived in England ☐ three days ago and are staying ☐ with friends.
☐ the day before yesterday ☐ at the Station Hotel.
☐ a week ago yesterday ☐ at your penfriend's.
☐ a week ago

While you are ☐ walking round the town you notice that your ☐ wallet has been stolen.
☐ visiting a museum ☐ purse
☐ sitting in a pub ☐ handbag

You had ☐ small change ☐ identity card in it.
☐ notes ☐ passport
☐ eurocheques ☐ driving licence
☐ eurocheque card ☐ car papers
☐ credit card ☐ receipts
☐ traveller's cheques

You go straight to the police station to report the theft.

You are very worried because ☐ you wanted to stay in England for another two weeks.

☐ you have to return home within a week.
☐ you are returning to _____ in two days' time.
the day after tomorrow.

You think it was stolen ☐ in the hotel ☐ sometime this afternoon.
☐ in the city centre ☐ just after breakfast.
☐ on the bus

You ask the police officer for advice as to what you should do.

Theft Report

Surname .... Christian Name(s) ....
Description of stolen article ....
Where stolen .... When stolen ....
Contents ....
....
Other remarks .... Signature ....

I need the money urgently A 2

- I've got a problem. My wallet has been stolen with all my money and papers.
- I see. Have you reported it to the police?
- Yes, I've just been there. They said I should give you this copy of the report.
- OK. What can we do for you?
- Well, I had traveller's cheques worth £250 in the wallet. Can you replace them?
- Certainly. Have you got the receipt from your bank?
- No, not on me. I left that at home in Germany.
- Well, I'm sorry, but I can't give you any new traveller's cheques without the receipt.
- But I need the money urgently, otherwise I won't be able to settle my hotel bill and get back to Germany.
- The only thing we could do is to phone your German bank and ask them to send you the money, but we

can't give you the money when it arrives here unless you can prove your identity.
- But all my papers were in the stolen wallet! How can I prove my identity?
- If you go to your consulate, they'll let you have new papers.
- I see. How long will it take to get the money here from Germany?
- If they send it by telegram or telex, it'll be here by the time you get back from the consulate.
- Good. My account is with the Westdeutsche Bank in Frankfurt. Here's my name, address and account number. Would you telex them to send me £250 to this branch right away?
- Certainly. We'll see to it at once.
- OK. Thanks for your help.
- That's all right. Goodbye.

I can't cash your traveller's cheques	if you don't bring unless you bring without	your passport.
You must bring your passport,	otherwise	I won't be able to cash your cheques.

I won't be able to settle my hotel bill	if I don't get unless I get without	money from my German account.
I need the money urgently,	otherwise	I won't be able to settle my hotel bill.

If you went to the bank with the following problems, what would the bank clerk say?

- Your traveller's cheques have been stolen. You'd like to have new ones, but you haven't got the receipt with you.
- You'd like to cash a eurocheque, but your cheque card has been stolen.
  You'd like to cash a traveller's cheque, but your passport/identity card has been stolen.

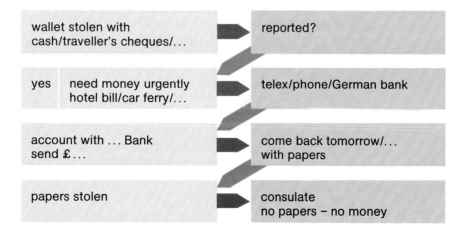

B 1 a Many banks and private companies offer credit cards and produce advertisements to try and attract new customers.

Here is an example of such an advertisement. Read the advertisement carefully and number the answers in the correct order.

Your Questions:

Our Answers:

1 Why should I have an EXCESS card?

2 Where can I use an EXCESS card?

☐ Anywhere. Next time you are in the High Street, look how many good shops, garages, hotels and restaurants have the EXCESS sign. And remember, it's like this in every High Street in the country and at most British Rail stations. In other words, whether you are buying furniture or a television, travelling or simply buying clothes, just use your EXCESS card.

3 Can I use it abroad?

☐ Yes – within your credit limit. You can get cash at 10,000 bank branches in the United Kingdom. When travelling abroad you can have up to £100 a day in the local currency.

4 How much will it cost me to get a card?

☐ As much as you wish up to the agreed credit limit on your EXCESS account. The bank will let you know from time to time what your limit is.

5 How much can I spend with an EXCESS card?

☐ Of course! Just use your EXCESS card as you do in this country.

6 What is meant by 'credit limit'?

☐ It makes shopping a lot easier (especially these days when a pound doesn't go very far). And you won't have to worry about whether you're carrying enough cash on you. After a short time with your EXCESS card, you'll wonder how you ever managed without one.

7 Can I get cash with my EXCESS card?

☐ We send you a clear statement with full details every month to show the total amount you owe us and your credit limit.

8 How do I know how much I have spent?

☐ The 'credit limit' is the maximum amount that you can owe. You are given your credit limit when you receive your card. You decide how much and how often you use it.

9 How much do I have to pay back each month?

☐ If you are 18 years of age or over, just fill in the application form and send it to us today.

10 So how do I apply for a card?

☐ This is the big advantage of an EXCESS card. Because you can choose how much you pay back each month. Pay as little as £5 or 5% of the total amount you owe, whichever is the greater. Or more if you wish, and you have 25 days for your payment to reach EXCESS.

☐ Nothing. Just send in the application form. You don't even need a stamp.

b According to the advertisement, what are the advantages of a credit card? Make a list of the promises made in the advertisement.

c What impression does the advertisement try to give about using credit cards? Find examples in the text to show how this impression is given.

d The following newspaper article describes the experiences 18-year-old Brian Thompson had with his new credit card. Which do you think is the best headline for the article?

MORE AND MORE SHOPS ACCEPT CREDIT CARDS

BUY NOW, PAY LATER

JUDGE WARNS OF DANGERS OF CREDIT CARDS

HOW TO LIVE WITHOUT CASH

PRISON SENTENCE FOR 18-YEAR-OLD

18-year-old Brian Thompson of Smith Street, Norwich, went on a spending spree in London. With the credit card he had just received from his local bank, he took a train to London (paying by credit card) and bought himself new clothes from various department stores in Oxford Street (using his credit card). He spent the evening at an expensive London nightclub (again using his credit card) and booked a room for the night at a first-class West End hotel. Everything else (taxis, tips, drinks, etc) he paid for in cash with money he got from various banks, again with his credit card.

"It was all so simple," said Brian in court yesterday. "None of the shops asked any questions. They took the credit card, gave me a receipt, and I walked out with the goods." It made him feel really good to be able to buy new clothes for the first time in his life without having any money in his pockets. He was able to enjoy a whole weekend in London without even having the feeling of spending money. It was only a month later, when the bank statement arrived, that Brian realized what a fool he had been. The bill was for £456, an amount far too high for a young unemployed person who had just left school to be able to pay. He tried to borrow money (with his credit card) in order to pay the money back to the bank, but it was impossible. After only a few months the bank took Brian to court.

Before sentencing Brian to the minimum fine of £10, the judge attacked the banks, who in his opinion were just as guilty because they make it too easy for people to spend more money than they can afford. Anybody over the age of 18 can apply for and receive a credit card. There is then nothing to stop them from going into the nearest shop and spending as much as they want, up to the limit of their card. They can then do exactly the same in the next shop. Brian Thompson was given two years to pay back the money, on condition that he did not apply for another credit card in that time.

e Now compare the article about Brian Thompson with the promises in the credit card leaflet. Does the advertisement give a full and true picture of credit cards?

f Have you ever used a credit card? Why?/Why not?

Review

a This is a game for two. One player thinks of one of the persons in the pictures. His/Her partner tries to find out in as few questions as possible which person it is.

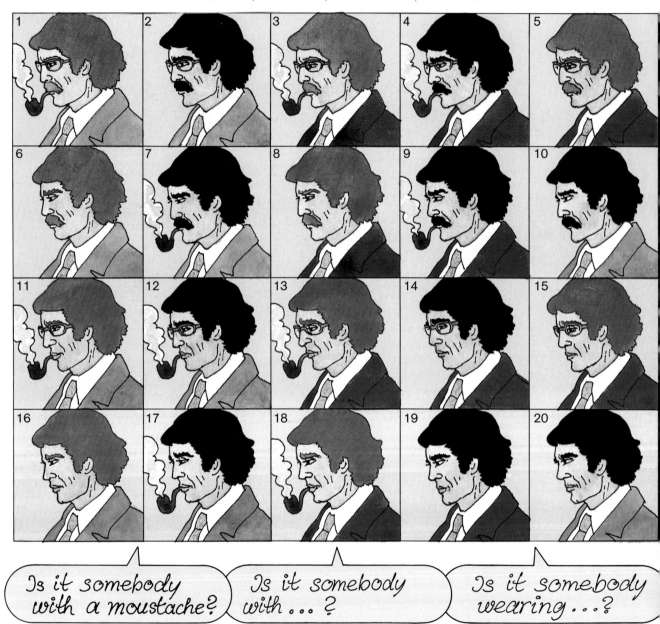

Is it somebody with a moustache?

Is it somebody with ... ?

Is it somebody wearing ...?

b Someone has stolen your wallet/purse. You know the thief; it's one of the men in the pictures. Describe him till your partner recognizes him.

Roy Rogers is back in films – in two television commercials with which the gun lobby is fighting to prevent new laws which would make it more difficult to buy guns and make it necessary to register them. "I wouldn't feel safe if I didn't have a gun in my house. It's one of the most important freedoms this country has." This country also has over 10,000 deaths caused by guns every year, and people living in one of the 50 biggest cities have a 1 in 33 chance of being murdered. (The chances of an American soldier being killed in World War II were 1 in 50.) Nobody wants to take Mr Rogers' gun away. They simply want to register it. But he says, "They'll have to shoot me first to take my gun."

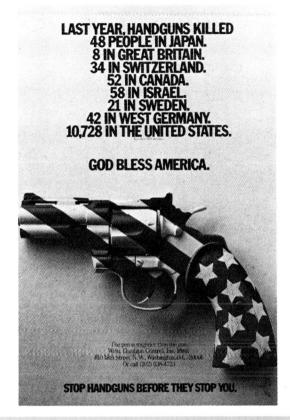

LAST YEAR, HANDGUNS KILLED
48 PEOPLE IN JAPAN.
8 IN GREAT BRITAIN.
34 IN SWITZERLAND.
52 IN CANADA.
58 IN ISRAEL.
21 IN SWEDEN.
42 IN WEST GERMANY.
10,728 IN THE UNITED STATES.

GOD BLESS AMERICA.

The pen is mightier than the gun.
Write Handgun Control, Inc. 20001
810 18th Street N.W., Washington, D.C. 20006
Or call (202) 638-4723

STOP HANDGUNS BEFORE THEY STOP YOU.

"I always carry a gun for reasons of personal safety. I feel safer when I know I can defend myself if I'm attacked."

"For me it's part of the American way of life. It's one of the freedoms a man has. That's why I own a gun. I just hope I'll never need to use it."

"The reason I always carry a gun is to protect myself and my family. This is a problem area of the city, and it's dangerous to go out alone in the evenings."

"Well, I live alone in a large apartment building. Only last week one of my neighbors was attacked in her bed in the middle of the night. So I always have a weapon to protect myself if anything happens."

The reason I always carry a gun is …
I always carry a gun for reasons of …

… So/That's why I always carry a gun.

a What reasons do the people give for carrying and owning guns? What do you think of the reasons they give?
b What do you think the poster is trying to say?
c Do you own a gun? Why?/Why not?
d Do the police in your country have guns? Do you think this is a good thing? Why?/Why not?

A 4

SCIENTIST ATTACKED IN TOWN CENTRE

Shortly after nine o'clock yesterday morning, the well-known Canadian scientist, 56-year-old Graham Brown, was attacked as he was getting out of his car in a car-park near the city library. A blue Mini suddenly stopped next to his Rover, and a young couple got out and ran towards him. "The man had a gun, the woman was carrying a grey case," Graham Brown told the police afterwards. "They attacked me, took my wallet with all my papers and drove away at high speed in my Rover. I was too surprised to defend myself or shout for help," he said. Fortunately, the scientist was discovered a few minutes later by 60-year-old Anne Lorne. She called the police and an ambulance. When the police arrived, they found a bunch of keys, a metal comb and a silver ball pen the couple had dropped. The blue Mini which the couple left behind had been reported stolen in Birmingham the day before. The search for the missing Rover, which is silver-grey and has the licence number COH 142T, has moved to the West Midlands. Anybody who was near the car-park at the time of the attack is asked to get in touch with the police as soon as possible.

a Can you say what you see in the pictures?

| That's the couple | whose keys were found. who attacked Graham Brown. the police are trying to find. |
| Those are the keys | found by the police. which were found by the police. (which) the couple dropped. |

b Here is a list of people, places and things that have been mentioned so far in ON THE WAY 3. Ask your partner if he/she remembers who, where or what they are.

Ronald Thorpe	Janet Steen	Elsie Barnet
The Last Taboo	Norman Barry	Avenger
Brian, Edgar,	The Sally	Pickfords
Maureen & Anita	Mrs Jones	Glastonbury

B 2 Capital punishment: for and against

The last people to be sentenced to death and hanged in a British prison were Peter Allen and Gwynne Evans in 1964, both for the murder of John West.

The following year Parliament decided to stop capital punishment in Britain. At that time the average number of murders per year was 286 and there were 14,000 cases per year of violence against the person. Since then there has been a rise in the figures each year, and in 1982 the criminal statistics for England and Wales included 559 murders and 100,200 other violent crimes.

As a result of this development, many people believe that sooner or later hanging will have to be brought back. They say it is the only sure deterrent and it is the only punishment certain criminals deserve.

In a recent radio programme, Jim Davison, a well-known lawyer, argued with Sir Timothy McNamara of Scotland Yard about whether capital punishment should be brought back or not. First you hear Sir Timothy.

a What do Sir Timothy McNamara and Jim Davison think of capital punishment?

b Listen to the interview once again and write down the arguments they give for and against capital punishment.

Tom Paxton is a popular American songwriter and folk-singer. He has written love songs, humorous songs and children's songs, but he is perhaps best known for his protest songs, in which he attacks war, corruption, social injustice etc. The following song, which he wrote in 1962, belongs to this category, though you have to 'read – or listen – between the lines' to understand what he is really saying.

The song is a kind of dialogue.
Listen to the cassette and read the text.

a Who do you think the two people in the dialogue are?

b Every verse begins with the same question, which is also the title of the song. Underline the important words in the answers given in each verse.

c What is Paxton saying about the kind of things children learn at school?

d Does he agree with what children are taught at school? Which line in each verse clearly shows his opinion?

c Which of the arguments given do you agree/disagree with? Give reasons.

d Is there capital punishment in your country? Do/Would you support it for certain crimes?

What did you learn in school today?

What did you learn in school today,
Dear little boy of mine?
What did you learn in school today,
Dear little boy of mine?
I learned that Washington never told a lie,
I learned that soldiers seldom die,
I learned that everybody's free,
And that's what the teacher said to me,
And that's what I learned in school today,
That's what I learned in school.

What did you learn in school today,
Dear little boy of mine?
What did you learn in school today,
Dear little boy of mine?
I learned that policemen are my friends,
I learned that justice never ends,
I learned that murderers die for their crimes,
Even if we make mistakes sometimes,
And that's what I learned in school today,
That's what I learned in school.

What did you learn in school today,
Dear little boy of mine?
What did you learn in school today,
Dear little boy of mine?
I learned that war is not so bad,
I learned of the great ones we had had,
We fought in Germany and in France,
And someday I might get my chance,
And that's what I learned in school today,
That's what I learned in school.

What did you learn in school today,
Dear little boy of mine?
What did you learn in school today,
Dear little boy of mine?
I learned our government must be strong,
It's always right and never wrong,
Our leaders are the finest men,
And we elect them again and again,
And that's what I learned in school today,
That's what I learned in school.

R 1 There are a number of differences in the two pictures. You have half a minute to find and mark as many of them as possible. Of course you won't find all the differences in only half a minute, but it is important that you don't work for more than 30 seconds.

You should then describe one of the differences you have found, so that the others can mark it in their books. The most important rule of the game is not to point at a difference you have found or to show it to the others, but to describe it.

Here is an example:

"I've found a difference on the table in the middle of the room. In the bottom picture, there's coffee in one of the cups instead of tea."

R 2

a Listen to the six
conversations on the
cassette and decide
which three conversa-
tions go with these
pictures.

b Now listen to the cassette again and try to say where the people are, who is
speaking to whom (friend, stranger, member of the family, etc), and what they
are talking about. Give reasons for your answers.

	place	speaker 1	speaker 2	event
1				
2				
3				
4				
5				
6				

R 3

Here's a letter a working wife wrote to the Women's
Page of a national daily newspaper in Britain.
If you read the letter carefully, you will find that it
includes 9 words which do not belong in this text.
Find these words and write them down. You can form
a statement with these words which expresses an
opinion about the question discussed in the letter.

a The 9 words that don't belong in the text:

_____   _____   _____

_____   _____

The statement they form:

_____.

b Does this statement express the opinion of the
woman who wrote the letter?
What example does she give to support her opinion?

c What's your opinion?

Family life and working hours

IT WAS with great interest that I read your article concerning family life and working hours. In Sweden, where I come from, I had a well-paid, responsible and highly qualified full-time job. I started work, like most other people, at 8 a.m., finishing at 2.45 p.m. in the summer months job, at 3.45 during the rest of the year. This meant that I could pick up my son from the kindergarden at 3 o'clock in the sunniest five months of the year, at 4 in the remaining seven the months.

Working hours like these make it possible for both parents to be have full-time jobs, while still having enough time for their family. Mum may be less bored, lonely and frustrated (and brings home a good income), Dad has a much better chance to get to know his children and take part in their life, the which may bring both parents to a better understanding of one another.

As a family married woman in Britain it has been impossible for me to understand and accept a family life which means that Dad only sees his children at weekends. As a result of this life I have spent a lot of time with hungry and very tired than children, waiting for the family to be together for the main meal of the day.

"What I don't like about Daddy is that he always puts us to bed," said our youngest son one day when he wanted to have a game after supper. Lots of should British children can't even say that much about their more fathers.

A change of working hours is not the whole answer. But it is a good start, and can be followed by other changes to make it possible for both parents to enjoy their family more: job-sharing, flexi-time, part-time work for both parents and so important on. —
Karen Bergman,
Forest Row, Sussex.

R 4

WHEEL OF FORTUNE

THROW AGAIN!

A thief has stolen my TV.

I've decided to go and live in Australia.

GO BACK TWO SPACES!

Next month is our 25th wedding anniversary.

I'm flying to America soon.

My rich uncle has died.

I've just bought an expensive new car.

MISS A TURN!

START

THROW AGAIN!

explain the purpose

express surprise

say you are sad and why

GO FORWARD TWO SPACES!

The government wants to build a nuclear power station near our town.

make a promise

ask when

express a warning

express your worries

A friend of mine is going camping for 3 weeks in Scotland.

A good friend of mine has just stopped smoking.

express congratulations

express your good wishes

One of my colleagues has just been fired.

say how important and why

say why you are pleased

make a suggestion

STAY WHERE YOU ARE!

MISS A TURN!

My dog has just died.

My TV has broken down.

START & FINISH

My car's been stolen.

My father's starting to learn French.

THROW AGAIN!

Rules of the game

1 This is a game for two players. They need a dice and three counters: one counter each for the outer circle, and one counter for both players together for the inner circle.
2 The aim of the game is to go round the outer circle twice and to reach the finish first.
3 The first player throws the dice and moves his counter around the outer circle. If he lands on a situation space he reads out the situation. The second player then throws the dice and moves the counter around the inner circle. According to the instructions he finds there, he must then give a

suitable reply to the first player's statement. (The second player only moves around the inner circle if the first player lands on a situation space.)
4 If the reply is correct, the second player moves his counter on the outer circle two spaces forward. If his reply is wrong or no reply is possible, he moves two spaces back.
5 Then it is the second player's turn. He throws the dice and moves around the outer circle and the game continues in the same way as above.
6 The player who reaches the finish first after two rounds on the outer circle is the winner.

"Do you know that we only use one third of our brain?"

"I wonder what happens to the other third?"

Which word in each of the groups does not go with three of the others?

The odd word out game R 5

1 a pay
   b cheque
   c sign
   d cash
   e letter

2 a pyjamas
   b bed
   c wear
   d carry
   e sleep

3 a passenger
   b wait
   c call
   d travel
   e bus stop

4 a drive
   b petrol
   c car
   d fill
   e room

5 a camera
   b photos
   c take
   d film
   e watch

6 a sail
   b boat
   c water
   d drink
   e sea

7 a hurt
   b hospital
   c leg
   d rule
   e break

8 a table
   b eat
   c plate
   d dinner
   e order

R 6 a Look at the following list of recorded information services offered by British Telecom.

1 What would you hear if you dialled 8071
  – on Wednesday at 8.00 p.m.?
  – on Thursday at 4.30 p.m.?
  – on Saturday at 8.00 p.m.?
  – on Sunday at 12.05 p.m.?

2 What number would you dial if
  – you were in London and did not know what events were taking place?
  – you wanted to know the snow conditions at the Aviemore Winter Sports Centre in Scotland?
  – you were planning to go sailing in the Bristol Channel?

Recorded information services

Bedtime Stories

From 6pm each night **8071**

Motoring Information

The information given covers roads within 50 miles of each of the following centres:
Belfast **0232 8021**
Birmingham . . . . **021 – 246 8021**
Bristol **0272 8021**
Cardiff **0222 8021**
Leeds, Bradford, Sheffield
  and Doncaster **0532 8021**
London . . . . **01 – 246 8021**
Manchester and
  Liverpool . . . . **061 – 246 8021**
Newcastle and
  Middlesbrough **8021**
Scotland (whole) . . . . . . **031 – 246 8021**
Southampton **0703 8021**

Recipe
Monday to Friday 8am-6pm **8071**

Skiing Information
(1 Dec-30 April; but may be extended)
Skiing conditions at the principal
Scottish ski centres . . . . **031 – 246 8031**

Time
For the Speaking Clock **8081**

Gardening Information
Saturday and
Sunday 8am-6pm **8071**

What's On
For a daily selection of the main events and places of interest in and around
London: in English . . . . . . **01 – 246 8041**
London: in French . . . . . . **01 – 246 8043**
London: in German . . . . . **01 – 246 8045**
Edinburgh (in English only)
  (1 May-30 Sept) . . . . . **031 – 246 8041**

Weather Forecast

Bedford area (40 mile
  radius) . . . . **01 – 246 8099**
Belfast area **0232 8091**
Birmingham area . . . . . . **021 – 246 8091**
Bristol area (including
  Weston-super-Mare) **0272 8091**
Cardiff area **0222 8091**
Devon and Cornwall **0752 8091**
Edinburgh area . . . . **031 – 246 8091**
Essex coast . . . . **01 – 246 8096**
Glasgow area . . . . **041 – 246 8091**
Kent coast . . . . **01 – 246 8098**
Lancs, Merseyside,
  Greater Manchester
  and Cheshire . . . . **061 – 246 8091**
Leeds, Bradford and
  Huddersfield area **0532 8091**
London area . . . . **01 – 246 8091**

b Listen to the cassette and decide what number you would have to dial to hear each of the recordings.

c Listen to the cassette again and make a note of the important information in each recording.

R 7

Charlene Wood, a 26-year-old secretary from Liverpool, has been a good friend of yours for some time. You first met her during a holiday in Austria a few years ago, where she worked for an American company in Salzburg. Although she speaks German quite well, you always write to one another in English. She is single, has no children, and you have visited each other several times over the last few years.

Now you get the following letter from her:

27 Southport Road
Liverpool
August 27th

Dear...,

Forgive me for not writing to you for such a long time, but since I last wrote I've had a lot of problems to deal with. Trade was so bad that the travel agency I was working for closed down last month, and so I'm now one of the millions of people who are out of work. I've been looking round for a job anywhere, but there's no work in sight. There are so many unemployed secretaries that over a hundred people apply for every job that's in the newspaper! It's all rather disappointing, what with all the qualifications and experience I've got. If there's no sign of a new job soon, I'll probably have to leave this flat and look for something cheaper.

How are things with you? I'd love to hear from you. If things were better, I'd try to come and visit you this year. But as the situation is at the moment, I don't think I'll be able to afford it.

Sorry this is such a short letter, but I'm off for another interview this morning. Perhaps I'll have a bit more luck this time!

Looking forward to hearing from you soon,

Regards,

Charlene

A few days after you receive the letter you see this advertisement in your newspaper. You think Charlene might be interested in the job and decide to send her the advertisement with a letter.

Include the following details in your letter:
- Thank her for her letter.
- Say what you think about the news.
- Express your hopes and best wishes for her.
- Say what is enclosed and why.
- Say why you think she may be suitable for the job.
- Offer your help if she gets the job.
Start and finish the letter in the usual way.

Sir–It was with great interest that I read the article on advertising in your magazine last month. I fully agree with what you say about the ways in which advertisers try to influence customers. There are of course so many similar products on the market today that it is very difficult for people to decide between them. But what really makes me angry is when advertisers actually try to make me buy things I don't want or don't need.

For example, even though they keep telling us we can't really live without XYZ sherry, I personally feel it is not necessary for anybody to drink a glass in order to relax. Nor do I like the way they try to suggest that you have to smoke at least one packet of ABC cigarettes a day in order to be a 'real person'. This is just not true.

Last week I took my five-year-old daughter with me to the supermarket. She wanted me to buy a particular brand of toothpaste that she has seen advertised on TV and which is twice as expensive as the brand we have been using for years. When I refused to buy it, she told me I was not a good mother: "Mothers who really love their family buy TOOTHSHINE." She repeated the exact words she had heard on TV.

In this way people are made to think that they have to buy things they don't need, that are just not necessary. I'm glad your magazine has helped to bring this problem to people's notice. **(Mrs) Gill Turner,** Heathfield.

Vivarin keeps you going when the going gets rough.

Working overtime? Beginning to feel the strain? Take a Vivarin Stimulant Tablet. Vivarin's active ingredient is caffeine. It's like having two cups of coffee squeezed into one little tablet. Whether you're studying, driving, or working late, you'll stay alert for hours.

Getting round to Spring Cleaning? There's only one name to remember for all your cleaning needs. Ajax.

All around your house, you can Spring Clean with an Ajax product–from floor to windows and walls to every kind of sink and cooker, even to giving your pots and pans a real going over!

Ajax is the name you know. The name you trust. So, whatever you need to clean your home, Spring into action with Ajax.

Clean up with AJAX

a What does Mrs Turner complain about in her letter?
b Why is she angry about the advertisements she mentions in her letter?
c What do the advertisements on this page try to say?
  Do you accept what they say?

It's (not) necessary (for me) to have …
This product is (not) necessary (for me).

I must have this …
I (don't) have to have …
I have got to have …

I need to/needn't buy …
I (don't) need this product.

That's just not true.
They're wrong when they say …
I don't think you can say that.

Everybody needs a Poncho Cape.

The ingenious hooded weatherproof cape made of strong lightweight vinyl in soft lovat green will protect you from the heaviest downpour. Used flat it's a groundsheet, buy two and make a tent! 84" x 54".

Only £1.95 (plus p&p)

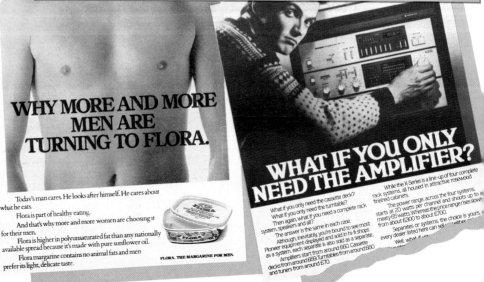

WHY MORE AND MORE MEN ARE TURNING TO FLORA.

Today's man cares. He looks after himself. He cares about what he eats.

Flora is part of healthy eating.

And that's why more and more women are choosing it for their men.

Flora is higher in polyunsaturated fat than any nationally available spread because it's made with pure sunflower oil.

Flora margarine contains no animal fats and men prefer its light, delicate taste.

FLORA. THE MARGARINE FOR MEN.

WHAT IF YOU ONLY NEED THE AMPLIFIER?

What if you only need the cassette deck? What if you only need the turntable? Then again, what if you need a complete rack system, speakers and all?

The answer is the same in each case. Although, inevitably, you're bound to see most Pioneer equipment displayed and sold in hi-fi shops as a system, each separate is also sold as a separate. Amplifiers start from around £60. Cassette decks from around £69. Turntables from around £60 and tuners from around £70.

While the X-Series is a line-up of four systems, all housed in attractive rosewood finished cabinets.

The power range, across the four systems, starts at 20 watts per channel and shoots up to a meaty 65 watts. Whereas the price range rises slowly from around £300 to about £700.

Separates or systems, the choice is yours, every dealer listed here can sell you either.

What we really need is ... A 1

– I think the government should provide more money for industry because we need more robots and computers.
– That's nonsense! What we really need is a shorter working week. Unemployment is costing the country millions. A shorter working week would mean more new jobs.

– In my opinion the government should hurry up and build more nuclear power stations to produce the energy we need for the future.
– I'm sorry, I don't agree at all. What the government really ought to do is make a greater effort to save energy.

That's exactly
That's just
> what we do need.
> what the government should do.
> ought to do.

I (don't) think
> we need ...
> we ought to ...
> the government should ...
> the government ought to ...

I agree with you.

That's nonsense!
I don't agree at all.
I doubt that very much.
I don't altogether agree.

What we really need is ...
What the government ought to do is ...
> should do is ...

a Support one of the following ideas. The others can then either agree or express the alternative opinion.

increase industrial production	protect the environment
improve social services	reduce the number of people working for the state
more teachers	better teachers
earlier retirement age	shorter working week

b Look at the following ideas. Write down possible alternatives.

put up taxes on alcohol
    and cigarettes
higher pensions
save energy
nuclear power stations
better road system
more money for the arts
less money on weapons
job-sharing
free medical services
higher income tax

better information in schools about dangers of alcohol and cigarettes

c Which of those ideas do you support? What are the opinions of other people in your class?

I think the government should increase income tax.

That's nonsense! What they really ought to do is reduce government spending.

A 2 The state of the country – a public opinion poll

An interesting aspect of political life is the way in which political leaders often become unpopular after they have been elected. This happened, for example, to both Jimmy Carter and Ronald Reagan not long after their election to the White House. How quickly public opinion can change can easily be seen by comparing the results of two public opinion polls for Ronald Reagan. They were carried out in October and December 1982, less than two years after he came into power in January 1981. At that time he had been supported by a large majority of the American voters, not only by the well-off and the middle-class but also by trade-unionists and blacks. They all thought he would be able to improve their standard of living and the quality of life in the United States. He had not been in power two years, however, before they started to change their minds. Opinion polls showed how in only three months – that is to say between October and December 1982 – the President lost a lot of his popular support.

a Compare the polls of October and December 1982.

	October 1982 YES	December 1982 YES
Do you support President Reagan's defense policy?	66%	56%
Are you satisfied with President Reagan's tax policies?	42%	37%
Are you in favor of President Reagan's peace policies?	26%	16%
Are you satisfied that President Reagan is leading the country well?	36%	30%

b Fill in the following opinion poll for your government.

	completely satisfied	fairly satisfied	not altogether satisfied	dissatisfied	don't know
economic policy					
defence					
employment					
education					
housing					
transport					
environment					
energy					
health					

c Compare your results with the opinions of other people in your class.

Do you support
Are you in favour of
How satisfied are you with
the present government's ... policy?

d What does your class as a whole think of the various policies of your government?

NAME Constituency	BORN	EDUCATED	JOB/BACKGROUND
ABSE, Leo Torfaen, Wales Labour	1917	London School of Economics	Lawyer
ATKINS, Humphrey Spelthorne Conservative	1922	Wellington College	Officer in the Royal Navy
CHALKER, Lynda Wallasey Conservative	1942	London University	Manager
CLAY, Bob Sunderland North Labour	1946	Cambridge University	Bus Driver, Trade Union Official
DORRELL, Stephen Loughborough Conservative	1952	Oxford University	Company Director
JOHNSTON, Russel Inverness, Scotland Liberal	1932	Edinburgh University	Teacher

B 1

a
Which of these Members of Parliament do you think is most typical of the majority of MPs in the House of Commons?

THE MEN IN POWER

If you take the average MP, you'll find a professional man about 48 years old. He'll probably be well educated and a good talker.

He could be either Labour or Tory and it's a fifty-fifty chance that he went to a private school. But he will not look or sound anything like the great majority of British people.

The British MP, a book published recently by a Bradford University lecturer, shows how Parliament is in danger of getting completely out of touch with the lives of ordinary people.

It shows that 46·7 per cent of all MPs elected in the last ten general elections were educated at public schools. Among Tory MPs the figure was 77·8 per cent, amazing when you remember that only 5·6 per cent of children in Britain go to public schools.

The author also points out that neither of the two main parties makes much effort to give women a fairer share of seats in Westminster. There were twenty-four women MPs in 1945. Now there are twenty-seven. JUST THREE MORE IN FORTY YEARS! What progress!

That is SHOCKING!

Who else is under-represented? The number of manual workers occupying Labour seats fell from 39·2 per cent in 1945 to only 4·6 per cent at the last general election.

Compared with 1945, there are many more teachers, university lecturers, journalists and public relations experts in Parliament, probably as a result of their ability to make excellent speeches and influence the voters. Another group which is well represented in Westminster is lawyers, with about 20 per cent of all MPs.

These figures show that our MPs are totally unrepresentative of the British people. Unrepresentative of ordinary workers. Unrepresentative of women.

Unrepresentative, also, of the growing black population. There is NOT ONE black MP.

In the last century, Benjamin Disraeli described Britain as TWO NATIONS! The rich and the poor, the haves and the have-nots. It still is when you examine the House of Commons.

What we need in Parliament are MPs that really represent the people of this country. More women. More manual workers. More factory managers. More people without old school ties and university degrees.

If more people from the real world outside got into Parliament, perhaps we would have better, more democratic governments.

b
Now read the article.

Which groups does the author think are under-represented and which are over-represented?

Why does he think so? Do you agree?

c
How does the situation compare with your country? How many women/workers/civil servants are elected members of your parliament?

d
Are you satisfied with the situation? What changes do you think are necessary?

Special

S 1 With today's trend towards holidays further and further away from home, it is becoming more and more important to pay attention to the various health risks that you could run. Here is a list of practical tips for travellers:

a
Which of these tips are for what you should do before/during/after your holiday?

TIPS FOR TRAVELLERS

- Avoid alcohol, ice cream and ice-cold drinks in the midday heat.
- Be careful what you eat. Avoid uncooked meat, pork, salads, etc.
- Take simple medical items and medicine for coughs and colds along with you.
- Inquire about health insurance in good time. Don't forget to read the small print, to make sure you are fully covered.
- Do not spend too much time in the sun in the first few days.
- Avoid heavy meals, alcohol and coffee when travelling.
- Go and see your doctor before long journeys.
- When you return home, give yourself time to get used to the climate again. If you feel ill, go to your doctor for a thorough examination.
- Take it easy during the first few days of your holiday. Lie down for an hour in the afternoon.
- Drink only bottled water.
- When you sweat, your body needs extra water and salt.
- Don't forget to have any necessary injections.
- If you get ill during your holiday, see a local doctor. If he cannot help you, he can send you to the nearest hospital for special treatment.

b
You are going to hear an interview from a radio programme about holidays and health.

Well, doctor, what do you think are the most important things our listeners should pay attention to if they are planning a holiday abroad?

First listen to the interview.
Then read the sentences 1–10 on the opposite page.
After that you will hear the interview again in three parts.
After each part you will have time to mark whether the sentences are true -T- or not true -NT-.

Example:

The doctor thinks you should not go on holiday if you are in good health.

The answer is not true, so you mark NT .

1 When planning a journey to a foreign country, the doctor thinks you should always have a word with your family doctor.

2 If you need injections for the country you are visiting, you should have them just before you leave.

3 You can get first-aid kits from your doctor.

4 You should always take a travel-sickness tablet before your journey.

5 Coffee is not good for you just before your journey.

6 You should spend no more than two hours in the sun at the beginning of your holiday.

7 You should only drink bottled mineral water.

8 It's safer to avoid swimming in the sea.

9 You should always take out private insurance.

10 You should have a few days' rest after your holiday.

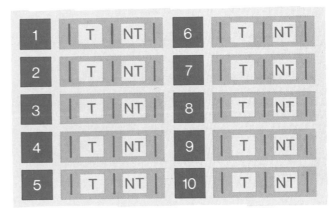

1	T	NT	6	T	NT
2	T	NT	7	T	NT
3	T	NT	8	T	NT
4	T	NT	9	T	NT
5	T	NT	10	T	NT

c
Listen to the interview once more and take notes on the information that is not mentioned in the list of tips.

Has the weather changed?

S 2

Whenever people, especially older people, talk about the 'good old days', they often make them sound so much better than today. They say this is even true of the weather, which according to them is no longer what it used to be. The winters were always freezing cold and icy with frequent periods of frost. The summers were really hot with weeks of bright sunshine and only one or two thunderstorms. Today the seasons seem more and more alike. You get windy or foggy or rainy days all the year round. You can even get snow showers in summer and warm days in the middle of winter.

sun	*Sunny*		thundery
	foggy	winter	
	icy	shower	
storm			rainy
frost			windy

a
Complete the box.

b
Do you agree with the opinion expressed in the text? Describe the typical weather of each of the four seasons in your area.

S 3

a Build words with **-y** in the same way as in *S2* from the following:

beef	fruit	noise	sand
cream	grass	nut	smoke
dirt	hill	oil	soap
dust	meat	rock	stone
fish	milk	salt	taste

b Decide which of the new words from *a* will fit into one or more of the following sentences.

1 Most of their food has a/an ... taste.
2 It's a poor little fishing port with fifty yards of ... beach.
3 We noticed a/an ... smell coming from the kitchen.
4 The countryside's different here. Where I live it's very ....

S 4 Letter Writing

You hear that a good friend of yours in England has just passed a language exam. You decide to send him a letter.

Include the following points:

a How you heard of his success
b Express congratulations
c Say you are taking an exam/your driving test
d Describe the exam/test (include where and when)
e Express your hopes

Begin and end the letter in the usual way.

a The following chart lists eight parties that had candidates in the UK general election in June 1983. You also find the percentage of votes they received in the whole of the UK.
Guess how many of the 650 seats in the House of Commons they each won.

General election 1983

Party	Total votes	% of votes	Number of seats your guess	actual number
Conservative Party	13,012,161	42.4		
Labour Party	8,456,828	27.5		
SDP/Liberal Alliance	7,781,121	25.3		
Scottish Nationalists	334,675	1.6		
Plaid Cymru (Wales)	125,309	0.4		
Unionist Parties (N. Ireland)	435,572	1.4		
SDLP (N. Ireland)	137,012	0.4		
Sinn Fein (N. Ireland)	100,450	0.3		

b Read the following text and compare the actual results with your guess.

Although Prime Minister Margaret Thatcher could have waited almost another year (her maximum period of office of five years not ending until May 1984), she decided to take advantage of the difficult situation that the other main parties were in and called an election on June 9th 1983. The above table shows the percentage of votes the parties received. It proved to be a very successful election for the Conservative Party who, although they lost almost 700,000 votes compared to the previous election in 1979, still managed to increase their number of seats in the House of Commons from 335 to 397. The Labour Party came second, losing about 10% of their 1979 votes, and the number of seats they had in Parliament dropped from 268 to 209. The most interesting result was that of the SDP/Liberal Alliance who, although they got over 25% of the votes (just 2% less than the Labour Party), only won 23 seats (compared with the 209 seats of the Labour Party). Of the other parties, the Scottish Nationalists and the Welsh party Plaid Cymru got two seats each, with 17 seats going to the Northern Ireland parties, 15 of these to the Unionist Parties. These nationalist parties only have candidates in their particular part of the United Kingdom.

This situation is the direct result of the British electoral system, where the candidate who gets the most votes in his/her constituency wins the seat ('direct representation'). As a consequence, there is a more personal relationship between the Member of Parliament and the people in his/her constituency, and they even call him/her 'their MP'. Very few countries in Europe have this kind of system, most of them having some kind of proportional representation, where the number of seats each party receives depends on the number of votes it gains at the general election. The situation in the United Kingdom has led to a movement to introduce proportional representation. Whether this reform will be possible or not will depend on the two largest parties (Conservative and Labour). They enjoy the advantages of the present system, which puts all the smaller parties at a great disadvantage.

c What are the differences between the parliamentary system in your country and the system in the United Kingdom as described in the above text?
Does your country have direct representation or proportional representation? What do you think are the advantages and disadvantages of the two systems?

Review

1 What do the following mean?

CND. That must be the Campaign for Nuclear Disarmament.

EEC BST MP
UK PTO UN
DIY VIP
TUC
VAT GMT
BBC NHS

please turn over
do it yourself
bed and breakfast
European Economic Community
Value Added Tax
British Summer Time
British Broadcasting Corporation
Trades Union Congress
Greenwich Mean Time
very important person
Automobile Association
United Kingdom
National Health Service
Member of Parliament
United Nations

That's probably...

... seems to be...

2

A Canadian friend of yours has written that she is coming to Europe for two weeks next summer.
You may feel you ought to correct some of her ideas.

> Of course I want to make sure I see everything. From Norway to Gibraltar if possible. After all, I'll be there for almost two weeks. I was thinking of bringing lots of warm clothes with me. You never know what the weather'll be like, and I don't want to risk catching a cold. I hope four suitcases will be enough. I was also wondering whether to bring some tinned food with me, as I'm not sure if I'll like European food. By the sound of it, you eat nothing but pork and potatoes in your country. From the postcards you've sent, it seems like such a pretty country. So I think I'll bring my movie camera and get some really good home movies. Is there any point in bringing my lights and other studio equipment with me? The problem is that it weighs about 10 kilos.

Write down the advice you would give your friend in a letter.

If I were you, I wouldn't ...
It's important not to ...
You shouldn't ...

A 1

NEW PAY OFFER TURNED DOWN BY HEALTH UNIONS
DAY OF ACTION GOES ON

TUC
DAY OF ACTION
Before

September 17, 1982

For several months in 1982 there was a disagreement between workers in the National Health Service in Britain and the employers. The government refused to give the workers the pay rise they had asked for. So the TUC took the unusual step of organizing a Day of Action on September 22, 1982. Workers from all sectors of the economy were asked to show their support for the nurses and other workers in hospitals.

a

What is the trade unionist advised not to do?

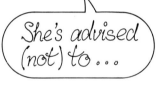

She's advised (not) to ...

– You'd better not stop people from going into the hospital if they want to. Just talk to them and explain the situation. Ask them not to go to work until the strike is over.
– Yes, but what about people who are afraid to strike?
– You could try telling them it's not a good idea to go to work when everyone else is on strike.

b

After reading the following leaflet, what kind of advice would you give your colleagues?

**DOs AND DON'Ts
ON DAY OF ACTION**   **Metropolitan Police**

● Trade unionists are asked not to travel to London by car.

● They are advised not to take their children with them on the demonstration.

● They ought not to carry anything which looks as if it might be a dangerous weapon.

c

What would you say to a colleague or friend who is thinking of
– leaving the union?
– going on strike?
– changing jobs?
– taking part in a demonstration?
– taking early retirement?
...

● Trade unionists are also advised not to argue with the police.

● They are advised to follow the official route.

● Drivers in central London are advised to avoid the Hyde Park area because of the demonstration.

A 2

TUC
DAY OF ACTION
On the day

September 22, 1982

Several hundred thousand workers in the NHS went on strike or stopped work for several hours in their fight for higher pay.

a Alexandra Richards talked to three people taking part in the industrial action.

– ... Yes, I'm a nurse, and we have to work what are known as unsocial hours. But for the work we have to do after 8 o'clock, all we get is 30% more than for normal hours. And it's the same on Saturday and on night duty too.
– So in other words, you think nurses should get more money.
– Yes.

– What's your feeling about the day of action?
– Obviously the last thing we nurses want is to hurt the people in our care; that would be completely against our principles. But the government has always exploited this in the past, and I feel that if we don't fight for our rights, they'll simply carry on exploiting us.
– So, if I've understood you correctly, what you're saying is that normally you wouldn't go on strike as a nurse, but this is a special case and you're willing to make an exception.
– That's right.

– Dave, you're a trade union official. How do you see the position of your union on this?
– Our members expect us to get them a fair day's pay for a fair day's work. Now, we believe in negotiating, in talking to the management, and if it had been at all possible, we would have liked to avoid this kind of action.
– So you believe the unions have been forced into a strike.
– One hundred percent.

What a terrible situation it would be if workers were unable to make an organized protest against management decisions.

It is only the right to strike that gives the worker a voice in his own working life.

People like doctors and nurses have a duty to the rest of society to stay at work whatever happens.

Without the unions, the economic situation of the workers today would be a catastrophe!

In other words ...

So you believe ...

So you're saying ...

If I've understood you correctly, what you're saying is that ...

... people in responsible positions should never go on strike.

... all workers should be allowed to take industrial action.

... unions are necessary to give workers an acceptable standard of living.

... conditions of work would never have improved if it hadn't been for the unions.

b Read these statements about working conditions.
Choose the statement closest to what you think.
Tell other people in your class; listen to check
whether they have understood you properly.

"You can't be happy when you have to work with dangerous machines all day and there's always the fear of getting hurt."	"How can anyone be happy at work if the air is full of dust and smoke and they've always got a cough!"
"What's the point of having good working conditions when you know that your wages at the end of the week are not going to be enough to pay the bills."	"I pity the poor shiftworkers. It's no fun working all night and then spending all day trying to sleep. People aren't robots; they just can't live like that!"
"Who thinks about working conditions when they see how many people are out of work and know that one day it could happen to them."	"I hate the thought of going to work – all those good-looking, boring people, all that stupid typing, and then making coffee for the bloody boss. It makes me sick."
"The millions of people out of work at the moment are only interested in finding a job. They don't care about anything else, and I can fully understand how they feel."	"What about the poor housewife? I bet you wouldn't like to be on duty from sunrise till long after sunset, seven days a week! And see your work undone almost as soon as it's finished, so you have to start it all again the next day! And no pay!"

In other words, you think a housewife's life is hell.

So you're saying you're worried about the high cost of living.

So (if I've understood you correctly,) what you're saying is that the risk of accidents is too high in some jobs.

B 1

TUC DAY OF ACTION

After

a

In the article

- Len Murray says the TUC ...
- Frank Chappell says the movement ...
- Norman Fowler says the government ...

b

Say whether the following statements are true or false.

c

"Public service workers should never go on strike!"

What do you think of this opinion?

d

When do you think it is right for workers to go on strike?

---

23 September 1982

MILLIONS IN ACTION
Murray: Now a new pay offer must be on the way

Millions of workers all over Britain yesterday followed the call to take part in the TUC's day of action for the health service workers. So it must have been a greatly satisfied TUC general secretary, Mr Len Murray, who spoke to the press in the evening. He said the day had been a great success and he warned the government that it was not a good idea to ignore such a demonstration of solidarity with the health workers. In fact, he was expecting a new pay offer to be made in the near future. Otherwise the TUC was going ahead with plans for further action.

Support for the day of action was strongest in Scotland, Wales, Northern Ireland and the north of England. In some parts of the country, teachers and cleaning staff and other workers took part in the day of action, which meant that thousands of children had a day's holiday. But most schools were open for part or all of the day. Most ferry services were stopped and many city bus services were interrupted. But air and train services were not disturbed at all. Most support for the health workers came from the coal mines, docks, shipyards, engineering and printing industries and the public services. In other words, most sectors of the economy were affected by sympathetic action of some kind. And there were demonstrations in most cities and towns, where health workers showed wide support for the unions' call for action.

In the capital, about 120,000 people took part in a large demonstration. Starting from the Embankment, the march took three hours to reach Hyde Park at 2 o'clock to listen to speeches from trade union leaders. It included many young people and families and was quiet and peaceful.

In Hyde Park, Frank Chappell told the marchers that the unions were going to continue the struggle for the health workers. Another leader said: "We will not give in until the health workers win. The government had better not go on cheating the nurses. Let us remind them that this is not going to be the last day of action!"

However, according to the cabinet minister at the centre of the protest, Mr Norman Fowler, the government is not thinking of improving the offer. He said that there was no reason for the government to think over its decision.

---

true | false

1 The day of action was only supported in Scotland and the north of England.

2 The writer of the article is sure that Len Murray was pleased with the day of action.

3 Most schoolchildren were unable to go to school.

4 Though most people were sympathetic, they only marched in a few cities.

5 There was no public transport on the day of action.

6 In most industries there was some form of action.

7 London had a very big demonstration.

8 One trade union leader warned the government against not helping the nurses.

9 The government is going to make a new offer to the health workers.

People with no children are childless. This word is built up of the word child plus -less.
Toothless is built up in the same way and means 'without teeth'.

a

Remind yourselves of the meanings of the following words:

cloud	sense
colour	shape
end	sleep
expression	smoke
fault	sound
friend	star
home	taste
meaning	use

Now fill in the sentences using the correct word.

1 It was a beautiful day; the sun shone warmly in a/an _____ sky.
   (cloudless/starless/colourless/endless)

2 They shook hands, but there was no sign of a welcome in her _____ face.
   (friendless/meaningless/homeless/expressionless)

3 The oranges were nice, but I'm afraid the apples were _____ .
   (tasteless/shapeless/senseless/faultless)

4 All was still in the factory. The robots stood in _____ rows waiting
   for the workers to arrive. (sleepless/useless/soundless/smokeless)

Form sentences using some of the other words.

b

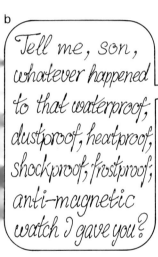

c If something you can believe is believable, what is something you
can move/enjoy/exchange/wash/understand/replace?

d Going a step further, if something you cannot break is unbreakable, e.g. a sheet of
unbreakable glass, what might you describe as unrecognizable/unforgivable/
unpronounceable/unavoidable/unbeatable?

e Build a word from one of those given to complete the sentences.
You may use -y, -less, -proof or -able with or without un-.

1 The crowd was _____ and gave the police a rough time.
   (control/taste/bottom)

2 The young people have to play their instruments in a _____ room in
   the basement of the house. (colour/sound/use)

3 Baby clothes should always be _____ . (shape/noise/wash)

4 It's important to give young people a _____ diet. (count/health/value)

5 The guard saw the _____ body sink below the surface and
   disappear for ever into the depths of the North Sea. (like/accept/life)

S 2 You are going to hear an interview with James Roberts, who used to be a member of the Moonies' religious sect. He will be talking about some of his experiences with the Moonies.

First listen to the interview. Then read the sentences on the right. After that you will hear the interview again in three parts.

After each part you will have time to mark whether the sentences are true -T- or not true -NT-.

Example: James Roberts was a member of the Moonies.
The answer is true, so you mark .

1 James comes from a very religious family.
2 James was a very unhappy person before he joined the Moonies.
3 James was drinking a lot and using drugs when he joined the Moonies.
4 His friends asked him not to join the Moonies.
5 The Moonies were not able to help him with his problems.

6 His first contact with the Moonies was in a pub.
7 He joined the Moonies right away.
8 James had to work very hard with the Moonies.
9 He visited his parents every weekend.
10 It was easy for him to leave the Moonies.

11 James feels that religious sects offer no advantages to their members.
12 Living together in a group is one thing which attracts many young people to religious sects.
13 Most young people in religious groups don't like their leaders making decisions for them.
14 Religion was like a drug for James.
15 James thinks his experience with the Moonies was more negative than positive.

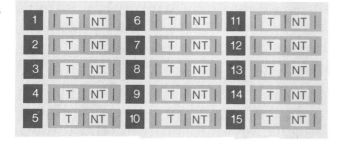

In ON THE WAY you have already met several examples of how Americans speak English. You will have noticed that the way they speak is different from that of people from Britain.

It is not important for you to learn to speak like Americans, unless you want to. Americans will understand you if you use British pronunciation. But it may be helpful to be able to understand Americans and to get used to the way they speak.

a
Listen to the following speakers. Can you recognize which are American and which are not?

b
Listen to the cassette again and take notes on what you think are the main differences between the American and the British speakers. Discuss these in pairs and with your teacher.

Here are two aspects you will probably have noticed.

1 The r
Apart from at the beginning of words, or after b or t etc, British speakers do not pronounce r's. The American r is pronounced everywhere and affects the sounds before it in words like the following:

air	beer	far	hear	search	wear
are	bird	fire	more	sure	work
arm	ear	hair	pair		

2 In some words a different part (syllable) is stressed in American English.

BE		AE	
address	[əˈdres]	address	[ˈædres]
cigarette	[ˌsɪgəˈret]	cigarette	[ˈsɪgəret]
detail	[ˈdiːteɪl]	detail	[dɪˈteɪl]
garage	[ˈgærɑːdʒ]	garage	[gəˈrɑːdʒ]
magazine	[ˌmægəˈziːn]	magazine	[ˈmægəziːn]

Can you find any further examples?

c Spelling can be different in American English.
Look at the following list of words. Which are American and which are British English?

	BE/AE?	The equivalents are spelt:
1 color		
2 centre		
3 (traveler's) check		
4 (driving) licence		
5 theater		
6 catalog		
7 tyre		
8 gray		
9 defense		

Also you may see signs like:

d In American and British English you will also find different words for the same thing.
Find the British English equivalent for the following:

automobile _____
airplane _____
movie _____
gas _____
elevator _____
sidewalk _____
trailer _____
campground _____
vacation _____

holiday pavement
camping site car
film
caravan aeroplane
lift petrol

e You will also find words for things that do not exist in Britain:

carhop

luncheonette

pizza parlor

Can you remember what they are?
Do you know any other American words?

123

1 Review

Do you suffer from stress?

The following test shows whether you suffer from stress and how great the risk of stress is for you. Mark each statement as follows:

1 point if the statement is (almost) always true
2 points if the statement is often/usually true
3 points if the statement is sometimes true
4 points if the statement is occasionally true
5 points if the statement is rarely or never true
for you.

1 I eat at least one hot meal a day.
2 I have seven to eight hours sleep at least four nights a week.
3 I exercise to the point of sweating at least twice a week.
4 I smoke less than half a packet of cigarettes a day.
5 I drink alcohol less than five times a week.
6 I am the correct weight for my height.
7 I can pay my bills.
8 I am a member of a club and/or take part in social activities.
9 I have one or more friends with whom I can talk about personal problems.
10 I am in good health.
11 I am able to speak about my feelings when I am angry or worried.
12 I make sure I enjoy myself at least once a week.
13 I am able to organize my time.
14 I prefer fresh fruit to sweets or chocolate.
15 I find some quiet time for myself during the day.

	total

To get your result add up all your points.
If your total is over 35, you are running some risk of stress. The risk of stress is high if your total is between 50 and 75, and extremely high if it is over 75.

a
Look at the statements in the test. What advice could you give on how to reduce the risk of stress?

To reduce the risk of stress	you should … you ought to … it would be a good idea to …

b
Ask your neighbour about his/her marks for each statement and if necessary give some advice.
– Are you always in good health?
– Well, I occasionally catch a cold, but otherwise I'm usually in good health.

– Do you always eat at least one hot meal a day?
– No, not always.
– If I were you, I'd always try to get a hot meal every day.

– How often do you drink alcohol?
– I normally have a few drinks after work.
– Oh, I think you'd better try to drink less. It's not good for you.

ADVICE ON NUCLEAR SURVIVAL

Advice on how to protect our-selves and to survive a nuclear attack was published yesterday by the Civil Aid organization. Some of the information is very similar to the advice given – or rather kept quiet – in the secret government leaflet 'Protect and Survive' which the Home Office has refused to publish until a short time before the bomb drops.

One of the most important ideas in the Civil Aid leaflet is that of neighbours helping each other. Preparations should be made for neighbours to cook together, using one kitchen for several homes and families.

They also suggest it might be a good idea to get used once again to the more traditional ways of keeping food, since fridges will become useless without electric-ity.

Mr Robin Meads, vice-chair-man of Civil Aid, said at the press conference yesterday that after a nuclear attack people would have to eat whatever they could get when they ran out of the food they had saved. "If you saw a frog run-ning about, you would have to try and catch it, though you would have to wash away the nuclear dust before cooking and eating it."

The leaflet explains that people should expect to have to spend about 14 days in a shelter to avoid nuclear fall-out. The Civil Aid advice is to make sure you have some of those practical things you might need to sur-vive these first two weeks, e.g. matches for lighting fires, string, needles and cotton, etc. And without electricity, a small stove with coal or wood could be a very useful thing to heat tinned food or just to keep warm.

The Civil Aid people also have a word to say about the problem of polluted water. "If water has been polluted by radiation, it should be filtered through clean sand," they say.

a What advice is given in the Civil Aid leaflet?

"They suggest it might be a good idea for you to   "
"Their advice is to …"
"People should …"

What impression does the Civil Aid leaflet try to give?

b Now read the article about Dr Williams, a village doctor from Gloucestershire, and the rather different advice he gives. Then answer the questions.

What advice does Dr Williams give?
What is the difference between the advice given by Dr Williams and that given by Civil Aid?
Whose advice do you think is more realistic?
What other advice would you give?

c What advice would you give governments on how to prevent nuclear war?

"I'd advise them to …"
"My advice would be to …"
"If you ask me, they ought to …"

d Look at the picture of two demonstrators wearing 'Citizens' Survival Bags'. What do they think about survival after a nuclear attack? How do they express their opinion?

WHAT TO DO IF THE BOMB DROPS

"To stop the pain and misery of people suffering from radiation sickness after a nuclear attack, hit them over the head with a large stone." This is the advice of village doctor Barney Williams, who has produced a plan for 'survival' after the bomb. He also says: "If you are badly hurt, please try to die where your body will not pollute water or cause illness to others."

The 44-year-old doctor says that nuclear war is nothing to joke about, and his ten-point plan is no more black humour than the official leaflets planned by the government or Civil Aid. He also says that doctors have been asked by the Home Office to provide plans for patients after an atomic attack, and this is his contribution.

Two demonstrators with their own views about survival. Instructions on the 'survival bags' say: "In the event of nuclear attack: place bag over head; put fingers in ears; face the other way; kiss your loved ones goodbye."

A 2 a The text below is part of an interview with a member of the Campaign for Nuclear Disarmament.
Only the first half of the interview is in the book, but you can hear the whole interview on the cassette.

First look at the following ten statements.
After reading the text, form five sentences from these ten statements, using one of the words in the small box to join two statements together.

The first protests came as early as 1945		the US developed the H-bomb.
CND began in February 1958		the Americans were testing an H-bomb in the Pacific.
The Stockholm Peace Appeal received millions of signatures	after / when / while	a meeting was held in Central Hall, Westminster.
A Japanese fishing-boat was only about 85 miles away		millions of people were shocked by what happened to Hiroshima and Nagasaki.
Many members thought Great Britain would soon give up atomic weapons		CND was formed.

– Here in the studio this evening we welcome Colin Jones, who has been working with CND for over 25 years. Colin, when did CND actually start?
– It officially began in February 1958 when a meeting of interested groups took place in Central Hall, Westminster. But there had been organizations with similar ideas for many years before that. The first protests against the development of atomic bombs were as early as 1945, when millions of people all over the world were shocked by the news of the atomic bombs that had been used against Hiroshima and Nagasaki. Only then did the world realize the danger of these weapons.
– So the protest spread all over the world?
– Yes, it did. The Stockholm Peace Appeal received millions of signatures in 1950, especially after the US developed the even more powerful H-bomb, which greatly increased the fear of nuclear war. Amongst those who signed the appeal were people from Eastern European countries occupied by the Soviet Union. In Great Britain many groups hoped that this country would not follow the American example, risking the lives of millions of people. There were a great number of demonstrations, including one at Aldermaston, where many such demonstrations took place in

the sixties. But in 1952, despite these protests, Great Britain tested her first A-bomb, America the first H-bomb, and one year later, Russia her first H-bomb.
– Wasn't there a terrible accident during an H-bomb test?
– That's right. While the Americans were testing an H-bomb in the Pacific in 1954, a Japanese fishing-boat was about 85 miles away. Though the Americans tried to keep it a secret, it became known when all the crew got ill and one died. Only after that did opposition start to grow quickly in Great Britain. Various committees were formed to stop the testing of nuclear weapons and Labour MPs formed a committee to stop the production of the bomb in Great Britain. These and other groups came together in February 1958 to form CND.
– 1958? That was the year of the first Aldermaston March, wasn't it?
– That's right. But that march had been organized before CND was formed. When CND was formed, many members thought that it wouldn't take long to achieve their aims, that is, for Great Britain to give up production and use of atomic weapons. Never for a moment did they expect that the fight would last so long. Their plan was to organize local groups which would arrange public meetings in the hope of influencing Parliament.

b Now listen to the cassette and try to form four sentences from the following eight statements, using one of the words in the small box to join two statements together.

The most famous CND demonstration was in Trafalgar Square in 1961		they opened a peace camp outside the Greenham Common American base.
There were many demonstrations in the Glasgow area	**after**	32 demonstrators were arrested and sent to prison.
Cooperation between the CND and similiar organizations in Europe increased	**when**	Polaris submarines were stationed in Scotland.
"Women for Life on Earth" became well-known		America developed the neutron bomb.

c Find the sentences in the written text that mean the same as the following and write them on a separate piece of paper.
1 The world only then realized the danger of these weapons.
2 Opposition only started to grow after these events.
3 They never thought for a moment that CND would have to go on for so long.

d Now do the same while listening to the cassette.
1 There had not been open discussion of nuclear weapons before.
2 People only realized later how dangerous it was to live with the bomb.
3 Mrs Thatcher and President Reagan not only believed in the power of nuclear weapons to prevent war, they also greatly increased the amount of money spent on such weapons.

a What is this advertisement trying to say?
What does £16 a week mean to you and your family, and what could you do with an extra £16?
Does your country spend a similar amount of money on weapons?
Why do countries spend so much money on weapons?

B 1

ADVERTISEMENT

The average British family spent £16 a week on arms last year

DON'T FORGET THE H-BOMBS, MUM...

ADVERTISING FOR PEACE P.O. Box 24, Oxford OX1 3JZ

This advert is being used in a national billboard

b The article below deals with the amount of money spent for military purposes. Read the article and number the following points in the order in which they are mentioned in the text.

○ military spending in Third World countries

○ arguments for military spending

○ money spent in the world on weapons and money spent on education

○ comparison of spending in Third World countries and in Great Britain

○ dangers to world peace

○ amount of food and weapons available in the world

WORLD'S SPENDING ON WAR MATERIAL GOES UP AND UP

The countries of the world last year spent over £212,000 million on various forms of military activity, including £60,000 million on weapons. Each year the average amount of money spent on each of their soldiers is £9,000, compared with £130 a year on education for each school-age child.

The spending on weapons is now 70 per cent higher than it was in 1960, and for the last seven years the increase in spending on weapons has been greater than inflation. These figures have been published in a report by Mrs Ruth Leger Sivard, who works for a private organization. Her publishers, who include the British Council of Churches, say that this is the only report that compares military and social spending.

Another figure she publishes is that, expressed in tons, there is more war material on earth than food. The situation is particularly bad in the Third World countries. The poor nations have increased their military spending by 400 per cent, compared with 44 per cent among the developed nations. What this means in Ethiopia, as an example, is that it spent £64 million for military purposes, compared with £35 million on education and £13 million on health. In Pakistan the figures are £390 million on weapons, £141 million on education and £40 million on health. Britain by comparison spent

£5,537 million on its military needs, £6,673 million on education and £5,720 million on health.

The increase in numbers of weapons all over the world increases the power and the danger of the armed forces in the present situation, writes Mrs Sivard. In the developing nations in particular, the armed forces are often the largest group of trained people. As a result of this they are getting more and more political power, and in many nations they are in firm control of the government. In Latin America and among the new nations of Africa, one government in two is now under direct military control.

Military spending is often de-fended as a way of helping the economy of the country, a way of building the nation. It is also said that it increases investment and employment. "The point is, no-body has yet been able to show that military spending has a posi-tive effect on economic develop-ment," says Mrs Sivard. "Instead it is much more likely to make things worse, as it means that people, materials and money are used for the wrong purposes." There is no question, however, that military spending and the production of weapons for sale serve the interest of certain people and certain countries. In many parts of the world, the import and export of weapons has become big business.

c Answer the following questions.
1 How much did the countries of the world spend on weapons in the year before the article was written?
2 What is the average amount of money countries spend a year on each of their soldiers?
3 How much did Ethiopia spend on education and defence?

4 How much did Pakistan spend on health?
5 By how much have Third World countries increased their military spending since 1960?
6 Why have the armed forces got so much political power in many countries?
7 What is said about military spending and the economic development of a country?
8 What does the text say about the trade in weapons?

d Do you agree with your government's spending for military purposes?
What would you advise the government to spend money on instead of weapons?

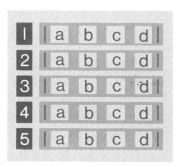

In each of the following five situations you will hear one person speaking. Listen to what the person says, then read the question, then listen again and decide which answer is correct. Mark your answer a, b, c or d in the box.

1 You are on a ferry from Calais to Dover. Just as you are approaching Dover you hear an announcement. Does it mean that
   a all passengers should now leave the ship?
   b all passengers should now go to their cars?
   c car passengers should now go to their cars?
   d car passengers should wait for the next announcement?

2 You come back to your hotel at half past six in the evening. The receptionist gives you a message. What does she tell you?
   a Mr Brown will phone later.
   b Mr Brown will be coming again tomorrow morning.
   c Mr Brown has asked you to come round to see him.
   d Mr Brown has been waiting for you for half an hour

3 You are in a town in England looking for the Hotel Antoinette. You decide to ask a policeman for help. He tells you that the Hotel Antoinette is
   a next to the theatre.   c near the park.
   b opposite the traffic lights. d in North Street.

4 You want to take a bus from the hotel to the station but are not sure which bus to take. A bus stops at the bus stop and you ask the driver if it goes to the station. What do you find out?
   a The 63 will take you straight to the town hall.
   b The 63 will arrive in about 5 minutes.
   c If you take this bus you will have to change.
   d The town hall is next to the station.

5 You are on a train. Another passenger speaks to you just as the train stops at a station. The passenger asks you
   a if you can help her with her luggage.
   b if you would look for a free seat for her.
   c if you would look after her luggage while she goes to the dining-car.
   d if you would make sure nobody takes the two seats while she is away.

How much is a housewife worth? S 2

A Sunday newspaper reported recently that an insurance company has calculated the cash value of a housewife's work at almost £220 per week, that is over £11,000 per year.

Form groups of three. Two people play the parts of the interviewers, one person answers the questions. The first interviewer's questions are in the green parts of the snake, and the second interviewer's questions in the blue parts.

1 What's your reaction to this figure? Are you surprised? (Why/Why not?)

2 They made a list of 17 different jobs that housewives have to do. Can you suggest what some of them were? (Anything else? Do you think that is realistic?)

3 Do you think that housewives should receive a weekly wage for their work? (Why's that?)

6 Some people say that complete equality between husband and wife is not possible. What's your opinion? (Anything else? Does it make any difference if there is a family?)

5 Do you think the situation is the same for those wives who are in full-time or part-time paid employment? (In what way?)

4 If the idea of a weekly wage for housewives were introduced, who do you think should pay? (The husband perhaps?/The state?/Who else?)

7 Do you think children suffer if both parents go out to work? (What makes you think that?)

8 After we have finished you will have to tell the class what we have been talking about. What will you say?

9 The insurance company has also worked out the cost of the work a husband does in the home. My friend here read the report. Ask him/her for this information.

10 (£68 a week)

S 3

1 You shouldn't put all your _____ in one basket.
   a eggs
   b apples
   c wishes
   d sweets

2 Don't _____ your bridges before you come to them.
   a build
   b buy
   c cross
   d burn

3 A penny _____ is a penny earned.
   a bought
   b saved
   c spent
   d lent

4 First come, first _____.
   a go
   b served
   c arrived
   d leave

5 A _____ in the hand is worth two in the bush.
   a pencil
   b bird
   c tiger
   d photograph

a Complete the five proverbs. The sentences in the box below will help you to understand the meaning. Mark your answer a, b, c or d in the second box.

1 It is important not to risk everything at one time.
2 Don't make your decisions until it is necessary.
3 If you spend less, you'll have more money in your pocket.
4 If you want something, it is best to ask for it before anyone else.
5 It is better to have a little than to have only the hope of getting more.

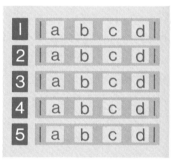

b Choose a, b, or c to complete the following text. Mark your answers in the box.

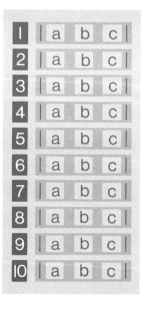

THE NEW YORK SHELTON GUEST CARD

The New York Shelton is pleased *1 a)* to welcome *b)* welcome *c)* in welcoming you to New York City. We are happy to have you as our *2 a)* stranger *b)* guest *c)* visitor and our wish is to make your *3 a)* stay *b)* journey *c)* rest both enjoyable and memorable. To avoid any *4 a)* money *b)* problems *c)* cash at check-out time we wish to advise you of the hotel credit policy. You may *5 a)* settle *b)* solve *c)* give up your bill by cash, traveler's checks or major credit cards, including American Express, Diners Club and Master Charge. Persons *6 a)* who would pay *b)* paying *c)* to pay by personal check should visit with the Lobby Credit Manager 24 hours before they *7 a)* were leaving *b)* will leave *c)* leave. If you *8 a)* would wish *b)* will wish *c)* wish to have credit, you are requested to talk to the Lobby Credit Manager when you check in. Please do not hesitate *9 a)* asking *b)* to ask *c)* ask for assistance *10 a)* some *b)* a *c)* any time we can be of service to you. Thank you.   The Management

Blowin' in the wind

Bob Dylan is one of the best known representatives of the protest song movement which started in the sixties among young people in the United States and Great Britain. The protest was directed against war and weapons in general and against the war in Vietnam and nuclear armament in particular. But the protest also included other aspects of society and was directed against what was called the establishment. "Blowin' in the wind" is probably Bob Dylan's best known song. It has been translated into many languages and has thus become very popular all over the world.

How many roads must a man walk down
Before you call him a man?
Yes, 'n' how many seas must a white dove sail
Before she sleeps in the sand?
Yes, 'n' how many times must the cannon balls fly
Before they're forever banned?
The answer, my friend, is blowin' in the wind,
The answer is blowin' in the wind.

How many times must a man look up
Before he can see the sky?
Yes, 'n' how many ears must one man have
Before he can hear people cry?
Yes, 'n' how many deaths will it take till he knows
That too many people have died?
The answer, my friend, is blowin' in the wind,
The answer is blowin' in the wind.

How many years can a mountain exist
Before it's washed to the sea?
Yes, 'n' how many years can some people exist
Before they're allowed to be free?
Yes 'n' how many times can a man turn his head,
Pretending he just doesn't see?
The answer, my friend, is blowin' in the wind,
The answer is blowin' in the wind.

Listen to the song.

a Which of the following questions goes with which verse of the song?
  1 When will people take a greater interest in the way other people are treated?
  2 When will there be an end to war?
  3 When will people become more aware of human misery caused by war?
b Does Bob Dylan give an answer to the questions he asks in the song?

Review

1 Unidentified flying objects

– Now then, Mr Brooks, could you just tell us again what you saw?
– I was on the train in the sleeping-car. I had just turned out the lights and was taking a last look out of the window when I suddenly noticed something strange in the sky. Now it was just after sunset, about eight o'clock, and there wasn't much light, but it was enough for me to see that the object was moving slower than a plane would. It's very difficult to describe what it looked like really, but it reminded me of a very large cigar.

a
Which of these UFOs do you think it was that Mr Brooks saw?

b
Imagine you have seen one of the strange objects in the pictures above. It was such an unusual sight that you thought it would be a good idea to report it to the British UFO Research Association. Fill in the form.

c
Other people in your class have seen similar objects. Talk to them about it and try to find someone who has seen the same thing as you.

Unidentified Flying Object

Report no. ....
Name.. Date of birth..............................
Address ....
Time of observation .... Your position..........................
Position of object.................................... Distance from you ....
How long in sight?...
Description of object (shape, size etc) ....
....
Position of any lights/motors/windows..
Was object moving?.............. If so, in what direction? ....
Speed of object .... Did it make any sound?/What?..............
....
What else did you notice? ....
....
Was object photographed? .... Are prints available?...............

It was similar to...

It was moving more quickly than a...

It was (something) like a...

It disappeared faster than I could follow with my eyes.

d
People who have seen the same thing should prepare a report together for the rest of the class. Listen to the reports and say which of the objects they are about.

Apartheid A 1

In South Africa the 2 million whites are in control of a government which rules over 15 million blacks. The system of apartheid separates the population into three classes: whites, coloureds and blacks. The class a person belongs to determines where he can live, whether he is allowed to vote and what his basic civil rights are. This system has a number of extremely unpleasant aspects.

Those people who have never been near Soweto, or who live in places where all people are treated as people, if there is any such place in the world, cannot imagine what a Soweto hostel is like.

The long straight rows of grey huts with rough, asbestos roofs remind you of a Nazi concentration camp.

It was the first time that I had been to the hostel to visit someone, and naturally my senses were sharp. The first thing that told you you were in a different place was the smell hanging in the air – a mixed smell of spoilt food, rubbish, urine, dirty water and toilets. It was like a cowshed. It made me sick and ashamed to think that it was humans who let other humans live like that, treating them worse than wild animals: and yet it is their sweat that keeps the economy of the country going.

Inside, the men are crowded together in the narrowest of spaces. You have no private life here. You sleep in one corner of a small dark room 80 short centimetres from the man next to you and almost touching the man below you, sixteen men to a room, forty-eight men to one hut only forty metres long.

a Which of the following statements are correct?

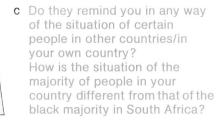

The author

is giving arguments for and against apartheid.

is telling a story.

is giving advice to visitors to South Africa.

is describing a scene.

wants the reader to have certain feelings.

is complaining about the way some people treat their homes.

b Which words in the text helped you to decide?
What do these words tell you about the living conditions of the black workers in South Africa?

c Do they remind you in any way of the situation of certain people in other countries/in your own country?
How is the situation of the majority of people in your country different from that of the black majority in South Africa?

A 2

Aborigines

All over the world, racial minorities are being badly treated and exploited. Those people who are least able to defend themselves are being cheated and robbed by the strong, the organized and the rich.

In Australia the situation is no different. The original inhabitants of the country, a black race of people known as the Aborigines, have suffered great harm through the kind of treatment they have been receiving from the whites. One of the main problems is the question of land. The whites are only interested in what they can get out of it. But to the Aborigines, the land is a living thing, and for many thousands of years it has had a deep religious meaning for them. And the sad fact is that the Aborigines are continually being forced off their land – through legal tricks and as a direct result of white government policy.

There are other problems. Although the Aborigines are only 0.35 % of the total population of Australia:

● In New South Wales prison sentences are being given to 34 times as many Aborigines arrested for being drunk as are being given to whites arrested for the same thing.

● In Victoria Aborigines have 45 times more chance of going to prison than whites, and Aborigine children are 26 times more likely to be taken away from their parents and put into children's homes than white children.

● In Western Australia death rates among black children are now six times higher than among white children.

● In the continent as a whole there is 20 times as much chance of an Aborigine going blind as there is for a white. And the death rate among whites is less than half as high as among the Aborigines.

	whites	Aborigines
numbers of people	14.85 mill.	50,000
unemployment rate	5.7 %	57 %
average weekly wage	$160	$35
cases of leprosy	30	820
rate of diabetes	2 %	30 %
average life expectancy	70 years	50 years
share of budget	99.35 %	0.65 %

adapting to 'civilization'

corrugated iron huts

unemployed Aborigines in Alice Springs

Aborigine wood-carving

Aborigine in ritual war-paint

a
Compare aspects of white and Aborigine life.

There	is/are	twice	as much ... as whites.
		half	many ... Aborigines.
Aborigines	are	20 times	high ...
Whites	have		
	earn	45 times	more chance of ...ing ...
	live	...	more likely to ... than ...
	...	...	longer than ...
			more/less than ...

b Complete these four statements about the situation in Australia, using 'most' or 'least'.

1 For the Aborigines, land is one of the _____ important things in life.
2 Politically, the Aborigines are the _____ powerful group in Australia.
3 One of the _____ serious Aborigine problems is unemployment.
4 The Aborigines are the _____ respected race in Australia.

c Read these statements and say what you think about them.

1 Perhaps the most positive aspect of the situation in Australia is the way the whites look after Aborigine children.
2 Generally speaking, the Aborigines are one of the most fairly treated minorities in Australia.
3 Aborigines are very tough and strong. I think that health is probably the least urgent of their problems.
4 We've got to stop spoiling the Aborigines. In my opinion we give them far too much help.
5 Some of the most successful people in Australia are Aborigines.
6 The whites are most interested in protecting Aborigine culture.

How can anybody say that when Aborigine children are being forced to grow up in homes, away from their parents?

Their rights needs ...	are/aren't being	respected protected lookod after destroyed	by the whites.
Their culture land ...	is/isn't being	stolen ...	

Today we're discussing the native people of New Zealand...

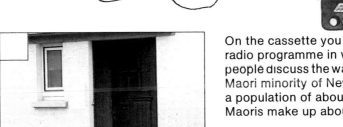

Maoris B 1

On the cassette you will hear a radio programme in which two people discuss the way of life of the Maori minority of New Zealand. In a population of about 3 million the Maoris make up about 8 per cent.

a
The pictures are of things mentioned in the programme. Number them in the right order.

135

b Now listen to the cassette again and say whether the following statements are true or false.

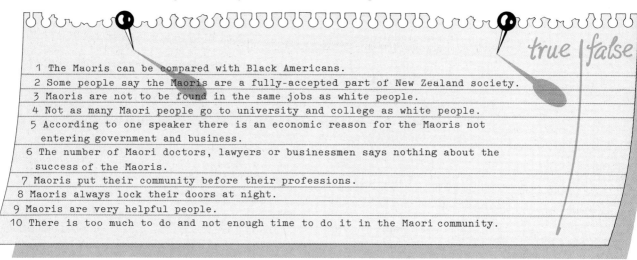

true / false

1 The Maoris can be compared with Black Americans.

2 Some people say the Maoris are a fully-accepted part of New Zealand society.

3 Maoris are not to be found in the same jobs as white people.

4 Not as many Maori people go to university and college as white people.

5 According to one speaker there is an economic reason for the Maoris not entering government and business.

6 The number of Maori doctors, lawyers or businessmen says nothing about the success of the Maoris.

7 Maoris put their community before their professions.

8 Maoris always lock their doors at night.

9 Maoris are very helpful people.

10 There is too much to do and not enough time to do it in the Maori community.

c 1 Do you think the Maoris are right to criticize Western society for being too restless?

2 Is it better for a minority group to be peacefully integrated into the majority or to remain separate? Are there any dangers?

3 Are there different national groups and races living in your country? Does this cause any problems?

4 What do these groups contribute to life in your country?

Special

S 1 You are planning a four-week holiday in Britain in July and have put your name down for a summer holiday course in Bangor. A friend of yours in Wigan has written you a letter inviting you to stay with her for a while during your holidays.

Write her a letter and include the following points:

a Thank her for her invitation

b Describe the course

c Say when you would like to visit her

d Ask how to get to Wigan

e Ask what you should bring with you to Britain

Begin and end your letter in the usual way.

UNIVERSITY COLLEGE OF NORTH WALES
COLEG PRIFYSGOL Y GOGLEDD
YSGOL HAF BANGOR
BANGOR SUMMER SCHOOL

Courses available this summer:

1 English Language, July 5-26, £234
2 English Literature, July 5-26, £234
3 Introducing Wales – Past and Present, July 12-26, £156
4 Dysgu Cymraeg (Learning Welsh), July 12-19, £78
5 Practice in English Conversation, July 12-19, £78
6 American Slang, July 12-19, £78

Fee for the course includes tuition, accommodation and full board.
A deposit of £25 must be sent with each application.

Address: Summer School Secretary, University College of North Wales, Bangor, Gwynedd, LL57 2 DG

Send stamped addressed envelope for further information, including detailed timetable.

a First read the article, then choose the answers to the questions 1–3 and mark the correct letter (a, b, c or d) in the box.

Angry Beverley accuses supermarket of discrimination

Left speechless...

By AUBREY CHALMERS

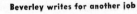
Beverley writes for another job

HOUSEWIFE Beverley Reddel thought a part-time job in a supermarket would be just right for her.

But after what seemed like a satisfactory interview, things suddenly went wrong.

While 20-year-old Beverley was filling in an application form, a personnel officer noticed she was left-handed.

And that, says Beverley, lost her the chance of the £19-a-week job filling shelves on three nights a week at Sainsbury's in Tamworth, Staffordshire.

Beverley, the mother of a two-year-old girl, said yesterday at home in Stoneydelph, Tamworth:

Girl unfit for 'right-handed' job

'The personnel officer told me that being left-handed was a problem.

'She said that although I had applied for a job as a shelf-filler they were occasionally asked to operate checkout tills* – and they were built for right-handed people.

'She asked me to ring her the next day, when I was told: "Sorry, you cannot reach our standards because you are left-handed."'

Beverley was left speechless!

She said: 'I never thought that anything like this could happen. I felt I'd been discriminated against. I wasn't even given a chance to prove I could do the job.'

The manager of the Sainsbury's store, Mr Stephen Plowright, who was away on holiday when the interview took place, refused to discuss the problem yesterday.

But at the London office of the company, a spokesman said: 'We have a number of left-handed people working in our shops and the company's policy is quite clear. We do not discriminate between left-handed and right-handed people.'

He added: 'I suppose that there must have been some sort of misunderstanding at the interview and we are looking into it.'

*checkout till = where you pay in a supermarket

1 The supermarket would not give Beverley the job because
   a the company only wanted right-handed people.
   b she could not use a telephone properly.
   c shelf-fillers were not allowed to handle cash.
   d the tills were not suitable for left-handed people.

2 Beverley was told she had not got the job
   a when she filled in the application form.
   b at the end of the interview.
   c when she phoned the personnel officer the next day.
   d when the manager returned from his holiday.

3 In London they said they
   a didn't really know what had happened at the interview.
   b supposed that people are generally right-handed.
   c didn't discuss whether people were right- or left-handed.
   d had a policy of only employing a certain number of left-handed people.

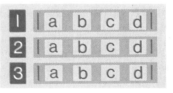

b Which of the following reports deals with the same news as "Left speechless..."?

GREAT Grandmother Doris Pickering entered a television quiz show and won £50, a clock and the chance of seeing her long-lost sister Gertrude Woodmansey again.

Gertrude, 80, of Bridlington, Humberside, and Doris, 74, Collingham, Yorks, parted 53 years ago when Gertrude left home to get married.

But Gertrude recognized Doris when she appeared on the Mr and Mrs show, and now both of them are looking forward to getting together again.

A ten-year-old girl saved the life of a widow who lay helpless in her home for five days after she had fallen while going upstairs.

Beverley Shelton noticed papers and letters piling up on the doorstep at the home of 87-year-old Irene Lewenden.

Beverley told the police, who broke in and found Mrs Lewenden lying on the floor at the foot of her stairs with a broken hip.

Mrs Lewenden of Tamworth, Staffs had wrapped herself in newspapers when she got cold and had kept herself alive on a few pieces of bread and a few drops of milk which she had put out for the cat in the hall. Now Beverley is to receive a Citizen of the Month award from the police.

Mrs Lewenden said: "I call her my darling girl. I was lying there and I couldn't get up.

"I kept on calling out, but no-one could hear my shouts. Beverley is really bright. It's thanks to her that I am still here."

A WOMAN claimed yesterday that she was turned down for a job filling supermarket shelves because she was left-handed.

Beverley Reddel, 20, applied for a part-time job at Sainsbury's in Tamworth, Staffs.

She said: "They told me there might be difficulties because it was possible I would have to work on check-out tills and they were designed for people who are right-handed."

Last night Sainsbury's were holding an inquiry. A spokesman said: "We don't discriminate against people for being left- or right-handed."

GREAT grandmother Gertrude Woodmansey, 80, of Bridlington, Humberside, was watching a TV quiz show when she recognized one contestant as her sister Doris, 74, whom she hadn't seen for more than 50 years.

WIDOW, Irene Lewenden, 87, lay helpless on the upper floor of her home in Tamworth, Staffs for five days after breaking a hip...until Beverley Shelton, ten, saw newspapers piled up on the doorstep and phoned the police.

c Find other articles that belong together in pairs. What additional information is there in the longer article that is not in the shorter article?

How important is this information? What other differences are there between the two articles?

S 3 Choose a, b or c to complete the following text and mark the correct letter in the box.

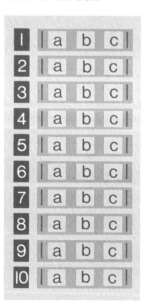

Everybody makes mistakes

A man *1a)* was *b)* were *c)* has been in a hotel restaurant when the bill came. He signed his name to it, but couldn't *2a)* remind *b)* remember *c)* think his room number. So he looked at his watch!

In getting ready for a party, someone else carefully prepared a cake and a salad, then put the cake in the fridge and the salad in the oven.

Mistakes like this happen to all of us once in a while and, *3a)* if *b)* because *c)* unless they cause embarrassment, usually seem to be a strange, but harmless part of our life. But in certain jobs they can be *4a)* helpful *b)* dangerous *c)* lucky. By accident, an air-traffic controller once gave a plane the signal to take off on the left runway when he meant the right one. Although confusing right and left is one of the *5a)* most common *b)* quickest *c)* lightest mistakes people make, in the case of the plane, it could have caused a very *6a)* serious *b)* difficult *c)* heavy accident.

7a) Even when *b)* Also when *c)* Although Freud believed that we express our secret feelings and wishes through our mistakes, modern scientists feel that they can be better explained by looking *8a)* after *b)* at *c)* for the human mind as a computer. Sometimes it is defeated by too *9a)* many *b)* few *c)* much information. People often make mistakes when they are thinking about a lot of things at the same time.

A friend of mine reported that before starting to work at his desk at home, he first went into the bedroom. There he realized that he had forgotten what he had gone there for. "I just stood there," he *10a)* meant *b)* told *c)* said, "hoping that something in the bedroom would remind me." He finally returned to his desk, realized that his glasses were dirty and, smiling to himself, went back into the bedroom to pick up the handkerchief he needed to clean them.

What would you say in the following situations?

An English friend has come to stay with you for a few days.

a You want to show him an interesting place in your area. Tell him what it is and describe it.

b It's his birthday. What do you say? Suggest a way of spending the evening.

c In a department store your friend sees a present for his wife. You have seen the same article at a much lower price in your local second-hand shop. What advice do you give him? Give reasons.

d You go out for a meal together and he wants to pay for everything. Refuse and give reasons.

e The day before he wants to return to England your car develops engine trouble, so that you can't take him to the airport. Explain the problem and tell him how to get to the airport.

f He wants to say cheerio to your brother before he goes, but due to an important business appointment, your brother has had to leave the house early. Explain the situation.

Interview with an American Indian

Interviewer: Rolling Thunder, let's talk about the problems that have existed – and unfortunately – continue to exist between Indians and the other peoples that have come to live in this country. How did all the trouble start?

Rolling Thunder: Probably the best way to begin would be to tell you about the history of just one of the many treaties made between the United States Government and the _____ Indian tribes in this country. The story of the Shoshone Treaty, as our people remember it, is a very sad one to tell. It was signed by the principal Indian chiefs, approved by the Congress of the United States and paid for by the Indians, in blood, in a most horrible manner. At that time you see, the white people in these parts were few in number, and they came to the Shoshone people _____ for a peace treaty. The United States was at war within itself, the North against the South, and President Lincoln _____ gold from California in order to pay his soldiers. But the North couldn't spare any soldiers to protect all the stagecoaches carrying the gold across the _____. That is why they wanted to sign a peace treaty with the Indians through whose lands the stagecoaches had to _____. Therefore, the US Government announced that it would like to meet with the chiefs of the Western Shoshone Nation for the purpose of _____ such a treaty. Once a date was agreed upon, the Indians were informed that there would be a big meeting and feast and that they should come without their weapons. On the day of the _____ the Shoshone people and their leaders gathered in the Ruby Valley. So did the Government officials. The soldiers who came with them left their rifles in big piles. However, as soon as everyone was in place, the white soldiers brought out an Indian prisoner who was accused of robbing a stagecoach, picked up their weapons and _____ him. That killing would serve as a lesson, they said, to any other Indian who might have been thinking of trying to stop white people from traveling _____ Indian lands. Then they cut up the dead Indian and cooked him in a big iron pot! Finally, the other Shoshone people were forced to eat their dead brother. After that _____ event, the Treaty of 1863 was signed.

asking	meeting	continent
needed		travel
	shot	various	signing
terrible		through

a Complete the text, using the words in the box.

b Now listen to the original interview on the cassette and compare it with your answers.

c How does this interview help to explain the bad feelings that many American Indians have towards the US government today?

R 1 Nancy Reynolds is a 10-year-old girl living in Davenport, Pennsylvania. On the cassette, a radio reporter describes the situation that she and her family are in. Like many other families in their area, they are suffering because of the difficulties in the local steel industry.

a While you are listening to the report, take notes of the information you hear about Nancy and her family.
– What was Nancy doing when the reporter first saw her?
– Why are the steelworkers and their families so angry?
– Why is the situation so difficult for the children in particular?
– What effect does the situation have on family life?
– What do the families most hope for?
– What do you think is the most interesting and the most surprising piece of information in the report?

b As you have good friends in Pennsylvania, you decide to write to them to ask what further information they can give you about the situation described in the radio programme. Include the following points in your letter:
– Tell your friends about the report.
– Say what you found interesting and/or surprising.
– Give your own opinions and make comparisons with your own experience.
– Ask what your friends think about the information given in the programme and ask for more information.

R 2 What would you do in the middle of a party at your home if you discovered that you hadn't provided enough drinks? In a case like that, the people of Colchester can take advantage of an offer from a local taxi firm.

a Read the advertisement on the opposite page and then write down the kind of things AAB minicabs can do for housewives/the elderly/car-owners/others.

b Now say whether these statements are true or false.

true/false

1 If you have a car, this service is not much use to you.
2 You can send your children alone in an AAB taxi.
3 You have to pay more if you want to take a cab at 2 a.m.
4 You can take an AAB cab for the whole day if you want to.
5 If you are ill in bed, there's nothing the taxi service can do for you.
6 For a small group, a trip in a taxi may be as cheap as going by bus or by train.
7 You can ask an AAB taxi-driver to go shopping for you.

c Have you ever used a taxi service in ways like these?
In what other ways could you use this kind of taxi service?
Is there a similar kind of service where you live?
Do you think there is/would be a demand for it?

Colchester's Unique Service

Everyone knows our reputation as the largest, most reliable 24 hour cab company in East Anglia, but many do not realize that taking people from point A to point B is only a small part of our service. We can all find ourselves in a situation where we have to fight against time, or bother a friend or neighbour – no need just RING

Colchester 76226-7-8
42233, 44454 or 70500

Housewives
Can't reach the school to pick up the children in time?
Why not arrange with friends to go shopping or to the theatre?
Must get a message to someone not on the telephone?
Need an item of shopping or left an article in a store? **Ring us.**

Motorists
You need us too – in event of breakdown, out of petrol, a tow home or assistance on a jump start. We will pick up spares for the 'do-it-yourself' man. Convey you to and from the garage during servicing.

Businessmen
Cut out wasted staff and vehicles, we can take messages, documents, cash or even large parcels. We will undertake the transport of yourself, your staff and your clients.
Call us and open an account tomorrow.

Senior Citizens
Something heavy to be moved? Keep your independence, **ring us.** We will also go to the doctor pick up a prescription, take it to the chemist to be made up and deliver it to your door.

Mr, Mrs or Miss Citizen
Forgotten anniversary or guilty conscience, we will purchase, wrap and deliver any gift.
Rushing out? We can collect clothes from the cleaners or buy a pair of tights.
Cosy indoors? We can deliver cigarettes, food or drink.

How does it work?
24 hours per day our team of telephonists and radio controllers are awaiting your call. When you request a car or an estate car the details are transmitted by radio to the nearest car to you, out of our 45 vehicle fleet.

What will it cost?
The best is not always the most expensive! We operate an extremely efficient owner-driver system which enables us, with the lower overheads, to run at very reasonable rates. (If you use your car on short journeys only, we are probably cheaper.)

Example Fares
To give you an idea of the cost of hiring an AAB MINICAB:
1 Anywhere within the town boundary to the centre is around 85 p.
2 Brightlingsea or West Mersea to Colchester centre is £2.80.
3 A car for central London is approximately £18.
4 An 8 hour tour of Constable Country with only minimal local mileage would be in the region of £30.

If you are planning a trip, ring us for an estimate beforehand, you will find it will compare very favourably with public transport, especially if there are 3 or 4 in your party to share the cost, and there are no hidden extras for persons, VAT or luggage. Nor any fare increase after midnight.

Remember we provide a service which is unique, just

RING 76226

You are planning to join a group of people who are going to occupy the same house and share the work of running the home for three years. There are naturally things you like doing and things you don't, and you are interested in finding a group where the work you will have to do is pleasant for you.

R 3

a Mark each of the following with 1, 2 or 3.

1 = work you would not mind doing or learning to to
2 = work you would rather not do
3 = work you wish to avoid at all costs!

	handling the accounts
	buying food supplies
	keeping the house tidy
	growing food
	repairing machinery
	looking after children
	taking care of animals
	cooking and making jam
	earning money

	washing and repairing
	knitting and sewing
	decorating and painting
	doing house repairs
	looking after the sick
	organizing holidays
	answering letters/phone
	planning leisure activities

b Now form groups of 3 or 4 and find out if you could live together. Discuss the kind of work you are prepared to do and try to come to an agreement. If this is impossible for you, go and join another group. The game is over when all members of the class are in a group where they feel comfortable.

c Report back to the class about the problems you had in forming the groups and if/how you solved them (for example, deciding to share certain tasks, etc.).

WHO-WHERE-WHAT-GAME

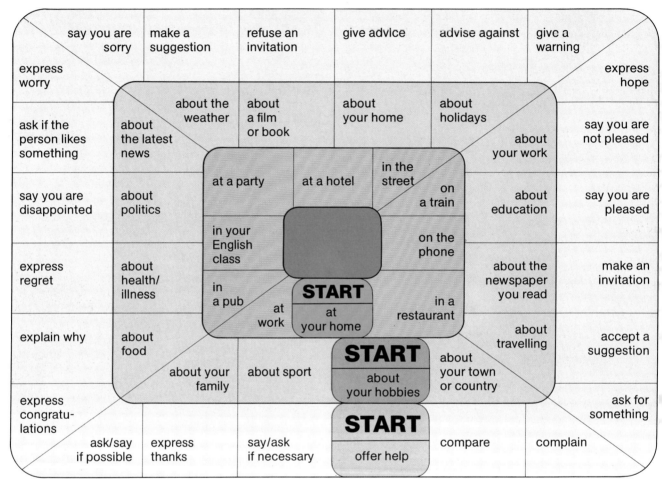

| say you are sorry | make a suggestion | refuse an invitation | give advice | advise against | give a warning |

express worry · express hope

| ask if the person likes something | about the latest news | about the weather | about a film or book | about your home | about holidays | about your work | say you are not pleased |

| say you are disappointed | about politics | at a party | at a hotel | in the street | on a train | about education | say you are pleased |

| in your English class | on the phone |

| express regret | about health/ illness | in a pub | START at your home | in a restaurant | about the newspaper you read | make an invitation |

at work

| explain why | about food | about travelling | accept a suggestion |

| about your family | about sport | START about your hobbies | about your town or country |

| express congratu-lations | ask for something |

| ask/say if possible | express thanks | say/ask if necessary | START offer help | compare | complain |

Rules of the game

1 This is a game for two or more players.
2 Each player needs a board, one dice and three counters, one for each ring of the board, and a slip of paper to note the score.
3 To start the game, place one counter on each of the squares marked START.
4 Each player throws the dice and moves all three counters around the rings the same number of spaces. To avoid difficult combinations, each counter can be moved either forwards or back-wards.
5 The player must then try to make a statement or

question that includes all the information in the three squares he/she has landed on.
If the number on the dice is a 1, 2 or 3, the player must imagine he/she is talking to a stranger, some-one he/she doesn't know very well, or his/her boss. If the number is 4, 5 or 6, the player is talking to someone he/she knows very well, e.g. a good friend, colleague etc.
6 If the player can make a suitable statement or question, he/she receives 2 points.
7 The player with the highest number of points after ten rounds (i.e. ten throws of the dice) is the winner.

AUSTRALIAN ADVENTURE GAME

R 5

You wish to travel from Alice Springs across the continent of Australia to Hamelin Pool **on foot.** On your journey you must go via Ayers Rock and Lake Gregory.

Form teams of 2 or 3 people. You take with you these basic things: 2 camels, food, water, camping equipment, blankets, a compass and some general maps. Now study the map of Australia on page 144/145 and read the key to the numbers on the map.

Discuss with the other members of your team which **four** extra pieces of equipment you would like to take with you in order to avoid trouble later. You may choose from: a spare camel, a storm tent, extra water, tools, extra food, extra blankets, guns and ammunition, detailed maps.

Now make a list of the things (basic and extra) you will have with you on your journey. Keep a record of these things during the game.

To play the game

a Your teacher throws a dice and all teams look at their map of Australia and make up their minds which direction – north, south, east or west – they would like to move in.

b All teams move the **same number** of squares.

c On one throw of the dice the teams may go **in one direction only,** except
  – when they are standing on the green route. In this case they may follow the green route. (To get on the green route your teacher must throw the exact number needed to reach it at any point.)
  – when they come to the edge of the map. In this case they may turn either left or right.

d They may change direction on the next throw of the dice.

e Red lines: The red lines you find here and there on the map are only important if you are standing on a square with a 2 (see no. 2 in the 'key to the numbers on the map').

f The first team to land exactly on the FINISH square at Hamelin Pool with at least one camel wins. If the throw of the dice is higher than the team needs to land exactly on the FINISH square, they may stay where they are.

Key to the numbers on the map

1 **River in flood.** Pick up water and/or extra water if needed, but unless you have tools to build a raft with, you lose all your maps and your compass in the river while crossing.

2 **Extremely rough country.** Camels can carry maps and compass, but no more than 3 other pieces of equipment each. The rest must be thrown away. Without both detailed maps and a compass, you cannot find your way out of here across a red line.

3 **Mountain path.** Your camels can carry maps and compass, but only 2 other pieces of equipment each. Throw the rest away.

4 **Freezing nights.** Without camping equipment, blankets and extra blankets, you are forced to give up the expedition.

5 **Extreme desert conditions.** You must drink either all your water or your extra water. Otherwise, unless you have got tools to make a water-hole with, you lose a camel.

6 **You are attacked by wild camels.** You must either use up all of your ammunition to protect yourselves against them or free one of your camels so that the wild ones follow it away into the desert. If you can do neither, you must give up the expedition.

7 **No kangaroos here.** You use up either your food or your extra food. Otherwise you must either use up all your ammunition shooting rabbits, or kill one of your camels for food.

8 **You lose your compass.** Return to Ayers Rock or Lake Gregory (whichever you passed through last) and pick up a compass and either another piece of equipment or a camel.

9 **You get caught in a sandstorm** and one of your camels escapes into the desert. And unless you have got a storm tent, your compass and all your food (and extra food) is ruined by sand as well.

10 **Water-hole.** Pick up water and/or extra water if needed. If you like, you may stay here in safety for one turn.

11 **Sheep station.** You can pick up one piece of equipment, but not a camel.

12 **Aborigine camp.** You can exchange either food or water for either tools or blankets.

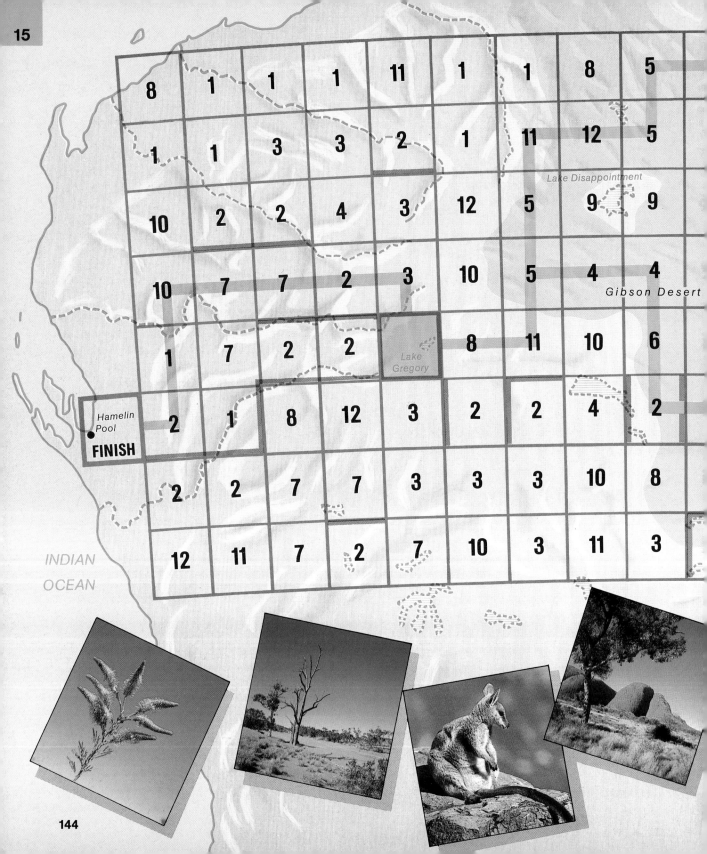

8	1	1	1	11	1	1	8	5
1	1	3	3	2	1	11	12	5
10	2	2	4	3	12	5	9	9
10	7	7	2	3	10	5	4	4
1	7	2	2		8	11	10	6
2	1	8	12	3	2	2	4	2
2	2	7	7	3	3	3	10	8
12	11	7	2	7	10	3	11	3

Lake Disappointment

Gibson Desert

Lake Gregory

Hamelin Pool

FINISH

INDIAN

OCEAN

6	9	9	12	11	11	1
6	9	7	7	7	12	4
6	7	7	11	2	3	3
6	3	2	10	10	3	1
3	12	3	3		10	11
3	3	12	12	3	4	3
5	5	5	6	9	9	4
10	5	5	6	9	9	3

Lake Mackay

Macdonnell Range

START

Alice Springs

Ayers Rock

Musgrave Range

Great Victoria Desert

Ayers Rock

Alice Springs

R 6 Unit 15 has tried to give you an idea of the level of English you have reached by the end of this book. You may feel that this is the level you wanted to reach when you first started learning English. On the other hand, it is equally possible that you may want to continue learning English, either individually or as a group. Whatever your personal feelings may be, there is still the question as to what you could do to maintain or improve your present level of English. The following box shows you a number of possibilities that have proved to be useful.

a Check the list of possibilities for further English practice and mark with a cross those which are available in your area and/or are possible for you.

☐ newspapers		☐ pen-friends	
☐ books		☐ English-speaking friends	
☐ radio		☐ language courses abroad	
☐ TV/films/theatre		☐ travelling	
☐ English club		☐ records/cassettes	

b Which of these activities will help you to practise speaking the language, understanding the language, reading or writing?
Which of them will give you information about English-speaking countries?

c Now read the statements on the right and choose one or two that are nearest to your own situation and/or opinions.

d Talk to the other people in your class and find out what their ideas are about continuing learning English, attending courses or taking examinations. Take notes of what the others say.

e Form a group with those people who have similar interests to you. If you think other members of the class or other groups should join you, try to convince them.

f Find out if the kind of course you would like to go to is available at your college or in your area. If not, discuss with your teacher what you could do to get the course you want.

1 You would like to practise speaking English, but you realize that this is not easy to do if you are learning by yourself and not in a course. So you would prefer to attend some kind of conversation course.
2 You would like to improve your English, but you would prefer not to continue in a course. Your idea is to increase your vocabulary by reading English newspapers, magazines or books.
3 You need English for your job and would like to take a course in business correspondence. You feel an examination is not absolutely necessary for you.
4 You have enjoyed the course and you not only want to continue learning English, but you would also like to continue learning with the same group of people.
5 You feel it would help you in your job to have a certificate in business English. So you wish to take a course preparing for an examination of that kind.
6 You feel you have learnt enough general English and would now like to specialize in technical English to help you in your job.
7 You would like to take a course leading to a higher examination, e.g. the First Certificate Examination of the University of Cambridge.
8 You feel that you would like to improve your knowledge of general English, but are not interested in taking any examinations.
9 You would like to learn more about life in the various English-speaking countries.
10 You think you should now go to an English-speaking country, either for a holiday or a language course, to further improve your understanding of the language and to practise speaking.
11 You would now like to concentrate on reading English and would prefer to take a course dealing with British and American literature.
12 You feel you no longer have enough time to attend a course regularly and would prefer to work on your own at home with cassettes and textbooks.
13 ...

1. Nouns   Hauptwörter   (→ ON THE WAY 1, Grammar 1/ON THE WAY 2, Grammar 1)

Singular or plural verb form   Einzahl- oder Mehrzahlform des Zeitworts

Einzahl	Einzahl oder Mehrzahl
Darling, this is Mr and Mrs Evans.	My company is/are moving me to another office. My family lives/live in Cardiff. The government says/say that smoking is dangerous.

2. Adjectives   Eigenschaftswörter   (→ ON THE WAY 1, Grammar 5/ON THE WAY 2, Grammar 5)

2.1. Word-formation   Wortbildung

Hauptwort + -y		Hauptwort + -less		Hauptwort + -proof	
storm	stormy	child	childless	dust	dustproof
sun	sunny	tooth	toothless	heat	heatproof
ice	icy	colour	colourless	water	waterproof

Zeitwort + -able		un- + Zeitwort + -able
move	movable	
believe	believable	unbelievable
break	breakable	unbreakable
wash	washable	

2.2. Comparative phrases   Vergleichsausdrücke

The Aborigines are	the least powerful the least respected	group in Australia. race in Australia.	...die am wenigsten einflußreiche... ...die am wenigsten respektierte...
One of	the most serious	Aborigine problems is unemployment.	...der ernstesten...

3. Adverbs: comparative forms and phrases   Umstandswörter: Vergleichsformen und Vergleichsausdrücke   (→ ON THE WAY 1, Grammar 6/ON THE WAY 2, Grammar 5–6)

Umstandswörter auf -ly: **more ... -ly (than)**	The new system does the job more quickly/easily/efficiently (than workers).
much → more little → less well → better fast → faster soon → sooner	The more I talk, the less they listen to my point of view. The new system can't do the work better than workers can. Technical progress is destroying jobs faster than it can create new ones. Report the loss of your traveller's cheques to your bank as soon as possible – the sooner the better, in fact.

4. Verbs   Zeitwörter   (→ ON THE WAY 1, Grammar 7/ON THE WAY 2, Grammar 7)

4.1. Tenses of regular verbs   Zeitformen regelmäßiger Zeitwörter

Zeitform	**Lang- und Kurzformen: bejaht**		**Lang- und Kurzformen: verneint**	
past perfect simple	I/you/he/she/it we/you/they	had/'d learned	I/you/he/she/it we/you/they	had not/hadn't learned
future continuous	I/you/he/she/it we/you/they	will/'ll be working	I/you/he/she/it we/you/they	will not/won't be working

4.2. Tenses of irregular verbs   Zeitformen unregelmäßiger Zeitwörter

bet [bet]	bet, betted [bet, 'betɪd]	bet, betted	wetten
build [bɪld]	built [bɪlt]	built	bauen
deal [diːl]	dealt [delt]	dealt	umgehen mit
fight [faɪt]	fought [fɔːt]	fought	kämpfen
forgive [fə'gɪv]	forgave [fə'geɪv]	forgiven [fə'gɪvn]	verzeihen
hang [hæŋ]	hung, hanged [hʌŋ, hæŋd]	hung, hanged	hängen; henken
hurt [hɜːt]	hurt [hɜːt]	hurt	verletzen
knit [nɪt]	knitted, knit ['nɪtɪd, nɪt]	knitted, knit	stricken
lean [liːn]	leant, leaned [lent, liːnd]	leant, leaned	lehnen
lend [lend]	lent [lent]	lent	leihen
light [laɪt]	lit, lighted [lɪt, 'laɪtɪd]	lit, lighted	anzünden
overtake [ˌəʊvə'teɪk]	overtook [ˌəʊvə'tʊk]	overtaken [ˌəʊvə'teɪkən]	überholen
prove [pruːv]	proved [pruːvd]	proved, proven ['pruːvən]	beweisen
sew [səʊ]	sewed [səʊd]	sewed, sewn [səʊn]	nähen
shake [ʃeɪk]	shook [ʃʊk]	shaken ['ʃeɪkən]	schütteln
shine [ʃaɪn]	shone [ʃɒn]	shone	scheinen, leuchten
spoil [spɔɪl]	spoilt, spoiled [spɔɪlt, spɔɪld]	spoilt, spoiled	verderben; verwöhnen
stand [stænd]	stood [stʊd]	stood	stehen
swear [sweə]	swore [swɔː]	sworn [swɔːn]	fluchen

5. can – be able to – could/might, need, ought to, would
(➜ ON THE WAY 1, Grammar 9/ON THE WAY 2, Grammar 8)

can could be able to	What time can you pick me up? I wonder if you could do me a favour. I'm afraid I won't be able to take you home in the car on Sunday.	Wann kannst du/können Sie...? ...Gefallen tun könntest/könnten? ...werde dich am Sonntag nicht heimfahren können.
might	It might be possible, though, to fit you in at the end of this month.	Es könnte vielleicht klappen,...
need	What other things do you need to remember? You needn't take down pictures.	...mußt du/müssen Sie denken? Ihr braucht/Sie brauchen nicht...
ought to	You ought to buy beer, milk and soft drinks in glass bottles which are re-usable. You ought not to carry anything which looks as if it might be a dangerous weapon.	Du solltest/Sie sollten... Du solltest/Sie sollten nichts...
would	A shorter working week would mean more new jobs. She would never have dreamt that anyone in America would choose to live so far behind the times.	...würde ... bedeuten. ...hätte sich nie träumen lassen... ...sich dafür entscheiden würde,...

6. Tenses and time: summary   Zeitformen und Zeit: Zusammenfassung
(➜ ON THE WAY 1, Grammar 10/ON THE WAY 2, Grammar 11)

Zeitformen	Beispiele	Bedeutung	Vergangenheit	jetzt	Zukunft
Past perfect simple	S: "Mr Smith said he had taken part in some evening classes since he left school."	Der Sprecher S berichtet die Äußerung einer Person über zurückliegende Ereignisse.	"Mr Smith said he had taken part in..."	←S	

Zeitformen	Beispiele	Bedeutung	Vergangenheit	jetzt	Zukunft
Past continuous	I **was sitting** in the park…	Der Sprecher stellt eine Handlung als **zeitlichen Ablauf** in der Vergangenheit dar.	…was sitting…		
Past simple	…when the accident **happened**.	Der Sprecher stellt ein **Ereignis** dar, das zu einem **bestimmten Zeitpunkt** in der Vergangenheit eintrat.	…accident happened.		
	Ilse and Heinrich **lived** in Canada for three years, from 1970 to 1972.	Der Sprecher stellt eine Handlung dar, die in der Vergangenheit **abgeschlossen** wurde. (= Ilse und Heinrich leben jetzt nicht mehr in Canada.)	1970 1972 …lived in Canada…		
Present perfect continuous	I'**ve been waiting** here for hours. I'**ve been living** in the United States for 15 years now/ since 1967.	Der Sprecher stellt eine Handlung als **zeitlichen Ablauf** dar, der in der Vergangenheit begann und **jetzt noch** von **aktueller Bedeutung** ist oder **andauert**. (Ich lebe nun schon seit 15 Jahren/seit 1967 in den Vereinigten Staaten.)	I've been waiting… I've been living…		
Present perfect simple	– Would you like a drink? – No, thank you. I'**ve** just **had** one. We'**ve been** very busy lately.	Der Sprecher stellt dar: 1. **abgeschlossene Handlung(en)** oder **Vorgänge**, deren **Folgen in der Gegenwart** betont werden; 2. in der **Vergangenheit begonnene** Handlungen/Vorgänge, die jetzt noch **andauern**;	I've just had one. S We've been very busy lately. S		

Zeitformen	Beispiele	Bedeutung	Vergangenheit	jetzt	Zukunft
Present perfect simple	I've moved more than 20 times in the past 15 years and have had about the same number of jobs.	3. eine **Abfolge einzelner Handlungen**, die in der Vergangenheit begann und sich **jetzt** (oder **in Zukunft**) **noch fortsetzt**.	I've moved… ⊢▸ ➔ ➔ – ➔ ➔ ➔ – ➔ …and have had… 15 years		
Present continuous (present meaning)	– What are you doing here? – I'm waiting for Cyril. They're just giving him an X-ray.	1. Die Sprecher stellen Handlungen als **gleichzeitige zeitliche Abläufe** in der **Gegenwart** dar.	What are you doing…? I'm waiting… They're just giving…		
(future meaning)	My company is sending me to the German Boat Show from October 10th to 14th.	2. Der Sprecher stellt eine **zukünftige Handlung** als **fest geplant** dar.		S ➔	…is sending me…
Present simple	– How long does the ferry take from Ostend to Dover? – It takes 4 ½ hours.	Der Sprecher stellt dar: 1. feststehende Tatsachen;		S ↓ It takes…	
	I go to my French class on Mondays.	2. immer wiederkehrende Handlungen/ Gewohnheiten;	●●●●● ◂●◂ S ●▸● ●●●●● I go to my French class on Mondays.	S ↓	
	I'm here on business.	3. augenblicklichen Zustand;		S ↓ I'm here on…	
	– What time does the coach leave tomorrow? – It leaves at 8 o'clock.	4. durch Fahrpläne, Kalender usw. offiziell festgelegte zukünftige Vorgänge.		S ➔	It leaves at 8 o'clock.

Zeitformen	Beispiele	Bedeutung	Vergangenheit	jetzt	Zukunft
be going to future	We're going to buy a cottage. David's going to put in central heating.	Der Sprecher drückt eine feste Absicht oder Erwartung für die nähere Zukunft aus.		S→	...are going to buy...
future continuous	While you're paying for motorways, I'll be buying duty-free goods.	Der Sprecher stellt eine zukünftige Handlung als zeitlichen Ablauf dar. Im Nebensatz steht das **present continuous.**		S→	~~~~→ I'll be buying
will-future	I'll give you some tablets. The south of England will be cold and dry.	Der Sprecher stellt eine zukünftige Handlung dar: 1. als neutrale Tatsache; 2. als sichere Vorhersage.		S→ S→	I'll give you... ...will be cold...

7. Sentences with -ing forms   Sätze mit -ing-Formen   (➔ ON THE WAY 2, Grammar 12)

a Hauptwort + Verhältniswort + -ing-Form:

For us it's an interesting way of spending our free time.

b Ergänzung + -ing-Form:

She's worried to death about them getting into trouble.
She's very unhappy about them not going to church.

8. The passive   Das Passiv   (→ ON THE WAY 2, Grammar 13)

8.1. be + past participle

The Language Centre promises that their offices	can be contacted	round the clock.	**present simple**
It	can't be helped,	I suppose.	**present simple**
The Aborigines	are being forced	off their land.	**present continuous**
Their culture	is being destroyed	by the whites.	**present continuous**
The Language Centre promises that the groups	will be brought	straight to the centre.	**will-future**
Two years later Marilyn Monroe	was given	a small role.	**past simple**

8.2. have / get + past participle

We'll send it back and	have	it	repaired	for you.	…und werden es für Sie reparieren lassen.
You should	get	the meters	read.		Sie sollten die Meßuhren ablesen lassen.

9. Reported speech   Berichtete Rede   (→ ON THE WAY 2, Grammar 15)

Bericht-Einleitung: past simple	Berichtete Information: past continuous	
Three out of five said	they were taking part in an evening class at the moment.	Bericht-Einleitung und berichtete Information sind gleichzeitig.

Bericht-Einleitung: past simple	Berichtete Information: past perfect simple	
Two out of five said	they had learned to drive a car since they left school.	Berichtete Information liegt zeitlich hinter der Bericht-Einleitung zurück.

10. Statements Aussagesätze (→ ON THE WAY 1, Grammar 13/ON THE WAY 2, Grammar 16)

10.1. Main clause + conjunction + main clause Hauptsatz + Bindewort + Hauptsatz

You must bring your passport,	otherwise	I won't be able to cash your cheques.

10.2. Main clause + conjunction + subclause Hauptsatz + Bindewort + Nebensatz

I can't cash your traveller's cheques	if	you don't bring your passport.
	unless	you bring your passport.
The Stockholm Peace Appeal received millions of signatures	after	the US developed the H-bomb.
A Japanese fishing-boat was only about 85 miles away	while	the Americans were testing the H-bomb.

10.3. Main clause + if-subclause Hauptsatz + Nebensatz mit if

if	Nebensatz: past perfect	Hauptsatz: would(n't) + have + past perfect
If	the rats hadn't become a problem,	he wouldn't have brought in the mongooses.

10.4. Main clause (+ relative pronoun) + subclause Hauptsatz (+ bezügliches Fürwort) + Nebensatz

Hauptsatz	Bezügl. Fürwort	Nebensatz	
He's the only man	who/that	isn't in politics.	**Bezug auf Personen** who/that, whose
That's the couple	whose	keys were found.	
That's the couple	(who/that)	the police are trying to find.	
Those are the keys	(which/that)	the couple dropped.	**Bezug auf Sachen** which/that, what
Those are the keys	which/that	were found by the police.	
Those are the keys	---	--- found by the police.	
That's exactly	what	we do need.	
New Year's Day is the day	on which/when	many people decide to give up bad habits.	**Bezug auf Zeit/Termine:** on which/when

11. Tag questions   Frageanhängsel   (➡ ON THE WAY 1, Grammar 14/ON THE WAY 2, Grammar 17)

Aussage bejaht	➡	Frageanhängsel verneint	
You're one of the neighbours,		aren't you?	Sie sind einer der Nachbarn, nicht wahr?
There are a lot of people here,		aren't there?	Es sind eine Menge Leute da, nicht wahr?
It's a great party,		isn't it?	Es ist ein tolles Fest, nicht wahr?
You were at Ron's birthday party last year,		weren't you?	Sie waren letztes Jahr auf Rons Geburtstagsfest, nicht wahr?
They've got a nice house,		haven't they?	Sie haben ein schönes Haus, nicht wahr?

Aussage verneint	➡	Frageanhängsel bejaht	
I don't think you've met my husband,		have you?	Ich glaube nicht, daß Sie meinen Mann schon kennen, oder?

12. Elliptic sentences   Verkürzte Sätze   (➡ ON THE WAY 2, Grammar 18)

a Verkürzte Hauptsätze:

– Hello, could I speak to Helen Jones, please?
– (Helen Jones) Speaking.

b Verkürzte Nebensätze:

The reason (why/that) I'm phoning is (because/that) we're having a house-warming party on Saturday night. Maybe the manager didn't look far enough ahead. If he had (looked far enough ahead), he would have seen the danger.

13. to-infinitive   Grundform des Zeitworts mit to
(➡ ON THE WAY 1, Grammar 18/ON THE WAY 2, Grammar 19)

a Nach Zeitwörtern:

She's advised not to stop people from going into the hospital.

b Nach Zeitwörtern + direkter Ergänzung:

The demonstrators want Canada to stop killing the seals.
We'd love you to come.
I'd like you to meet Peter Snarles.

c Nach Zeitwörtern und anderen Ergänzungen:

I think it's a good way for people to let off steam.
It's not for the government to decide such things.

d Nach Eigenschaftswort + Hauptwort:

Armstrong was the first man to land and walk on the moon.
Armstrong is the only man (of the three) not to be in politics.

e in order to:

In order to produce paper copies of what is shown on the monitor, you need a printer.

Phonetic alphabet Lautschrift

[ː] bedeutet, daß der vorangehende Laut lang ist
[ˈ] bedeutet, daß die folgende Silbe eine Hauptbetonung erhält
[ˌ] bedeutet, daß die folgende Silbe eine Nebenbetonung erhält

[iː]	meet [miːt]	[ɒ]	job [dʒɒb]	[p]	pub [pʌb]	[s]	son [sʌn]
[ɑː]	father [ˈfɑːðə]	[ʊ]	good [gʊd]	[b]	bye [baɪ]	[z]	is [ɪz]
[ɔː]	daughter [ˈdɔːtə]	[ə]	father [ˈfɑːðə]	[t]	teacher [ˈtiːtʃə]	[ʃ]	she [ʃiː]
[uː]	school [skuːl]			[d]	daughter [ˈdɔːtə]	[ʒ]	television [ˈtelɪˌvɪʒn]
[ɜː]	firm [fɜːm]	[eɪ]	name [neɪm]	[k]	clerk [klɑːk]	[h]	he [hiː]
		[aɪ]	my [maɪ]	[g]	good [gʊd]	[m]	my [maɪ]
[ɔ̃]	restaurant [ˈrestərɔ̃ːŋ]	[ɔɪ]	toilet [ˈtɔɪlɪt]	[tʃ]	teacher [ˈtiːtʃə]	[n]	now [naʊ]
		[əʊ]	show [ʃəʊ]	[dʒ]	job [dʒɒb]	[ŋ]	evening [ˈiːvnɪŋ]
[ɪ]	in [ɪn]	[aʊ]	now [naʊ]	[f]	firm [fɜːm]	[l]	like [laɪk]
[e]	yes [jes]	[ɪə]	here [hɪə]	[v]	evening [ˈiːvnɪŋ]	[r]	room [ruːm]
[æ]	thanks [θæŋks]	[eə]	where [weə]	[θ]	thanks [θæŋks]	[w]	where [weə]
[ʌ]	son [sʌn]	[ʊə]	tourist [ˈtʊərɪst]	[ð]	this [ðɪs]	[j]	yes [jes]

[ɬ] kommt nur in walisischen Wörtern wie z.B. Dolgellau [dɒlˈgeɬaɪ] vor.

Vocabulary: contextual vocabulary Wortschatz: *Unit*-Wörterverzeichnis

Die mit einem * versehenen Wörter gehören nicht zum verbindlichen Lernwortschatz. Sie sind zwar zur Durchführung einzelner *Unit*-Abschnitte notwendig, müssen aber zu einem späteren Zeitpunkt nicht aktiv beherrscht werden. (Treten solche Wörter in einer späteren *Unit* wieder auf, so sind sie an dieser Stelle erneut ins *Unit*-begleitende Wörterverzeichnis aufgenommen.)
Alle anderen Wörter gehören zum verbindlichen Lernwortschatz. Sie wurden nur an der Stelle ins Wörterverzeichnis aufgenommen,
an der sie zum erstenmal in einer bestimmten Bedeutung vorkommen. Sie müssen aktiv beherrscht werden, denn sie werden in den folgenden *Units* als bekannt vorausgesetzt. Der Lernwortschatz aus ON THE WAY 1 und 2 wird ebenfalls als bekannt vorausgesetzt. Die unregelmäßigen Zeitwörter wurden mit einem * versehen. Die in ON THE WAY 3 erstmalig vorkommenden unregelmäßigen Zeitwörter sind auf Seite 148 mit ihren Zeitformen noch einmal aufgelistet.

Unit 1

review [rɪˈvjuː] — Rückblick
•term [tɜːm] — •Semester, Trimester
•my company are moving me to another office [maɪ ˈkʌmpənɪ_ə ˈmuːvɪŋ miː tʊ əˈnʌðə_ˈɒfɪs] — •meine Firma versetzt mich in ein anderes Büro

how does Janet Steen introduce herself? [haʊ dəz ˈdʒænɪt ˌstiːn ˌɪntrəˈdjuːs həˈself] — wie stellt Janet Steen sich vor?

introduce [ˌɪntrəˈdjuːs] — vorstellen

A 1
. . . have just moved into a new house [həv ˌdʒʌst muːvd_ˈɪntʊ_ə ˈnjuː ˈhaʊs] — . . . sind gerade in ein neues Haus gezogen

have* a party [ˈhæv_ə ˈpɑːtɪ] — eine Party geben
•house-warming party [ˈhaʊsˌwɔːmɪŋ ˈpɑːtɪ] — •Einzugsfest, Einweihungsparty
since [sɪns] — *hier:* da
a written invitation [ə ˈrɪtn_ˌɪnvɪˈteɪʃn] — eine schriftliche Einladung
from the other side of town [frəm ðɪ_ˈʌðə ˌsaɪd_əv ˈtaʊn] — aus einem anderen Teil der Stadt
Yours truly [jɔːz ˈtruːlɪ] — *etwa:* mit freundlichen Grüßen (*Briefschluß*)

would you like to come in? [wʊd jʊ ˌlaɪk tə kʌm_'ɪn]	kommen Sie doch bitte herein
we've got the painters in [wɪv gɒt ðə 'peɪntəz_ɪn]	wir haben die Maler im Haus
just for a glass of sherry [ˌdjʌst fr_ə glɑːs_əv 'ʃerɪ]	nur auf ein Glas Sherry
can you make it? [kən jʊ 'meɪk_ɪt]	kannst du kommen?

A 2

please call me Ken [ˌpliːz kɔːl mɪ 'ken]	nennen Sie mich bitte Ken
lounge [laʊndʒ]	Wohnzimmer
darling ['dɑːlɪŋ]	• Liebling
managing director ['mænɪdʒɪŋ dɪ'rektə]	• leitende(r) Direktor(in)
have you got a minute? [hæv jʊ ˌgɒt ə 'mɪnɪt]	hast du einen Augenblick Zeit?

B 1

shy [ʃaɪ]	schüchtern
enter a room ['entər_ə 'ruːm]	ein Zimmer betreten
nobody ['nəʊbədɪ]	niemand
hold* a conversation [həʊld_ə ˌkɒnvə'seɪʃn]	• plaudern, sich unterhalten
shyness ['ʃaɪnɪs]	• Schüchternheit
sip [sɪp]	• nippen, schlückchenweise trinken
a great help [ə 'greɪt 'help]	eine große Hilfe
flow* [fləʊ]	• fließen
for a short while [fr_ə 'ʃɔːt 'waɪl]	(für) eine kurze Weile
you've got a nice suntan [juːv gɒt_ə ˌnaɪs_'sʌntæn]	• Sie sind schön braun geworden
contribute some conversation [kən'trɪbjuːt sʌm ˌkɒnvə'seɪʃn]	• etwas zum Gespräch beitragen
importance [ɪm'pɔːtns]	Bedeutung, Wichtigkeit
make* a comment on . . . [meɪk_ə 'kɒment_ɒn]	• eine Bemerkung über . . . machen
and even if you can't think of much to say [ənd_'iːvn_ɪf juː 'kɑːnt θɪŋk_əv ˌmʌtʃ tə 'seɪ]	und selbst wenn Ihnen nicht viel zu sagen einfällt
say* something worth saying [seɪ 'sʌmθɪŋ wɜːθ 'seɪɪŋ]	etwas Sinnvolles sagen
paragraph ['pærəgrɑːf]	Abschnitt, Absatz
ring [rɪŋ]	Ring

Good Friday [gʊd 'fraɪdɪ]	• Karfreitag
New Year's Day ['njuː jɜːz 'deɪ]	• Neujahr(stag)
Christmas Eve ['krɪsməs_'iːv]	• Heiligabend
Christmas Day ['krɪsməs 'deɪ]	• 1. Weihnachtsfeiertag
Boxing Day ['bɒksɪŋ deɪ]	• 2. Weihnachtsfeiertag
New Year's Eve ['njuː jɜːz_'iːv]	• Silvester(abend)

• May Day ['meɪ deɪ]	der 1. Mai; Maifeiertag
public holiday ['pʌblɪk 'hɒlədɪ]	gesetzlicher Feiertag

be* short of cash [bɪ 'ʃɔːt_əv 'kæʃ]	nicht genug Bargeld haben
friendly ['frendlɪ]	freundlich
Englishman ['ɪŋglɪʃmən]	Engländer
as the name says ['æz ðə ˌneɪm 'sez]	wie der Name schon sagt
apart from [ə'pɑːt frəm]	außer, abgesehen von
religious [rɪ'lɪdʒəs]	religiös
• Whitsun ['wɪtsn]	• Pfingsten
• Whit Monday [ˌwɪt 'mʌndɪ]	• Pfingstmontag
• business ['bɪznɪs]	• hier: Handel
up to the 1970's [ʌp tə ðə 'naɪntiːn 'sevntɪz]	bis in die siebziger Jahre
thanks to the trade unions [θæŋks tə ðə treɪd 'juːnjənz]	dank den Gewerkschaften
• celebrate ['selɪbreɪt]	• feiern
employee [ˌemplɔɪ'iː]	Arbeitnehmer
no matter on what day of the week [nəʊ 'mætər_ɒn 'wɒt deɪ_əv ðə ˌwiːk]	gleichgültig an welchem Wochentag
spring [sprɪŋ]	Frühling
agree on [ə'griː_ɒn]	sich einigen über
traveller ['trævlə]	Reisende(r)
diary ['daɪərɪ]	(Termin-) Kalender, Tagebuch

A 4

hidden holidays ['hɪdn 'hɒlədɪz]	versteckte Feiertage
hide* [haɪd]	(sich) verstecken
end [end]	enden
• the lady of the house [ðə 'leɪdɪ_əv ðə ˌhaʊs]	• die Dame des Hauses
anniversary [ˌænɪ'vɜːsərɪ]	Jahrestag
• Corpus Christi [ˌkɔːpəs 'krɪstɪ]	• Fronleichnam(sfest)
• All Saints' Day [ˌɔːl 'seɪnts deɪ]	• Allerheiligen
• Ascension Day [ə'senʃn deɪ]	• Christi Himmelfahrt

A 5

• odd man out [ˌɒd mæn_'aʊt]	• etwa: einer paßt nicht in die Reihe
have* something in common [hæv 'sʌmθɪŋ_ɪn 'kɒmən]	etwas gemeinsam haben
. . . was shot [wəz 'ʃɒt]	. . . wurde erschossen
shoot* [ʃuːt]	(er-)schießen
political enemy [pə'lɪtɪkl_'enəmɪ]	politischer Feind
• period of office ['pɪərɪəd_əv 'ɒfɪs]	• Amtszeit
. . . was cut short [wəz ˌkʌt 'ʃɔːt]	. . . wurde vorzeitig beendet

the first man to land and walk on the moon
[ðə ˈfɜːst mæn tə ˈlænd‿ən ˈwɔːk‿ɒn ðə ˈmuːn]
der erste Mensch, der auf dem Mond landete und herumlief

moon [muːn]
Mond

• Highland Games
[ˈhaɪlənd ˈɡeɪmz]
• schottisches Nationalfest mit traditionellen Wettbewerben kultureller und sportlicher Art

• National Eisteddfod
[ˈnæʃənl‿aɪsˈteðvɒd]
• walisisches Nationalfest mit musikalischen und literarischen Wettbewerben in walisischer Sprache

• Olympic Games
[əˈlɪmpɪk ˈɡeɪmz]
• Olympische Spiele

• yacht [jɒt]
• Jacht

B 2
• celebration [ˌselɪˈbreɪʃn]
• Feier

common [ˈkɒmən]
üblich, verbreitet

• Hogmanay [ˈhɒɡməneɪ]
• Neujahrsfest in Schottland

• pagan [ˈpeɪɡən]
• heidnisch

custom [ˈkʌstəm]
Sitte, Brauch

• first footing [ˌfɜːst ˈfʊtɪŋ]
• schottische Neujahrstradition

midnight [ˈmɪdnaɪt]
Mitternacht

• first footer [ˌfɜːst ˈfʊtə]
• nach schottischer Tradition der erste Besucher, der das Haus am Neujahrstag betritt

according to the tradition
[əˈkɔːdɪŋ tə ðə trəˈdɪʃn]
der Tradition nach/zufolge

good luck [ˈɡʊd ˈlʌk]
Glück

bad luck [ˈbæd ˈlʌk]
Pech

fair hair [ˈfeə ˈheə]
blondes Haar

blind [blaɪnd]
blind

sharp [ʃɑːp]
scharf

dark-haired [ˌdɑːkˈheəd]
dunkelhaarig

• a lump of coal
[ə ˈlʌmp‿əv ˈkəʊl]
• ein Stück Kohle

coal [kəʊl]
Kohle

• Cumberland Reel
[ˈkʌmbələnd ˈriːl]
• Volkstanz aus dem Nordwesten Englands

• row [rəʊ]
• Reihe

• the top two couples
[ðə ˈtɒp ˈtuː ˈkʌplz]
• die ersten beiden Paare am oberen Ende (der Reihe)

• wheel [wiːl]
• Rad

• four steps forward
[ˈfɔː steps ˈfɔːwəd]
• vier Schritte nach vorn

• four steps back
[ˈfɔː steps ˈbæk]
• vier Schritte nach hinten

• the couple then separates
[ðə ˈkʌpl ðen ˈsepəreɪts]
• dann geht das Paar auseinander

• at the bottom end
[ət ðə ˈbɒtəm‿end]
• am unteren Ende (der Reihe)

• when they reach the top
[ˈwen ðeɪ ˈriːtʃ ðə ˈtɒp]
• wenn sie zum oberen Ende kommen

• the other couples form an arch
[ðiː‿ˈʌðə ˈkʌplz fɔːm‿ən‿ˈɑːtʃ]
• die anderen Paare bilden einen (Tor-)Bogen

• to the bottom [tə ðə ˈbɒtəm]
• zum unteren Ende

• dancer [ˈdɑːnsə]
• Tänzer(in)

Unit 2

the Continent [ðə ˈkɒntɪnənt]
das europäische Festland

ferry [ˈferi]
Fähre

• you get good value for money
[jʊ get ˈɡʊd ˈvæljʊ fə ˈmʌni]
• Sie bekommen (auch) etwas für Ihr Geld

• lager [ˈlɑːɡə]
• leichtes, helles Bier

choose* from [ˈtʃuːz frəm]
auswählen

sausage [ˈsɒsɪdʒ]
Wurst

taste [teɪst]
schmecken

• Continental (breakfast)
[ˌkɒntɪˈnentl]
• einfaches Frühstück mit Brötchen, Butter, Marmelade und Kaffee oder Tee

A 1
• grade [ɡreɪd]
• (US für:) Klasse(nstufe)

• elementary school
[ˌelɪˈmentəri skuːl]
• Grundschule (1. bis 6. Schuljahr)

• junior high school
[ˈdʒuːnjə ˈhaɪskuːl]
• Schule, die das 7., 8. und 9. Schuljahr umfaßt

• senior high school
[ˈsiːnjə ˈhaɪskuːl]
• Schule, die das 10., 11. und 12. Schuljahr umfaßt

• high school diploma
[ˈhaɪskuːl dɪˈpləʊmə]
• Abschlußzeugnis nach der 12. Klasse

must be something like . . .
[mʌst bɪ ˈsʌmθɪŋ laɪk]
muß etwas Ähnliches sein wie . . ./dürfte etwa . . . entsprechen

• two tier system
[ˈtuː ˌtɪə ˈsɪstəm]
• zweigliedriges (Schul-) System

• primary school
[ˈpraɪməri skuːl]
• Grundschule (1. bis 6. Schuljahr)

• first school
[ˈfɜːst skuːl]
• Grundschule (1. bis 4. Schuljahr)

secondary school
['sekndrɪ sku:l]
• Schule, die von Kindern im Alter von 11 bis 16 bzw. 18 besucht wird

middle school
['mɪdl sku:l]
• Schule, die von Kindern im Alter von 9 bis 13 besucht wird

high school
['haɪsku:l]
• Schule, die von Kindern im Alter von 13 bis 16 bzw. 18 besucht wird

sixth form college
['sɪksθ fɔ:m 'kɒlɪdʒ]
• Schule, in der in zwei Jahren auf das britische Abitur vorbereitet wird

college of further education
['kɒlɪdʒ_əv 'fɜ:ðər_edju:'keɪʃn]
• Fachhochschule

employment [ɪm'plɔɪmənt]
• Arbeitsverhältnis; Beruf

A 2

please sit down
['pli:z sɪt ˌdaʊn]
bitte setzen Sie sich

application [ˌæplɪ'keɪʃn]
Bewerbung

G.C.E. 'O' Level
['dʒi:'si:'i: 'əʊ ˌlevl]
• Schulabschluß (entspricht etwa der Mittleren Reife)

export salesman
['ekspɔ:t 'seɪlzmən]
Exportkaufmann

so I guess you went to Interchem because . . .
[səʊ aɪ 'ges jʊ went tʊ_'ɪntəkem bɪ'kɒz]
• ich nehme also an, Sie sind zu Interchem gegangen, weil . . .

you just don't seem to fit
[jʊ dʒʌst 'dəʊnt si:m tə 'fɪt]
Sie scheinen einfach nicht (zu uns) zu passen

A 3

are you a life-long learner?
[ɑ: jʊ_ə 'laɪflɒŋ 'lɜ:nə]
lernen Sie Ihr Leben lang?

questionnaire [ˌkwestɪə'neə]
• Fragebogen

social science ['səʊʃl 'saɪəns]
Sozialwissenschaft

social ['səʊʃl]
sozial, gesellschaftlich

skill [skɪl]
Fertigkeit

in answer to
[ɪn_'ɑ:nsə tə]
• als Antwort auf

this was not really the case
[ðɪs wəz nɒt 'rɪəlɪ ðə 'keɪs]
dies war nicht ganz zutreffend

consider [kən'sɪdə]
• hier: meinen

handle a bank account
['hændl_ə 'bæŋk ə'kaʊnt]
ein Bankkonto führen

handle ['hændl]
umgehen/fertigwerden mit

pocket calculator
['pɒkɪt 'kælkjʊleɪtə]
Taschenrechner

type [taɪp]
mit der Maschine schreiben, tippen

enter ['entə]
• hier: eintragen

sex [seks]
Geschlecht

library ['laɪbrərɪ]
Bücherei, Bibliothek

credit card ['kredɪt kɑ:d]
Kreditkarte

B 1

• auto(mobile)
['ɔ:təʊ ('ɔ:təməbi:l)]
• (US für:) Auto

• know-how ['nəʊhaʊ]
• (Fach-)Wissen, Können

• dollars and sense
['dɒləz_ən 'sens]
• Wortspiel: 'dollars and cents'

sense [sens]
Sinn, Verstand; hier: Köpfchen

• study smarter ['stʌdɪ 'smɑ:tə]
• rationeller lernen

• budgeting your personal cash
['bʌdʒɪtɪŋ jə 'pɜ:snl 'kæʃ]
• mit dem persönlichen Einkommen haushalten/wirtschaften

• how to manage your boss
[haʊ tə 'mænɪdʒ jə 'bɒs]
• wie man mit seinem Vorgesetzten umgeht

natural gardening
['nætʃrəl 'gɑ:dnɪŋ]
biologischer Gartenbau

• tire (US für: tyre) ['taɪə]
• Reifen

suitable ['su:təbl]
geeignet, passend

prepare a meal [prɪ'peər_ə 'mi:l]
ein Essen zubereiten

• how to balance your personal checkbook [haʊ tə 'bæləns jə 'pɜ:snl 'tʃekbʊk]
• wie man ein ausgeglichenes Bankkonto führt

control [kən'trəʊl]
kontrollieren, im Rahmen halten

prepare for exams
[prɪ'peə fr_ɪg'zæmz]
sich auf Prüfungen vorbereiten

relationship [rɪ'leɪʃnʃɪp]
Verbindung, Beziehung

introduce [ˌɪntrə'dju:s]
bekannt machen, einführen

fruit(s) [fru:t(s)]
Obst

poison ['pɔɪzn]
Gift

increase [ɪn'kri:s]
(sich) vergrößern/erhöhen, zunehmen

safe [seɪf]
ungefährlich

helpful ['helpfʊl]
hilfreich, nützlich

• source of trouble
[ˌsɔ:s_əv 'trʌbl]
• Quelle des Ärgers

(3)

duty ['dju:tɪ]
Pflicht

steps [steps]
Stufen

stairs [steəz]
Treppen

keep* quiet [ki:p 'kwaɪət]
(sich) ruhig (ver-)halten

do* the garden
[du: ðə 'gɑ:dn]
den Garten pflegen/betreuen

keep* pets [ki:p pets]
Haustiere halten

use the garden
[ju:z ðə 'gɑ:dn]
den Garten (mit-)benutzen

back yard [ˌbæk 'jɑ:d]
Hinterhof

A 4

could we have a word with you? ['kʊd wɪ hæv_ə 'wɜ:d wɪθ jʊ]
könnten wir Sie (kurz) sprechen?

landlady ['lænˌleɪdɪ]
Vermieterin, (Haus-)Wirtin

tenant ['tenənt] | Mieter(in)
that's out of the question | das geht nicht/kommt
[ðæts 'aʊt_əv ðə 'kwestʃən] | nicht in Frage
I hate to turn you down | es tut mir leid, Ihnen
[aɪ 'heɪt tə ˌtɜːn juː 'daʊn] | eine Absage geben zu
| müssen

turn down [ˌtɜːn 'daʊn] | ablehnen, zurückweisen
somehow ['sʌmhaʊ] | irgendwie
I wonder if we could . . . ? | wäre es möglich, daß
[aɪ 'wʌndər_ɪf wɪ kʊd] | wir . . . ?
the day after tomorrow | übermorgen
[ðə 'deɪ_'ɑːftə təˈmɒrəʊ] |
landlord ['lænlɔːd] | Vermieter, (Haus-)Wirt
front door [ˌfrʌnt 'dɔː] | Haustür
bicycle ['baɪsɪkl] | Fahrrad
hall [hɔːl] | Flur, Korridor
build* [bɪld] | bauen
cellar ['selə] | Keller
front of the house | Hausfront, Fassade
['frʌnt_əv ðə ˌhaʊs] |
yes, by all means | selbstverständlich
[ˈjes baɪˈɔːl ˈmiːnz] |
we've got to think of . . . | wir müssen an . . . denken
[wiːv 'gɒt tə ˌθɪŋk_əv] |

A 5

move house [ˌmuːv 'haʊs] | umziehen
needn't ['niːdnt] | braucht nicht, muß nicht
what you have to get done | was Sie machen lassen
[wɒt ju ˌhæv tə get 'dʌn] | müssen
arrange a day [əˈreɪndʒ_ə 'deɪ] | einen Tag festlegen
dishes ['dɪʃɪz] | Geschirr
take* the sheets and | die Betten abziehen
blankets off the beds |
[teɪk ðə 'ʃiːts_ɒn |
'blæŋkɪts ɒf ðə 'bedz] |
keep them yourself | behalten Sie sie bei sich
[kiːp ðəm jɔːˈself] |
put* together [pʊt təˈgeðə] | zusammenlegen
take them with you personally | nehmen Sie sie an sich
[teɪk ðəm 'wɪθ juː 'pɜːsnəlɪ] |
electrical [ɪˈlektrɪkl] | elektrisch
appliance [əˈplaɪəns] | (Haushalts-)Gerät
cooker ['kʊkə] | Herd
fix [fɪks] | hier: anbringen,
| installieren
meter ['miːtə] | Zähler, (Meß-)Uhr
tube [tjuːb] | Tube
closed tight [ˌkləʊzd 'taɪt] | fest zu
mirror ['mɪrə] | Spiegel
shelf (Mehrzahl: shelves) | Regal
[ʃelf, ʃelvz] |
unpack [ˌʌnˈpæk] | auspacken
take* up loose carpets | (lose) Teppiche
['teɪk_ʌp luːs 'kɑːpɪts] | zusammenrollen
loose [luːs] | lose

B 2

offer ['ɒfə] | Angebot
outside ['aʊtsaɪd] | hier: außen
aerial ['eəriəl] | Antenne
broken ['brəʊkən] | kaputt
screw [skruː] | Schraube
pipe [paɪp] | Rohr
block [blɒk] | verstopfen, (ver-)sperren
inside ['ɪnsaɪd] | hier: innen
dark [dɑːk] | dunkel
electric wire [ɪˈlektrɪk 'waɪə] | elektrische Leitung
wooden ['wʊdn] | hölzern, aus Holz
wall-paper coming off | Tapete löst sich
['wɔːlˌpeɪpə ˌkʌmɪŋ_'ɒf] | (von der Wand)
condition [kənˈdɪʃn] | Zustand
hot water system | Warmwasserversorgung
[hɒt 'wɔːtə 'sɪstəm] |
for the time being | im Augenblick, vorerst
[fə ðə 'taɪm 'biːɪŋ] |
move in [ˌmuːv_'ɪn] | einziehen
workman ['wɜːkmən] | Handwerker

a

home sweet home | etwa: trautes Heim,
['həʊm ˌswiːt 'həʊm] | Glück allein
Asia ['eɪʃə] | Asien
home of the tiger | Heimat des Tigers
['həʊm_əv ðə 'taɪgə] |
a good home [ə 'gʊd 'həʊm] | ein gutes Zuhause
wherever [weər'evə] | überall wo
. . . is home to me | . . . ist mein Zuhause
[ɪz 'həʊm tə 'miː] |
several thousand homes | einige tausend Wohn-
['sevrəl 'θaʊznd 'həʊmz] | häuser
children's home | Kinderheim, Waisen-
['tʃɪldrənz ˌhəʊm] | haus
go* home [gəʊ 'həʊm] | nach Hause fahren

b

the homeless [ðə 'həʊmlɪs] | die Obdachlosen
a year before [ə 'jɜː bɪˈfɔː] | ein Jahr zuvor
registered homeless people | gemeldete Obdachlose
['redʒɪstəd 'həʊmlɪs 'piːpl] |
box [bɒks] | Kiste, Karton
against the wall | gegen die Wand
[əˈgenst ðə 'wɔːl] |
many thousands | viele Tausende
['menɪ 'θaʊzndz] |

c

the Palace of Holyrood House | Residenz der königlichen
[ðə 'pælɪs_əv 'hɒliruːd 'haʊs] | Familie in Edinburgh,
| Schottland
Kensington Palace | Residenz der königlichen
['kenzɪŋtən 'pælɪs] | Familie in Kensington,
| London

Tonmaterialien zu ON THE WAY

Bei der Entwicklung des Lehrwerks ON THE WAY haben wir besonderen Wert darauf gelegt, daß die gesprochene Sprache im Mittelpunkt steht. Dazu gehört auch, daß Sie als Lerner so oft wie möglich im Unterricht und zuhause von Muttersprachlern gesprochenes Englisch hören und damit üben können.

Die 2 Compact-Cassetten zu ON THE WAY 3 enthalten daher
● alle dialogischen Texte in normalem Sprechtempo
● alle Hörverständnistexte (im Lehrbuch nicht abgedruckt)
● britische und amerikanische Lieder und Musik

Die Texte sind von britischen und amerikanischen Muttersprachlern gesprochen.

Hiermit bestelle ich zur sofortigen Lieferung per Nachnahme

ON THE WAY 3

☐ **2 Compact-Cassetten – Klett-Nr. 50037**
Preis 39,60 DM ⊗

Laufgeschwindigkeit 4,75 cm/sek, Gesamtsprechzeit ca. 165 Minuten. Die Compact-Cassetten sind auf beiden Seiten besprochen.

Lieferung durch jede Buchhandlung oder, wo dies auf Schwierigkeiten stößt, zuzüglich der Portokosten per Nachnahme vom Verlag. Preise freibleibend. Stand vom 1.9.1989.

⊗ unverb. Preisempf.

Ort und Datum

Unterschrift

Dieser Abschnitt gilt als Versandadresse; bitte deutlich schreiben

Vorname, Name

Straße, Hausnummer

Postleitzahl, Wohnort

2 Compact-Cassetten zu
ON THE WAY 3

Sprecher: Peter Bartlett, Judy Bennett, Barbara Bliss, Caroline Bliss,
Carole Boyd, Charles Collingwood, Blain Fairman, Denica Fairman,
William Gaminara, John Green, Garrick Hagon, Kate Harper, Brian Jameson,
Derrick Jenkins, Liza Ross, Kerry Shale, Jill Shilling, Dorrit Welles
Regie: Peter Bartlett und Ernst Klett Verlag
Tonstudio: Studio AVP, London
Musik: Jimmy Patrick

2 Compact-Cassetten – Gesamtsprechzeit ca. 165 Minuten – Klett-Nr. 50037

Ernst Klett Verlag

Bitte als
Postkarte
frankieren

**Ernst Klett Verlag
Stuttgart**
Abt. Information und Beratung
Expeditionslager
Postfach 1170

7054 Korb

K 5003

Buckingham Palace
['bʌkɪŋəm 'pælɪs]

*Haupt-Residenz der königlichen Familie in London

St James's Palace
[snt 'dʒeɪmzɪz 'pælɪs]

*Residenz der königlichen Familie in London

Balmoral [bæl'mɒrəl]

*Sommerresidenz der königlichen Familie in Schottland, nahe Aberdeen

Sandringham ['sændrɪŋəm]

*Landhaus der königlichen Familie in Norfolk, England

Unit 3

thriller ['θrɪlə]

*Reißer, Krimi

science fiction film
['saɪəns 'fɪkʃn fɪlm]

*Science-Fiction-Film, utopischer Film

what kind of films . . . ?
[wɒt kaɪnd_əv fɪlmz]

welche Art von Filmen . . . ?/was für Filme . . . ?

the above films
[ði:_ə'bʌv fɪlmz]

die oben genannten Filme

piece of music
[pi:s_əv 'mju:zɪk]

Musikstück

boring ['bɔ:rɪŋ]

langweilig

A 1

overdose ['əʊvədəʊs]

*Überdosis

she led a very unhappy life
[ʃi led_ə 'veri:_ʌn'hæpɪ 'laɪf]

sie führte ein sehr unglückliches Leben

foster family ['fɒstə 'fæmlɪ]

*Pflegefamilie

of all time [əv_'ɔ:l taɪm]

aller Zeiten

reach [ri:tʃ]

erreichen

she was cut out of the film altogether [ʃi wəz 'kʌt_'aʊt_əv ðə film ɔ:ltə'geðə]

*sie wurde gänzlich aus dem Film herausgeschnitten

from time to time
[frəm 'taɪm tə 'taɪm]

von Zeit zu Zeit

act [ækt]

spielen (Film, Theater)

career [kə'rɪə]

*Karriere, Laufbahn

threaten ['θretn]

(be-)drohen

nude [nju:d]

*nackt

. . . thought the world of her
[θɔ:t ðə 'wɜ:ld_əv hɜ:]

*. . . hielten große Stücke auf sie

in real life [ɪn 'rɪəl 'laɪf]

im wirklichen Leben, in Wirklichkeit

*Actors Studio
[,æktəz 'stju:dɪəʊ]

*Schauspielschule in New York

recognize ['rekəgnaɪz]

anerkennen

fine [faɪn]

hier: hervorragend, großartig

skilful ['skɪlfʊl]

geschickt, fähig

actress ['æktrɪs]

Schauspielerin

*performance [pə'fɔ:məns]

*Darbietung, Leistung

director [dɪ'rektə]

Regisseur

*a strong personality
[ə strɒŋ ,pɜ:sə'nælətɪ]

*eine starke Persönlichkeit

clever ['klevə]

klug; hier: begabt

. . . who keeps improving all the time
[hʊ ,ki:ps_ɪm'pru:vɪŋ_ɔ:l ðə 'taɪm]

. . ., die sich ständig steigert

name [neɪm]

(er-)nennen, bezeichnen

in spite of [ɪn 'spaɪt_əv]

trotz

*her marriage broke up
[hə 'mærɪdʒ brəʊk_ʌp]

*ihre Ehe ging in die Brüche

more and more
['mɔ:_n 'mɔ:]

immer mehr

actor ['æktə]

Schauspieler

turn up [,tɜ:n_'ʌp]

erscheinen, auftauchen

she was fired
[ʃi wəz 'faɪəd]

sie wurde gefeuert/entlassen

destroy [dɪ'strɔɪ]

zerstören

guess [ges]

(er-)raten

read* . . . aloud [ri:d ə'laʊd]

vorlesen

one by one ['wʌn baɪ 'wʌn]

einzeln, nacheinander

A 2

for and against
['fɔ:r_ən_ə'genst]

Pro und Contra

space [speɪs]

Weltraum

*roving reporter
['rəʊvɪŋ rɪ'pɔ:tə]

*etwa: Reporter, der ständig unterwegs ist

be* keen on
[bɪ 'ki:n_ɒn]

begeistert sein von, sehr viel übrig haben für

*I don't think they do any great harm
[aɪ 'dəʊnt θɪŋk ðeɪ dʊ_'enɪ greɪt 'hɑ:m]

*meiner Meinung nach richten sie keinen großen Schaden an

enjoyable [ɪn'dʒɔɪəbl]

angenehm, unterhaltsam

let* off steam [,let ɒf 'sti:m]

Dampf ablassen

go* mad [gəʊ 'mæd]

verrückt werden

worry ['wʌrɪ]

Sorge, Ärgernis

now and then ['naʊ_ən 'ðen]

von Zeit zu Zeit, ab und zu

open ['əʊpən]

eröffnen

*attract [ə'trækt]

*anziehen, anlocken

influence ['ɪnflʊəns]

Einfluß

over and over again
['əʊvər_ən_'əʊvər_ə'gen]

immer wieder

. . . who don't seem to mind if . . . [hʊ 'dəʊnt si:m tə 'maɪnd_ɪf]

. . . denen es anscheinend nichts ausmacht, wenn . . .

as long as [əz 'lɒŋ_əz]

solange

B 1

- there has been an increasing amount of sex and violence in films [ðeə həz bɪn_ən ɪn'kriːsɪŋ_ə'maʊnt_əv 'seks_ən 'vaɪələns_ɪn 'fɪlmz] — der Anteil von Sex und Gewalt in Filmen ist gestiegen

amount [ə'maʊnt] — (Gesamt-)Betrag, Menge
in particular [ɪn pə'tɪkjʊlə] — insbesondere, vor allem
scene [siːn] — (Film-)Szene
- entertainment [ˌentə'teɪnmənt] — • Unterhaltung
- mugger ['mʌgə] — • Straßenräuber
- break* into [breɪk_'ɪntʊ] — • einbrechen
- tear* the clothes off the housekeeper [teə ðə 'kləʊðz_ɒf ðə 'haʊsˌkiːpə] — • der Haushälterin die Kleider vom Leib reißen
- rape [reɪp] — • vergewaltigen; Vergewaltigung

hero ['hɪərəʊ] — Held
- handicapped ['hændɪkæpt] — • behindert
jump from a high window [dʒʌmp frəm_ə ˌhaɪ 'wɪndəʊ] — aus einem Fenster im oberen Stock springen
iron ['aɪən] — Eisen; eisern
- fence [fens] — • Zaun
what is supposed to be . . . [wɒt_ɪz sə'pəʊzd tə biː] — was angeblich . . . sein soll
object ['ɒbdʒɪkt] — Objekt
attack [ə'tæk] — angreifen, überfallen
- brutal(ly) ['bruːtəl(ɪ)] — • brutal, auf brutale Weise
murder ['mɜːdə] — ermorden
- sympathy ['sɪmpəθɪ] — • Mitleid, Mitgefühl
criminal ['krɪmɪnl] — Verbrecher
- indeed [ɪn'diːd] — • in der Tat, tatsächlich
take* the law into one's own hands [teɪk ðə 'lɔː ɪntə wʌnz_'əʊn 'hændz] — Selbstjustiz üben

support [sə'pɔːt] — Unterstützung
actually ['æktʃʊəlɪ] — wirklich, tatsächlich
stand* up ['stænd_'ʌp] — aufstehen
- cheer [tʃɪə] — • bejubeln
- hatred ['heɪtrɪd] — • Haß
- pleasure ['pleʒə] — • Freude, Vergnügen
- victim ['vɪktɪm] — • Opfer
ticket sales ['tɪkɪt seɪlz] — Verkauf von Eintrittskarten

I fully believe that . . . [aɪ 'fʊlɪ bɪ'liːv ðət] — ich glaube fest daran, daß . . .
- violent ['vaɪələnt] — • gewalttätig
experience [ɪk'spɪərɪəns] — erleben, erfahren
. . . that it served them right [ðət_ɪt 'sɜːvd ðəm 'raɪt] — . . . daß ihnen ganz recht geschah
nasty ['nɑːstɪ] — scheußlich, widerlich
- strip [strɪp] — • entkleiden, ausziehen
in order to . . . [ɪn_'ɔːdə tʊ] — um . . . zu
what might it do . . . ? ['wɒt ˌmaɪt_ɪt 'dʊ] — was mag er (der Film) bewirken . . . ?
connection [kə'nekʃn] — Verbindung, Zusammenhang

. . . will no doubt say . . . [wɪl 'nəʊ ˌdaʊt 'seɪ] — . . . werden zweifelsohne sagen . . .
doubt [daʊt] — Zweifel
cause [kɔːz] — verursachen
at first sight [ət 'fɜːst 'saɪt] — auf den ersten Blick
cause and effect ['kɔːz_ən_ɪ'fekt] — Ursache und Wirkung
power ['paʊə] — Macht, Befugnis
wise [waɪz] — weise, vernünftig, klug
- self-censorship [ˌself'sensəʃɪp] — • Selbstzensur
. . . wishes to be accepted as . . . ['wɪʃɪz tə biː_ək'septɪd_əz] — . . . als . . . anerkannt werden will
- responsible film-maker [rɪ'spɒnsəbl 'fɪlmˌmeɪkə] — • verantwortungsbewußter Filmemacher
- accept a responsibility to [ək'sept_ə rɪˌspɒnsə'bɪlətɪ tʊ] — • Verantwortung übernehmen für/gegenüber
sign [saɪn] — (An-)Zeichen
list [lɪst] — auflisten, aufschreiben
put* one's arguments to . . . [pʊt wʌnz_'ɑːgjʊmənts tʊ] — . . . seine Argumente darlegen
- in reply to [ɪn rɪ'plaɪ tʊ] — • als Antwort auf

if you'd be prepared to . . . [ɪf jʊd bɪ prɪ'peəd tə] — wenn Sie bereit wären, . . .
- confirm [kən'fɜːm] — • bestätigen
- reservation [ˌrezə'veɪʃn] — • Reservierung
. . . put you up in a single room [ˌpʊt_jʊ_'ʌp_ɪn_ə 'sɪŋgl ˌruːm] — . . . Sie in einem Einzelzimmer unterbringen
but it looks as though . . . [bʌt_ɪt 'lʊks_əz ðəʊ] — aber es sieht so aus, als ob . . .
check in ['tʃek 'ɪn] — sich eintragen/anmelden (Hotel)
separate ['seprət] — getrennt
night porter [ˌnaɪt 'pɔːtə] — Nachtportier
be* on duty [biː_ɒn 'djuːtɪ] — im Dienst sein, Dienst haben
stiff [stɪf] — steif
- safe [seɪf] — • Tresor

A 3

clean [kliːn] — sauber
pork [pɔːk] — Schweinefleisch
tough [tʌf] — zäh
- cook [kʊk] — • Koch, Köchin
cake [keɪk] — Kuchen
pear [peə] — Birne
sour [saʊə] — sauer
gone off [gɒn_'ɒf] — sauer/schlecht geworden
similar ['sɪmɪlə] — ähnlich
burnt [bɜːnt] — verbrannt, angebrannt
salty ['sɔːltɪ] — salzig
not done [ˌnɒt 'dʌn] — nicht durch(gebraten)
tasteless ['teɪstlɪs] — ohne Geschmack, fade

bitter ['bɪtə]   bitter
hard [hɑːd]   hart
smell* [smel]   riechen

A 4

• complaint [kəm'pleɪnt]   • Beschwerde,
    Reklamation
complain [kəm'pleɪn]   sich beschweren,
    reklamieren
there's something wrong   mit ... ist etwas nicht in
    with ...   Ordnung
    [ðeəz 'sʌmθɪŋ 'rɒŋ wɪθ]
• short wave ['ʃɔːt ˌweɪv]   • Kurzwelle
• station ['steɪʃn]   • (Rundfunk-)Sender
• medium wave ['miːdjəm ˌweɪv]   • Mittelwelle
• long wave ['lɒŋ ˌweɪv]   • Langwelle
receipt [rɪ'siːt]   Quittung, Beleg;
    Kassenzettel
send* back [ˌsend 'bæk]   zurückschicken
we'll have it repaired for you   wir lassen es für Sie
    [wiːl hæv ɪt rɪ'peəd fə juː]   reparieren
exchange [ɪks'tʃeɪndʒ]   umtauschen
I'd rather have my money back   ich würde lieber mein
    [aɪd 'rɑːðə hæv maɪ 'mʌnɪ bæk]   Geld zurückbekommen
spot [spɒt]   Fleck
typewriter ['taɪpˌraɪtə]   Schreibmaschine
socks [sɒks]   Socken
woollen stockings   Wollstrümpfe
    ['wʊlən 'stɒkɪŋz]
woollen ['wʊlən]   wollen, aus Wolle
shaver ['ʃeɪvə]   Rasierapparat
steam iron ['stiːm ˌaɪən]   Dampfbügeleisen
tights [taɪts]   Strumpfhose
cotton shirt ['kɒtn ˌʃɜːt]   Baumwollhemd
pure cotton [ˌpjʊə 'kɒtn]   reine Baumwolle
button ['bʌtn]   Knopf
ball pen ['bɔːl ˌpen]   Kugelschreiber
department store   Kaufhaus, Warenhaus
    [dɪ'pɑːtmənt ˌstɔː]
• teasmade ['tiːzmeɪd]   • kombinierter Wecker
    und Teekocher
try out [traɪ ˌaʊt]   ausprobieren
by separate post   mit getrennter Post
    [baɪ 'seprət 'pəʊst]
neither ... nor   weder ... noch
    ['naɪðə 'nɔː]
Yours faithfully   etwa: mit freundlichen
    [jɔːz 'feɪθfʊlɪ]   Grüßen, hochachtungs-
    voll (Briefschluß)
• item ['aɪtəm]   • Gegenstand, Artikel
product ['prɒdʌkt]   Produkt, Erzeugnis

B 2

look into [lʊk ˌɪntʊ]   sich befassen mit
court [kɔːt]   Gericht
• Consumer Advice Centre   • etwa: Verbraucher-
    [kən'sjuːmər ˌəd'vaɪs 'sentə]   zentrale

• criticize ['krɪtɪsaɪz]   • kritisieren
• rubbish ['rʌbɪʃ]   • Blödsinn, Quatsch
• bloodsport TV games   • Jagdsport-Videospiele
    ['blʌdspɔːt ˌtiːˈviː ɡeɪmz]
• what a load of bloody rubbish!   • so ein Mist/großer
    ['wɒt_ə 'ləʊd_əv ˌblʌdɪ 'rʌbɪʃ]   Blödsinn!
• rape [reɪp]   • Vergewaltigung
• robbery ['rɒbərɪ]   • Raub(überfall)
• appliance [ə'plaɪəns]   • (Haushalts-)Gerät
• switch off [ˌswɪtʃ 'ɒf]   • ausschalten
• screen [skriːn]   • hier: Bildschirm
• record [rɪ'kɔːd]   • aufnehmen (Video/
    Tonband)

Unit 4

• survival quiz [sə'vaɪvl kwɪz]   • Überlebensquiz
stream [striːm]   Bach, Flüßchen
sink* [sɪŋk]   (ver-)sinken
soft [sɒft]   weich
bottom ['bɒtəm]   Grund, Boden
• kick [kɪk]   • treten, strampeln
at last [ət 'lɑːst]   endlich, schließlich
• fork [fɔːk]   • Gabelung, Abzweigung
broad [brɔːd]   breit
feel* hungry [fiːl 'hʌŋrɪ]   hungrig sein
nut [nʌt]   Nuß
• camp fire ['kæmp ˌfaɪə]   • Lagerfeuer
pull ... from the burned skin   ... von der verbrannten
    [pʊl frəm ðə bɜːnd skɪn]   Haut abziehen
pull [pʊl]   ziehen, zerren
give* reasons [ɡɪv 'riːznz]   Gründe angeben,
    begründen

A 1

• seal [siːl]   • Seehund
• hunt [hʌnt]   • Jagd
protest ['prəʊtest]   Protest
• on the eve of   • am Tage vor, am Vor-
    [ɒn ðiː_'iːv_əv]   abend von
• EEC (= European Economic   • EG (= Europäische
    Community) [ˌiːˌiːˈsiː   Gemeinschaft)
    (ˌjʊərə'piːən ˌiːkə'nɒmɪk
    kə'mjuːnətɪ)]
environment minister   Umweltminister
    [ɪn'vaɪərənmənt 'mɪnɪstə]

animal lover ['ænɪml 'lʌvə] — Tierfreund
from all over Britain [frɒm 'ɔːl 'əʊvə 'brɪtn] — aus ganz Großbritannien
protest [prə'test] — protestieren
•Department of the Environment [dɪ'pɑːtmənt əv ðiː ɪn'vaɪərənmənt] — •Umweltministerium
Canadian [kə'neɪdjən] — kanadisch; Kanadier(in)
off Newfoundland [ɒf 'njuːfəndlənd] — vor (der Küste von) Neufundland
a total of 195,000 animals [ə 'təʊtl əv 'wʌn 'hʌndrəd ən 'naɪntɪ faɪv 'θaʊznd 'ænɪmlz] — insgesamt 195000 Tiere
total ['təʊtl] — (Gesamt-)Menge, (End-)Summe
•count [kaʊnt] — •Zählung
•fur [fɜː] — •Fell, Pelz
trade [treɪd] — Handel
end [end] — (be-)enden
•slogan ['sləʊgən] — •Schlagwort, Parole
•halt imports [hɔːlt 'ɪmpɔːts] — •Importe stoppen
cut* down [kʌt daʊn] — abholzen, fällen
lorry ['lɒrɪ] — Lastwagen

A 2
•mark [mɑːk] — •Note
fairly good ['feəlɪ gʊd] — ganz gut
I ought to try that [aɪ 'ɔːtə 'traɪ ðæt] — ich sollte es versuchen/ausprobieren
nonsense ['nɒnsəns] — Unsinn, Quatsch
soft drink [sɒft drɪŋk] — alkoholfreies Getränk
glass bottle [glɑːs 'bɒtl] — Glasflasche
re-usable [ˌriː'juːzəbl] — wiederverwendbar
refuse [rɪ'fjuːz] — ablehnen, sich weigern
•can [kæn] — •Dose
non-returnable [ˌnɒnrɪ'tɜːnəbl] — keine Rückgabe möglich
whenever [wen'evə] — wann (auch) immer; wenn
wrap [ræp] — einpacken, einwickeln
ride* a bike [raɪd ə baɪk] — mit dem Fahrrad fahren
do* without . . . [duː wɪ'ðaʊt] — ohne . . . auskommen
•pressure-group ['preʃə gruːp] — •Interessengruppe
keep* . . . out of your town [kiːp aʊt əv jɔː taʊn] — . . . aus Ihrer Stadt heraushalten
re-use [ˌriː'juːs] — Wiederverwendung
throw* away [θrəʊ ə'weɪ] — wegwerfen
tyre ['taɪə] — Reifen
•adventure playground [əd'ventʃə 'pleɪgraʊnd] — •Abenteuerspielplatz
feel* cold [fiːl 'kəʊld] — frieren
put* on a pullover [pʊt ɒn ə 'pʊləʊvə] — einen Pullover anziehen
turn the heating up [tɜːn ðə 'hiːtɪŋ ʌp] — die Heizung aufdrehen
•recycling [ˌriː'saɪklɪŋ] — •Wiederaufbereitung, Recycling
collect [kə'lekt] — sammeln

material [mə'tɪərɪəl] — Material
waste metal [weɪst 'metl] — Altmetall, Schrott
metal ['metl] — Metall
disagree [ˌdɪsə'griː] — nicht einverstanden/anderer Meinung sein
protect [prə'tekt] — schützen

A 3
•environmental problem [ɪnˌvaɪərən'mentl 'prɒbləm] — •Umweltproblem
•plantation [plæn'teɪʃn] — •Plantage
control [kən'trəʊl] — unter Kontrolle bringen
•rat [ræt] — •Ratte
•mongoose ['mɒŋguːs] — •Mungo
•crop [krɒp] — •Ernte
they did not cause very much damage [ðeɪ dɪd nɒt kɔːz 'verɪ 'mʌtʃ 'dæmɪdʒ] — sie richteten nicht sehr viel Schaden an
lizard ['lɪzəd] — •Eidechse
•rapidly ['ræpɪdlɪ] — •(sehr) schnell, rapide
•completely [kəm'pliːtlɪ] — •völlig
ruin ['ruɪn] — zerstören, vernichten, ruinieren
fault [fɔːlt] — Schuld
maybe the manager didn't look far enough ahead ['meɪbɪ ðə 'mænɪdʒə 'dɪdnt lʊk 'fɑːr ɪ'nʌf ə'hed] — vielleicht hat der Manager nicht weit genug vorausgeschaut
•it was most unfortunate [ɪt wəz 'məʊst ʌn'fɔːtʃnət] — •es war höchst bedauerlich
•ecology [iː'kɒlədʒɪ] — •Ökologie (Lehre von den Beziehungen der Lebewesen zur Umwelt)
•Pied Piper of Hamelin ['paɪd 'paɪpər əv 'hæmlɪn] — •Rattenfänger von Hameln
•spray [spreɪ] — •spritzen, (be-)sprühen
poison ['pɔɪzn] — vergiften
nature ['neɪtʃə] — Natur

B 1
•tale [teɪl] — •Geschichte, Erzählung
floods [flʌdz] — Überschwemmung, Hochwasser
snowstorm ['snəʊstɔːm] — Schneesturm
storm [stɔːm] — Sturm
order ['ɔːdə] — anweisen, befehlen
•the authorities [ðiː ɔː'θɒrətɪz] — •die Behörden
die of cold [daɪ əv 'kəʊld] — erfrieren
far below zero ['fɑː bɪ'ləʊ 'zɪərəʊ] — weit unter Null
thousands of people ['θaʊzndz əv 'piːpl] — Tausende von Menschen
•power line ['paʊə laɪn] — •Hochspannungsleitung
travel by rail ['trævl baɪ 'reɪl] — Reisen mit der Bahn
travel by air ['trævl baɪ 'eə] — Fliegen
alive [ə'laɪv] — lebend, am Leben

mouth [maʊθ] — Mund
stuck to his car door — an der Tür seines Autos angefroren
[stʌk tə hɪz ˌkɑː ˈdɔː]
•stick* [stɪk] — (an-)kleben
•breathe [briːð] — •atmen
frozen [ˈfrəʊzn] — gefroren
•lock [lɒk] — (Tür-)Schloß
•ice-covered [ˈaɪsˌkʌvəd] — •eisbedeckt
slip [slɪp] — ausrutschen
snow [snəʊ] — schneien
•catch* [kætʃ] — •hier: steckenbleiben
traffic jam [ˈtræfɪk dʒæm] — Verkehrsstau
cloud [klaʊd] — Wolke
high waters [haɪ ˈwɔːtəz] — Hochwasser
fight* against [ˈfaɪt əˈgenst] — kämpfen gegen
border [ˈbɔːdə] — (Landes-)Grenze
•pavement [ˈpeɪvmənt] — •Gehweg, Bürgersteig

(3)

evening out [ˈiːvnɪŋ ˈaʊt] — Ausgehabend
day out [ˌdeɪ ˈaʊt] — Tagesausflug
anybody [ˈenɪˌbɒdɪ] — (irgend-)jemand
suggestion [səˈdʒestʃən] — Vorschlag
•barbecue [ˈbɑːbɪkjuː] — •Grillparty

A 4

(Helen Jones) speaking — am Apparat
[ˈspiːkɪŋ]
•Glastonbury [ˈglæstənbərɪ] — •Stadt im Südwesten Englands
•W.I. (= Women's Institute) — •Frauenorganisation in Großbritannien
[ˈdʌbljuːˈaɪ]
(ˈwɪmɪnzˈɪnstɪtjuːt)
set* the date for . . . — den Termin für . . . vereinbaren/festsetzen
[set ðə ˈdeɪt fɔː]
•bowls [bəʊlz] — •Rasen-Bowling
possibly [ˈpɒsəblɪ] — vielleicht, möglicherweise
half the team [ˈhɑːf ðə ˌtiːm] — die halbe Mannschaft
captain [ˈkæptɪn] — Kapitän
• . . . to fit you in — • . . . euch unterzubringen
[tə ˈfɪt juː ˈɪn]
hold the line [ˌhəʊld ðə ˈlaɪn] — bleib am Apparat
a second [əˈsekənd] — eine Sekunde
lovely [ˈlʌvlɪ] — hier: prima
that's settled [ˌðæts ˈsetld] — abgemacht
parents-in-law — Schwiegereltern
[ˈpeərəntsˌɪn lɔː]
go* for a run in the woods — einen Waldlauf machen
[gəʊ fər_ə ˌrʌn_ɪn ðə ˈwʊdz]
game of cards [geɪm əv ˈkɑːdz] — Kartenspiel
•slide [slaɪd] — •Dia
make arrangements to meet . . . — bereiten Sie ein Treffen mit . . . vor
[meɪk əˈreɪndʒmənts tə ˈmiːt]
arrangement [əˈreɪndʒmənt] — Vorkehrung, Vorbereitung

A 5

what made you join the . . . ? — was hat Sie veranlaßt, . . . beizutreten?
[ˈwɒt meɪd juː ˌdʒɔɪn ðə]
•Constitutional Club — •Freizeitklub in Großbritannien
[ˌkɒnstɪˈtjuːʃənl klʌb]
ever since [ˈevə ˌsɪns] — seit(dem)
•bowling green — •Rasenfläche für Bowling
[ˈbəʊlɪŋ griːn]
I go along to . . . — ich gehe zum . . .
[aɪ gəʊ_əˈlɒŋ tə]
•Labour Club [ˈleɪbə klʌb] — •Freizeitklub in Großbritannien, vor allem für Anhänger der Labour Party
•folk club [ˈfəʊklʌb] — •Klub, in dem Folksänger auftreten
sing* along [sɪŋ_əˈlɒŋ] — mitsingen
keep* fit [ˌkiːp ˈfɪt] — fit bleiben

B 2

•Radmoor Social Club — •Radmoor Freizeitklub
[ˈrædmʊə ˈsəʊʃl klʌb]
•darts [dɑːts] — •Pfeilwerfen (Spiel)
•entertainment [ˌentəˈteɪnmənt] — •Unterhaltung

•Yukon River [ˈjuːkɒn ˈrɪvə] — •Fluß in Alaska
•pack (of cards) [pæk] — •Satz Spielkarten
•draw* [drɔː] — •zeichnen, skizzieren
•show [ʃəʊ] — •Vorstellung (Theater)
•marvellous [ˈmɑːvələs] — •wunderbar, phantastisch
•the Alps [ðiː_ˈælps] — •die Alpen
•set [set] — •hier: Kasten
•artist [ˈɑːtɪst] — •Maler, Künstler
•such a [sʌtʃ_ə] — •so ein(e)
•do* the bedroom — •das Schlafzimmer renovieren
[duː ðə ˈbedrʊm]

Unit 5/Revision

R 1

politician [ˌpɒlɪˈtɪʃn] — Politiker(in)
•musician [mjuːˈzɪʃn] — •Musiker(in)
imagine [ɪˈmædʒɪn] — sich (etwas) vorstellen
ocean [ˈəʊʃn] — Meer, Ozean
get* out of control — außer Kontrolle geraten
[get_aʊt_əv kənˈtrəʊl]
fall* down [fɔːl daʊn] — herunterfallen
out of the sky — vom Himmel (herunter)
[ˌaʊt_əv ðə ˈskaɪ]
sky [skaɪ] — Himmel

towards the water
[təˈwɔːdz ðə ˈwɔːtə]

in Richtung Wasser

on purpose [ɒn ˈpɜːpəs]

mit Absicht, absichtlich

what you all do for a living . . .
[ˈwɒt_jʊ_ɔːl ˌduː fər_ə ˈlɪvɪŋ]

wie Sie Ihren Lebens-
unterhalt verdienen . . .

profession [prəˈfeʃn]

Beruf

excuse [ɪkˈskjuːs]

Ausrede, Entschuldigung

R 2

•survey [ˈsɜːveɪ]

•Umfrage

publish [ˈpʌblɪʃ]

veröffentlichen

a short time ago
[ə ˌʃɔːt ˈtaɪm_əˈgəʊ]

vor kurzem

•percentage [pəˈsentɪdʒ]

•Prozentsatz

relative [ˈrelətɪv]

Verwandte(r)

•exercise [ˈeksəsaɪz]

•Sport treiben

•jog [dʒɒg]

•Dauerlauf machen,
joggen

•pursue a hobby
[pəˈsjuː_ə ˈhɒbɪ]

•einem Hobby nachgehen

•have sex [hæv ˈseks]

•mit jemandem schlafen,
Geschlechtsverkehr
haben

•questionnaire [ˌkwestɪəˈneə]

•Fragebogen

R 3

•snakes and ladders
[ˌsneɪks_ən ˈlædəz]

•Schlangen und Leitern
(Brettspiel)

dice (Mehrzahl: dice)
[daɪs]

Würfel

counter [ˈkaʊntə]

Spielmarke

in turn [ɪn tɜːn]

abwechselnd, der Reihe
nach

square [skweə]

Quadrat, (Spiel-)Feld

finish [ˈfɪnɪʃ]

Ziel, Ende

R 4

leaflet [ˈliːflɪt]

Prospekt, Broschüre

•comment [ˈkɒment]

•Bemerkung, Kommentar

•letter of complaint
[ˈletər_əv kəmˈpleɪnt]

•Beschwerdebrief

•four-course meal
[ˈfɔːkɔːs ˈmiːl]

•Essen mit vier Gängen

•nearby [nɪəˈbaɪ]

•in der Nähe, nahe gelegen

charge [tʃɑːdʒ]

berechnen, in Rechnung
stellen

•packed lunch
[pækt lʌntʃ]

•Imbiß-/Lunchpaket

•drive [draɪv]

•(Auto-)Fahrt

first-class menu
[ˈfɜːstklɑːs ˈmenjuː]

erstklassige Speisekarte

down to the river
[daʊn tə ðə ˈrɪvə]

zum Fluß hinunter

band [bænd]

(Musik-)Kapelle,
(Tanz-)Orchester

stage [steɪdʒ]

Bühne

charming [ˈtʃɑːmɪŋ]

entzückend, reizend

•open-air theatre
[ˌəʊpnˈeə ˈθɪətə]

•Freilichttheater

smell [smel]

Geruch, Gestank

unforgettable
[ˌʌnfəˈgetəbl]

unvergeßlich

R 5

•anagram game
[ˈænəgræm geɪm]

•Buchstabenversetzrätsel

R 6

degree [dɪˈgriː]

akademischer Grad
(Hochschulabschluß)

prisoner-of-war
[ˈprɪznər_əv ˈwɔː]

Kriegsgefangene(r)

•Allied bombers
[ˈælaɪd ˈbɒməz]

•Bombenflugzeuge der
Alliierten

•novel [ˈnɒvl]

•Roman

promising [ˈprɒmɪsɪŋ]

vielversprechend

step forward
[step ˈfɔːwəd]

Schritt voran/vorwärts

•marvellous [ˈmɑːvələs]

•herrlich, wunderbar

sunshine [ˈsʌnʃaɪn]

Sonnenschein

take* care of
[teɪk ˈkeər_əv]

aufpassen auf

•regulation [ˌregjʊˈleɪʃn]

•Vorschrift, Regelung

•CND (= Campaign for
Nuclear Disarmament)
[ˌsiːenˈdiː: (kæmˈpeɪn fə
ˈnjuːklɪə dɪsˈɑːməmənt)]

•Friedensbewegung in
Großbritannien

•member's pack
[ˈmembəz pæk]

•etwa: Paket mit Mit-
gliedsunterlagen

•rate [reɪt]

•hier: (Mitglieds-)Beitrag

loud(ly) [laʊd(lɪ)]

laut

I can't stand the noise
[aɪ ˈkɑːnt ˌstænd ðə ˈnɔɪz]

ich kann diesen Lärm
nicht ertragen/aus-
halten

•letter to the editor
[ˈletə tə ðiː ˈedɪtə]

•Leserbrief

notebook [ˈnəʊtbʊk]

Notizbuch

discover [dɪˈskʌvə]

entdecken

. . . will put themselves
to great trouble
[wɪl pʊt ðəmˈselvz
tə ˈgreɪt ˈtrʌbl]

. . . werden sich viel Mühe
machen

nice-looking [ˌnaɪsˈlʊkɪŋ]

nett/sympathisch
aussehend

R 7

•picture-link game
[ˈpɪktʃəlɪŋk ˌgeɪm]

•Spiel, in dem die Bilder
miteinander in Zusam-
menhang gebracht
werden müssen

Unit 6

refresher [rɪ'freʃə] — Erfrischung; *hier:* Entspannungsübung

gentle ['dʒentl] — sanft
exercise ['eksəsaɪz] — (Leibes-)Übung
close your eyes ['kləʊz jər_'aɪz] — schließen Sie die Augen

hang* down [hæŋ daʊn] — herunterhängen
hold* still [həʊld stɪl] — stillhalten
straighten up ['streɪtn_'ʌp] — sich aufrichten
... gently stretches the legs ['dʒentlɪ 'stretʃɪz ðə 'legz] — ... dehnt die Beinmuskulatur auf sanfte Weise

refreshing effect [rɪ'freʃɪŋ_ɪ'fekt] — erfrischende Wirkung
stand* straight [stænd streɪt] — gerade stehen
apart [ə'pɑːt] — auseinander
the body will come (right) over [ðə 'bɒdɪ wɪl kʌm 'raɪt_'əʊvə] — der Körper wird (ganz) herunterhängen

force [fɔːs] — (er-)zwingen
direction [dɪ'rekʃn] — Anweisung

original [ə'rɪdʒənl] — originell
sew* on buttons [səʊ_ɒn 'bʌtnz] — Knöpfe annähen
fix [fɪks] — reparieren, in Ordnung bringen

climb trees [klaɪm triːz] — auf Bäume klettern
poem ['pəʊɪm] — Gedicht
play [pleɪ] — (Theater-)Stück
grow* roses [grəʊ 'rəʊzɪz] — Rosen züchten
change one's mind [tʃeɪndʒ wʌnz 'maɪnd] — es sich anders überlegen, seine Meinung ändern

A 1

promise ['prɒmɪs] — Versprechen
specialist ['speʃəlɪst] — Spezialist(in), Fachmann
host-family accommodation ['həʊst,fæməli:_ə,kɒmə'deɪʃn] — Unterbringung in Gastfamilien
within easy reach of ... [wɪ'ðɪn 'iːzɪ 'riːtʃ_əv] — in unmittelbarer Nähe von ..., leicht erreichbar von ...
within [wɪ'ðɪn] — in, innerhalb
tube [tjuːb] — Untergrundbahn *(in London)*
at one time [ət wʌn 'taɪm] — zur selben Zeit
opportunity [ɒpə'tjuːnətɪ] — Gelegenheit, Chance
spoil* [spɔɪl] — verderben
adventure [əd'ventʃə] — Unternehmen, Abenteuer

to this end [tə ðɪs_'end] — deshalb, deswegen
assurance [ə'ʃʊərəns] — Zusicherung
guaranteed [,gærən'tiːd] — garantiert
round the clock [raʊnd ðə klɒk] — rund um die Uhr
under 16 years of age ['ʌndə 'sɪksti:n jɜːz_əv_'eɪdʒ] — unter 16 (Jahren)
admit [əd'mɪt] — zulassen, aufnehmen
assistant [ə'sɪstənt] — Assistent(in)
straight [streɪt] — direkt
information sheet [,ɪnfə'meɪʃn ʃiːt] — Informationsblatt
district ['dɪstrɪkt] — Bezirk
take* home [teɪk həʊm] — nach Hause bringen, mit nach Hause nehmen
a light meal [ə laɪt 'miːl] — ein kleiner Imbiß
talk [tɔːk] — Vortrag
explanation [,eksplə'neɪʃn] — Erklärung
postage ['pəʊstɪdʒ] — Porto
at all times [ət_'ɔːl 'taɪmz] — jederzeit, ständig
full-board ['fʊl'bɔːd] — Vollpension
at a small extra charge [ət_ə 'smɔːl_,ekstrə 'tʃɑːdʒ] — gegen geringen Aufpreis

A 2

I don't seem to be making any progress [aɪ 'dəʊnt siːm tə bɪ 'meɪkɪŋ_'enɪ 'prəʊgres] — ich scheine keine Fortschritte zu machen
the thing is [ðə θɪŋ_'ɪz] — das Problem ist; die Sache ist die
sheet of paper [ʃiːt_əv 'peɪpə] — Blatt Papier
test [test] — kontrollieren, testen
grammar ['græmə] — Grammatik
native speaker ['neɪtɪv 'spiːkə] — Muttersprachler(in)
knit* [nɪt] — stricken

B 1

enthusiasm [ɪn'θjuːzɪæzəm] — Begeisterung
choice [tʃɔɪs] — (Aus-)Wahl
in much the same way [ɪn 'mʌtʃ ðə seɪm 'weɪ] — auf ähnliche Weise
speed [spiːd] — Tempo, Geschwindigkeit
fail [feɪl] — keinen Erfolg haben, versagen
time and time again ['taɪm_n 'taɪm_ə'gen] — immer wieder
hesitate ['hezɪteɪt] — zögern
risk [rɪsk] — Risiko
satisfied ['sætɪsfaɪd] — zufrieden
regret [rɪ'gret] — bereuen
tick [tɪk] — abhaken, ankreuzen
Ms [mɪz] — Frau/Fräulein *(wie bei 'Mr' ist auch bei 'Ms' der Familienstand nicht erkennbar)*

· vehicle ['viːɪkl] — · Fahrzeug
· lean* out of the window — · aus dem Fenster
  [liˌɪˌaʊt_əv ðə 'wɪndəʊ] — (hinaus)lehnen
paint [peɪnt] — Farbe
unsuitable [ˌʌnˈsuːtəbl] — ungeeignet
go* near [gəʊ 'nɪə] — (sich) nähern, nahe
  herangehen

watch out! [ˌwɒtʃ_ˈaʊt] — aufpassen! Vorsicht!
· overtake* [ˌəʊvəˈteɪk] — · überholen
get* nervous [get 'nɜːvəs] — nervös werden
get* on a plane — in ein Flugzeug steigen
  [get_ɒn_ə 'pleɪn]

A 3

look out! [ˌlʊk_ˈaʊt] — Vorsicht!
mind your head! — Kopf einziehen!
  [maɪnd_jə 'hed]
mind [maɪnd] — aufpassen/achten auf
drunk [drʌŋk] — betrunken
· caution ['kɔːʃn] — · Vorsicht; Warnung
avoid [əˈvɔɪd] — (ver-)meiden, ausweichen
· for external use only — · nur äußerlich an-
  [fər_ekˈstɜːnl juːs 'əʊnli] — zuwenden
out of the reach of children — außer Reichweite von
  [aʊt_əv ðə riːtʃ_əv 'tʃɪldrən] — Kindern
· keep out [ˌkiːp_ˈaʊt] — · Betreten verboten
rock [rɒk] — Stein

A 4

mother cares ['mʌðə 'keəz] — Mutter macht sich Sorgen
admit [ədˈmɪt] — zugeben
... turning me grey — meine Haare werden
  ['tɜːnɪŋ mɪ 'greɪ] — grau davon
grey [greɪ] — grau
deal* with ['diːl wɪθ] — umgehen/fertigwerden
  mit

· pot [pɒt] — · hier: Marihuana
swear* [sweə] — fluchen
I am worried to death — ich sorge mich zutiefst
  [aɪm 'wʌrɪd tə 'deθ]
get* into trouble — in Schwierigkeiten
  [get_ˈɪntə 'trʌbl] — kommen
sex we came to an — über Sex haben wir uns
  agreement on — geeinigt
  ['seks wɪ keɪm tʊ_ən_
  əˈgriːmənt_ɒn]
agreement [əˈgriːmənt] — Übereinkommen
careless ['keəlɪs] — unvorsichtig, leichtsinnig
drug [drʌg] — Droge, Rauschgift
soft drugs [sɒft drʌgz] — weiche Drogen
  (z. B. Marihuana)
... would worry me sick — ... würde mich krank
  [wʊd 'wʌrɪ mɪ 'sɪk] — machen vor Sorge
take* notice of ... — Notiz nehmen von ...,
  [teɪk 'nəʊtɪs_əv] — beachten

the more I talk, — je mehr ich rede, desto
  the less they listen — weniger hören sie mir
  [ðə 'mɔːr_aɪ 'tɔːk — zu
  ðə 'les ðeɪ 'lɪsn]
point of view [ˌpɔɪnt_əv 'vjuː] — Standpunkt
do* next [dʊ 'nekst] — als Nächstes tun
... which seems beyond my — ... auf die ich an-
  control — scheinend keinen
  [wɪtʃ siːmz bɪˈjɒnd maɪ — Einfluß habe
  kənˈtrəʊl]
beyond [bɪˈjɒnd] — jenseits, außerhalb

A 5

· individual [ˌɪndɪˈvɪdjʊəl] — · Einzelne(r), Individuum
· drug-related problems — · Probleme, die mit
  [ˌdrʌgrɪˈleɪtɪd 'prɒbləmz] — Rauschgift zusammen-
  hängen
· get* down to brass tacks — · zur Sache kommen
  [get daʊn tə 'brɑːs 'tæks]
nuclear ['njuːklɪə] — Atom-; atomar
· hassle ['hæsl] — · etwa: Hin und Her,
  Theater
· cruel ['krʊəl] — · grausam
· de-humanized — · entmenschlicht
  [ˌdiːˈhjuːmənaɪzd]
stuff [stʌf] — Zeug, Stoff; hier: Rauschgift
· collapse [kəˈlæps] — · zusammenbrechen
· pour [pɔː] — · eingießen, einschenken
· roll a joint [rəʊl ə dʒɔɪnt] — · einen Joint (Marihuana-
  zigarette) drehen
· sniff coke [snɪf kəʊk] — · Kokain schnupfen
· switchboard ['swɪtʃbɔːd] — · Telefonzentrale
· pusher ['pʊʃə] — · Rauschgifthändler
· put their views — · ihre Meinung sagen
  [ˌpʊt ðeə 'vjuːz]

B 2

healthy (healthily) — gesund
  ['helθɪ(lɪ)]
a second time [ə 'sekənd taɪm] — ein zweites Mal
· lung cancer ['lʌŋ 'kænsə] — · Lungenkrebs
manage ['mænɪdʒ] — es schaffen, fertigbringen

1

· Guy Fawkes [ˌgaɪ 'fɔːks] — · Anführer der
  Pulververschwörung
  vom 5. 11. 1605
· celebrate ['selɪbreɪt] — · feiern
· failure ['feɪljə] — · Mißlingen
· Gunpowder Plot — · Verschwörung
  [ˈgʌnˌpaʊdə plɒt] — englischer Katholiken,
  König James I. und das
  gesamte Parlament in
  die Luft zu sprengen
· blow* up ['bləʊˌˈʌp] — · sprengen

light* [laɪt] • anzünden
stuff [stʌf] • stopfen
straw [strɔ:] • Stroh
roast chestnuts • Kastanien rösten
[rəʊst ˈtʃesnʌts]

2

Braemar Gathering • *die Hochlandspiele von*
[ˈbreɪmɑ: ˈgæðərɪŋ] *Braemar*
Balmoral [bælˈmɒrəl] • *Sommerresidenz der*
königlichen Familie in
Schottland, nahe
Aberdeen
piping [ˈpaɪpɪŋ] • Dudelsackspiel
bagpipe(s) [ˈbægpaɪp(s)] • Dudelsack
kilt [kɪlt] • Schottenrock
toss [tɒs] • werfen
caber [ˈkeɪbə] • *(Schottisch für:)* Pfahl,
Stamm
treetrunk [ˈtri:trʌŋk] • Baumstamm

3

pancake [ˈpænkeɪk] • Pfannkuchen
Lent [lent] • Fastenzeit
feastday [ˈfi:stdeɪ] • Fest-/Feiertag
flavour [ˈfleɪvə] • würzen
lemon [ˈlemən] • Zitrone
frying pan [ˈfraɪŋ pæn] • Bratpfanne

4

crown [kraʊn] • krönen
Maypole [ˈmeɪpəʊl] • Maibaum
covered [ˈkʌvəd] • bedeckt
perform [pəˈfɔ:m] • vorführen
ribbon [ˈrɪbən] • (buntes) Band
mass rallies [ˈmæs ˈræliz] • Massenkundgebungen

5

Llangollen Eisteddfod • *internationales*
[lanˈgolen ˌaɪsˈteðvɒd] *Musikfestival in Wales*
sound [saʊnd] • Klang
choir [ˈkwaɪə] • Chor

6

Hallowe'en [ˌhæləʊˈi:n] • Abend vor Allerheiligen
gift [gɪft] • Geschenk
barrel [ˈbærəl] • Faß
lantern [ˈlæntən] • Laterne
turnip [ˈtɜ:nɪp] • (Steck-)Rübe
candle [ˈkændl] • Kerze
term [tɜ:m] • Wort, Ausdruck
All Hallows' Eve • Abend vor Allerheiligen
[ˌɔ:l ˈhæləʊz ˈi:v]
All Saints' Day • Allerheiligen
[ˌɔ:l ˈseɪnts deɪ]
All Hallows' Day • Allerheiligen
[ˌɔ:l ˈhæləʊz deɪ]

Unit 7

apply for [əˈplaɪ fɔ:] sich bewerben um
... have just had a baby ... haben gerade ein
[həv ˈdʒʌst hæd_ə ˈbeɪbɪ] Kind bekommen
prize [praɪz] (Sieges-)Preis
• crossword [ˈkrɒswɜ:d] • Kreuzworträtsel
our weekend in Paris is off unser Wochenende in
[ˈaʊə ˌwi:kˈend_ɪn Paris muß abgesagt
ˈpærɪs_ɪz_ˈɒf] werden/ausfallen
sold out [ˌsəʊld_ˈaʊt] ausverkauft
... has just got divorced ... hat sich gerade
[həz ˈdʒʌst gɒt dɪˈvɔ:st] scheiden lassen
divorced [dɪˈvɔ:st] geschieden
my son's broken a leg mein Sohn hat sich das
[maɪ ˈsʌnz ˈbrəʊkən_ə ˈleg] Bein gebrochen
I've just been given my notice mir ist gerade gekündigt
[aɪv ˈdʒʌst bɪn ˈgɪvn maɪ ˈnəʊtɪs] worden
I didn't do very well in the exam Ich habe in der Prüfung
[aɪ ˈdɪdnt dʊ ˈverɪ ˈwel_ɪn nicht sehr gut
ði:_ɪgˈzæm] abgeschnitten
argument [ˈɑ:gjʊmənt] Streit, Auseinander-
setzung
arrest [əˈrest] verhaften

A 1

• engagement [ɪnˈgeɪdʒmənt] • Verlobung
• ... have great pleasure in • ... freuen sich ...
announcing ... bekanntzugeben
[hæv ˈgreɪt ˈpleʒər_ɪn_əˈnaʊnsɪŋ]
... have got engaged ... haben sich verlobt
[həv gɒt_ɪnˈgeɪdʒd]
actually [ˈæktʃʊəlɪ] *hier:* übrigens
• for the world [fə ðə ˈwɜ:ld] • um alles in der Welt
• coming of age • mündig/volljährig werden
[ˈkʌmɪŋ_əv_ˈeɪdʒ]
• marriage [ˈmærɪdʒ] • Heirat, Eheschließung

A 2

express letter [ˈɪkspres ˈletə] Eilbrief
• in answer to [ɪn_ˈɑ:nsə tʊ] • als Antwort auf
when I got back ... als ich zurückkam ...
[ˈwen_aɪ gɒt ˈbæk]
take* risks [teɪk rɪsks] Risiken eingehen
such a thing [sʌtʃ_ə θɪŋ] so etwas
shock [ʃɒk] Schock
• it's sure to take time • es wird sicher einige Zeit
[ɪts ˈʃʊə tə teɪk ˈtaɪm] dauern
in any way [ɪn_ˈenɪ ˈweɪ] auf jede Weise
I'd be glad [aɪd bɪ ˈglæd] ich würde mich freuen
there's room enough hier ist Platz genug
[ðeəz ru:m_ɪˈnʌf]
take* a few days off ein paar Tage freinehmen
[teɪk_ə fju: deɪz_ˈɒf]

• condolence [kənˈdəʊləns]
Beileid
leave* the past behind
die Vergangenheit hinter
[liːv ðə ˈpɑːst bɪˈhaɪnd]
sich lassen
move back [muːv ˈbæk]
zurückkehren
motorbike [ˈməʊtəbaɪk]
Motorrad
sharp bend [ʃɑːp bend]
scharfe Kurve
at high speed
mit hoher Geschwindig-
[ət ˈhaɪ ˈspiːd]
keit
lose* control of
die Gewalt verlieren über
[luːz kənˈtrəʊl‿əv]
. . . ran into the front of a lorry
. . . prallte frontal mit
[ræn‿ˌɪntə ðə ˈfrʌnt‿əv‿ə ˈlɒrɪ]
einem Lastwagen
zusammen
they ought to be home soon
sie müßten (eigentlich)
[ðeɪ‿ˈɔːtə bɪ həʊm ˈsuːn]
bald nach Hause
kommen

B 1
as to [ˈæz tʊ]
was . . . anbetrifft,
hinsichtlich
delay [dɪˈleɪ]
verzögern, hinauszögern
treatment [ˈtriːtmənt]
Behandlung
subject [ˈsʌbdʒɪkt]
Thema
• archbishop [ɑːtʃˈbɪʃəp]
• Erzbischof
make* a decision
eine Entscheidung fällen
[meɪk‿ə dɪˈsɪʒn]
• recover [rɪˈkʌvə]
• wieder gesund werden,
sich erholen
embarrassing [ɪmˈbærəsɪŋ]
peinlich, unangenehm
embarrass [ɪmˈbærəs]
in Verlegenheit bringen
• this point was made
• etwa: dies wurde unter-
[ðɪs ˌpɔɪnt wəz ˈmeɪd]
strichen
• after-dinner speech
• Tischrede
[ˈɑːftəˌdɪnə ˈspiːtʃ]
speech [spiːtʃ]
Rede
• Royal College of Nursing
• Schule für Kranken-
[ˌrɔɪəl ˈkɒlɪdʒ‿əv ˈnɜːsɪŋ]
schwestern
the problem facing the relatives
das Problem, dem die
[ðə ˈprɒbləm ˈfeɪsɪŋ ðə
Verwandten gegen-
ˈrelətɪvz]
überstehen
remain silent [rɪˈmeɪn ˈsaɪlənt]
schweigen
silent [ˈsaɪlənt]
schweigsam, still,
geräuschlos
• silence [ˈsaɪləns]
• (Still-)Schweigen
lonely [ˈləʊnlɪ]
einsam
actually [ˈæktʃʊəlɪ]
in Wirklichkeit
die in pain [daɪ‿ɪn peɪn]
schmerzvoll sterben
truth [truːθ]
Wahrheit
in other words [ɪn‿ˈʌðə wɜːdz]
mit anderen Worten
• honest [ˈɒnɪst]
• ehrlich
• if the care of the dying is to
• wenn die Pflege von
be improved [ɪf ðə ˈkeər‿əv
Sterbenden verbessert
ðə ˈdaɪɪŋ‿ɪz tə bɪˈɪmˈpruːvd]
werden soll
only if he is aware that . . .
nur wenn (es) ihm bewußt
[ˈəʊnlɪ‿ɪf hiːz‿ə ˈweə ðət]
ist, daß . . .
• extraordinary [ɪkˈstrɔːdnrɪ]
• außergewöhnlich
unconscious [ʌnˈkɒnʃəs]
bewußtlos

weak [wiːk]
schwach
. . . only serves to put off the
. . . dient nur dazu, den
time of death [ˈəʊnlɪ ˈsɜːvz
Zeitpunkt des Todes
tə ˌpʊt‿ˈɒf ðə ˌtaɪm‿əv ˈdeθ]
hinauszuzögern
• encourage [ɪnˈkʌrɪdʒ]
• ermutigen, unterstützen
• euthanasia [juːθəˈneɪzjə]
• Sterbehilfe
a clear difference
ein deutlicher Unter-
[ə ˈklɪə ˈdɪfrəns]
schied
useless [ˈjuːslɪs]
nutzlos, unnütz
• bring* about [brɪŋ‿əˈbaʊt]
• herbeiführen
its [ɪts]
sein/ihr

• definite plans
• feste Pläne
[ˈdefɪnɪt ˈplænz]
motorboat [ˈməʊtəbəʊt]
Motorboot
• up to Holland [ʌp tə ˈhɒlənd]
• nach Holland (hinauf)
climbing [ˈklaɪmɪŋ]
Bergsteigen
go* home [ˌgəʊ ˈhəʊm]
nach Hause gehen/fahren
go* for a ride on the bike
radfahren
[ˌgəʊ fər‿ə ˌraɪd‿ɒn ðə ˈbaɪk]
get* my hair cut
meine Haare schneiden
[get maɪ ˈheə kʌt]
lassen
take* things easy
sich ausruhen/ent-
[teɪk θɪŋz‿ˈiːzɪ]
spannen
tidy up [ˌtaɪdɪ‿ˈʌp]
aufräumen
hire [ˈhaɪə]
mieten
invite friends over
Freunde zu sich nach
[ɪnˈvaɪt ˈfrendz‿ˌəʊvə]
Hause einladen
take* the car in for a service
das Auto zur Inspektion
[teɪk ðə ˈkɑːr‿ɪn fər‿ə ˈsɜːvɪs]
bringen
service [ˈsɜːvɪs]
Service, Wartung,
Kundendienst
the spare bedroom
das Gästezimmer
[ðə ˈspeə ˈbedrʊm]
spare [ˈspeə]
extra, frei, übrig
I'm not certain
ich bin nicht sicher
[aɪm nɒt ˈsɜːtn]
go* swimming [ˌgəʊ ˈswɪmɪŋ]
schwimmen gehen
wouldn't you like to join us?
möchten Sie nicht mit-
[ˈwʊdnt jʊ laɪk tə ˈdʒɔɪn‿ʌs]
kommen?

A 3
if you could do me a favour
ob du mir einen Gefallen
[ɪf jʊ kʊd ˈduː miː‿ə ˈfeɪvə]
tun könntest
pick me up at the station
mich am Bahnhof
[pɪk miː‿ˈʌp‿ət ðə ˈsteɪʃn]
abholen
return ticket [rɪˈtɜːn ˈtɪkɪt]
Rückfahrkarte
single [ˈsɪŋgl]
Karte für einfache Fahrt
train services [ˈtreɪn ˈsɜːvɪsɪz]
Bahnverbindungen/-ver-
kehr

A 4
• speed trap [ˈspiːd træp]
• Radarfalle
mood [muːd]
Stimmung, Laune
• by the pool [baɪ ðə ˈpuːl]
• am Schwimmbecken

still 800 kilometres off
[stɪl ˈeɪtˌhʌndrəd
ˈkɪləˌmiːtəzˌˈɒf]
apartment block
[əˈpɑːtmənt blɒk]
retire [rɪˈtaɪə]

nuclear power
[ˈnjuːklɪə ˈpaʊə]
average family
[ˈævərɪdʒ ˈfæməlɪ]
polluted [pəˈluːtɪd]
have* equal rights
[hæv ˈiːkwəl ˈraɪts]
equal [ˈiːkwəl]
queue [kjuː]

noch 800 Kilometer
entfernt

Wohnblock

•aufhören zu arbeiten,
in Pension gehen
Atomkraft/-energie

Durchschnittsfamilie

•verschmutzt
gleichberechtigt sein

gleich
Schlange stehen,
anstehen

B 2

Northern Territories
[ˈnɔːðn ˈterɪtərɪz]
northern [ˈnɔːðn]
the wide open spaces
[ðə ˈwaɪd ˈəʊpən ˈspeɪsɪz]
Australian [ɒˈstreɪljən]

the outback [ðiːˌˈaʊtbæk]

keep* in touch with
[kiːpˌɪn ˈtʌtʃ wɪð]
cover [ˈkʌvə]
by means of
[baɪ ˈmiːnzˌəv]
radio base [ˈreɪdɪəʊ beɪs]
transmitter [trænzˈmɪtə]
operate [ˈɒpəreɪt]
settler [ˈsetlə]
otherwise [ˈʌðəwaɪz]
development [dɪˈveləpmənt]
mark with a cross
[ˈmɑːk wɪðˌəˈkrɒs]
cross [krɒs]
write* down [raɪt daʊn]

•Nordterritorium
    (in Australien)
Nord-; nördlich
etwa: das weite, offene
    Land
australisch;
    Australier(in)
•das Hinterland
    (in Australien)
in Kontakt bleiben mit

•bedecken; hier: umfassen
durch, (ver-)mittels

•Radiostation
•Sender
•bedienen
•Siedler
andernfalls, sonst
Entwicklung
ankreuzen

Kreuz
aufschreiben

🐾🐾🐾

British Rail [ˈbrɪtʃ ˈreɪl]

in about six weeks' time
[ɪnˌəˈbaʊt ˈsɪksˌwiːks ˈtaɪm]
valid [ˈvælɪd]
day of issue
[deɪˌəvˌˈɪʃuː]
available [əˈveɪləbl]

•staatliche Eisenbahn-
    gesellschaft in
    Großbritannien
•in ungefähr sechs
    Wochen
•gültig
•Ausgabetag

•erhältlich

Unit 8

(1)

•pedal-bin [ˈpedl bɪn]
it's a new idea of mine
[ɪtsˌə ˈnjuːˌaɪˈdɪəˌv maɪn]
•empty the bin [ˈemptɪ ðə ˈbɪn]

(2)

•riddle [ˈrɪdl]
quickly [ˈkwɪklɪ]
•accurately [ˈækjʊrətlɪ]
•take* a coffee-break
[teɪkˌə ˈkɒfɪbreɪk]

A 1

•fully automatic
[ˈfʊliːˌˌɔːtəˈmætɪk]
robot [ˈrəʊbɒt]
the system reminds you less
of a factory than ...
[ðə ˈsɪstəm rɪˈmaɪndzˌjʊ
ˈlesˌəvˌə ˈfæktərɪ ðæn]
row [rəʊ]
on the ground [ɒn ðə ˈgraʊnd]
all around [ɔːl əˈraʊnd]

shape [ʃeɪp]
computer-controlled
[kəmˈpjuːtə kənˈtrəʊld]
... can work by themselves
[kən ˈwɜːk baɪ ðəmˈselvz]
the biggest of its kind
[ðə ˈbɪgɪstˌəvˌɪts ˈkaɪnd]
•more efficiently
[mɔːrˌɪˈfɪʃəntlɪ]
•trade-union official
[ˌtreɪdˈjuːnjənˌəˈfɪʃl]
employer [ɪmˈplɔɪə]
we don't doubt
[wɪ ˌdəʊnt ˈdaʊt]
technical progress
[ˈteknɪkl ˈprəʊgres]
•create [krɪˈeɪt]
what will be different with ...?
[ˈwɒt wɪl bɪ ˈdɪfrənt wɪθ]

A 2

purpose [ˈpɜːpəs]
well-known [ˈwelnəʊn]
the idea behind the personal
computer is ...
[ðiːˌaɪˈdɪə bɪˈhaɪnd ðə ˈpɜːsnl
kəmˈpjuːtərˌɪz]

•Treteimer
es ist eine meiner neuen
Ideen
•den Abfalleimer leeren

•Rätsel
schnell
•genau
•eine Kaffeepause
machen

•vollautomatisch

Roboter
die Anlage erinnert
weniger an eine Fabrik
als ...

Reihe
auf dem Boden
überall (herum),
ringsherum
Form
rechnergesteuert

... arbeiten selbständig

der Größte seiner Art

•rationeller, wirtschaft-
licher
•Gewerkschafts-
funktionär(in)
Arbeitgeber
wir bezweifeln nicht

der technische Fort-
schritt
•schaffen
was wird mit ... anders
sein?

Zweck
bekannt
der dem Heimcomputer
zugrundeliegende
Gedanke ist ...

V Vocabulary

- technology [tek'nɒlədʒɪ] — Technologie
- hardware ['hɑːdweə] — alle technisch-physikalischen Teile einer Datenverarbeitungsanlage

- monitor ['mɒnɪtə] — Bildschirm
- calculation [ˌkælkjʊ'leɪʃn] — Berechnung
- keyboard ['kiːbɔːd] — Tastatur
- printer ['prɪntə] — Drucker
  produce [prə'djuːs] — herstellen
  copy ['kɒpɪ] — Kopie
- disc [dɪsk] — Diskette, Magnetplatte
- store [stɔː] — speichern
- disc drive ['dɪskdraɪv] — Diskettenlaufwerk
- microprocessor [ˌmaɪkrəʊ'prəʊˌsesə] — Mikroprozessor
- description [dɪ'skrɪpʃn] — Beschreibung
  be* sick and tired of ... [bɪ 'sɪk_n 'taɪəd_əv] — es satt haben, ...
  beat* [biːt] — schlagen
- master ['mɑːstə] — Meister
  quality ['kwɒlətɪ] — Qualität
- software ['sɒftweə] — alle nicht technisch-physikalischen Teile einer Datenverarbeitungsanlage, z. B. Einsatzanweisungen, Programme

  dream [driːm] — Traum
  come* true [ˌkʌm 'truː] — wahr werden
  super ['suːpə] — phantastisch
  generous ['dʒenərəs] — großzügig
- terms [tɜːmz] — (Zahlungs-)Bedingungen
  smooth [smuːð] — glatt, reibungslos
  trust [trʌst] — vertrauen
  in this field [ɪn ðɪs fiːld] — auf diesem (Fach-)Gebiet

  kiss ... goodbye [kɪs ˌgʊd'baɪ] — ... einen Abschiedskuß geben
  kiss [kɪs] — küssen
  usual [juːʒʊəl] — gewöhnlich
  dull [dʌl] — langweilig
- chess [tʃes] — Schach

B 1

  disadvantage [ˌdɪsəd'vɑːntɪdʒ] — Nachteil
- introduction [ˌɪntrə'dʌkʃn] — Einführung
  add up [ˌæd_'ʌp] — zusammenzählen, addieren
- profit most from ['prɒfɪt 'məʊst frəm] — am meisten profitieren von

  draw* [drɔː] — zeichnen, skizzieren
  I didn't care for [aɪ 'dɪdnt 'keə fə] — ich war nicht begeistert von

  I was very pleased with [aɪ wəz 'verɪ 'pliːzd wɪð] — ich war sehr zufrieden mit
  chocolate ['tʃɒklət] — Schokolade
  shoe-cream ['ʃuːkriːm] — Schuhcreme
  handkerchief ['hæŋkətʃɪf] — Taschentuch
  photograph ['fəʊtəgrɑːf] — Foto
  lend* [lend] — leihen

  thirsty ['θɜːstɪ] — durstig
  just now [dʒʌst 'naʊ] — im Moment
  stand* in a queue [stænd_ɪn_ə 'kjuː] — Schlange stehen, anstehen
  take* a bath [teɪk_ə 'bɑːθ] — baden, ein Bad nehmen
  change places [tʃeɪndʒ 'pleɪsɪz] — die Plätze tauschen
  performance [pə'fɔːməns] — (Theater-/Kino-)Vorstellung

A 3

  eastern ['iːstən] — Ost-; östlich
- Old Amish Order [əʊld_'eɪmɪʃ_'ɔːdə] — Sekte der Mennoniten in den USA
  I never realized [aɪ 'nevə 'rɪəlaɪzd] — mir ist nie bewußt gewesen
  realize ['rɪəlaɪz] — erkennen, sich klarwerden, begreifen

  come* from ... ['kʌm frɒm] — aus ... kommen
- Pennsylvania Dutch [ˌpensɪl'veɪnjə 'dʌtʃ] — Bezeichnung für Deutschstämmige in Pennsylvania und ihre Sprache
  their name is said to go back to ... [ðeə 'neɪm_ɪz ˌsed tə gəʊ 'bæk tʊ] — man sagt, daß ihr Name auf ... zurückzuführen ist
  leader ['liːdə] — (An-)Führer
- much as ['mʌtʃ_əz] — so wie
- the past two hundred years [ðə 'pɑːst 'tuː 'hʌndrəd 'jɜːz] — die letzten 200 Jahre
  dream* [driːm] — träumen
  behind the times [bɪ'haɪnd ðə 'taɪmz] — hinter seiner Zeit zurück (geblieben), veraltet
- carriage ['kærɪdʒ] — Kutsche, Wagen
  along the roads [ə'lɒŋ ðə 'rəʊdz] — die Straßen entlang
- in the style [ɪn ðə staɪl] — im Stil
  all the time [ˌɔːl ðə 'taɪm] — die ganze Zeit, immer
  the men have all got beards [ðə men həv_'ɔːl gɒt 'bɪədz] — die Männer tragen alle einen Bart
- cap [kæp] — Haube
  except for [ɪk'sept fə] — außer, mit Ausnahme von
  play an important part [pleɪ_ən_ɪm'pɔːtnt 'pɑːt] — eine wichtige Rolle spielen
  every two weeks ['evrɪ ˌtuː 'wiːks] — alle zwei Wochen

A 4

Dolgellau [dɒlˈgeɬaɪ]
County Gwynedd   •Grafschaft in Nordwales
   [ˈkaʊntɪ ˈgwɪnəð]
the latest attempt   •der jüngste Versuch
   [ðə ˈleɪtɪst_əˈtempt]
Sunday opening   •Öffnung (der Kneipen) an
   [ˈsʌndiː_ˈəʊpnɪŋ]   Sonntagen
be* in favour of   dafür sein
   [biː_ɪn ˈfeɪvər_əv]
absolutely bloody dead   •etwa: vollkommen tot
   [ˈæbsəluːtlɪ ˈblʌdɪ ˈded]
bloody [ˈblʌdɪ]   verdammt, verflucht
Middle Ages [ˈmɪdl_ˈeɪdʒɪz]   •Mittelalter
it's wrong [ɪts ˈrɒŋ]   es ist nicht richtig
get* drunk [get ˈdrʌŋk]   sich betrinken
I'm all in favour of . . .   ich bin ganz dafür, . . .
   [aɪm_ˈɔːl_ɪn ˈfeɪvər_əv]
shut [ʃʌt]   geschlossen
I don't think it makes   ich glaube nicht, daß es
   any difference   etwas ändert/ausmacht
   [aɪ ˈdəʊnt θɪŋk_ɪt
   meɪks_ˈenɪ ˈdɪfrəns]
ways and means   Mittel und Wege
   [ˈweɪz_ən ˈmiːnz]
I never go in them anyway   ich gehe sowieso nicht
   [aɪ ˈnevə gəʊ_ɪn ðəm_ˈenɪweɪ]   'rein
it makes no difference to me   das ist mir egal/einerlei
   [ɪt meɪks ˈnəʊ ˈdɪfrəns tə ˈmiː]
by-law [ˈbaɪlɔː]   •Verordnung
cut* the grass [kʌt ðə ˈgrɑːs]   den Rasen mähen

B 2

what are the feelings of the   wie empfindet die Jugend
   young towards . . . ?   . . . gegenüber?
   [ˈwɒt_ə ðə ˈfiːlɪŋz_əv
   ðə ˈjʌŋ təˈwɔːdz]
NB (= nota bene) [ˌenˈbiː]   •wohlgemerkt
chapel [ˈtʃæpl]   •nichthochkirchliches
      Gotteshaus in
      Großbritannien
established [ɪˈstæblɪʃt]   •etabliert
once [wʌns]   einst
people [ˈpiːpl]   hier: Volk
nation [ˈneɪʃn]   Nation
original [əˈrɪdʒənl]   ursprünglich
. . . are now in ruins   . . . sind jetzt Ruinen
   [ɑː ˈnaʊ_ɪn ˈruːɪnz]
congregation [ˌkɒŋgrɪˈgeɪʃn]   •(Kirchen-)Gemeinde
things have changed   die Verhältnisse haben
   [θɪŋz_əv ˈtʃeɪndʒd]   sich geändert
believe in [bɪˈliːv_ɪn]   glauben an
the poor [ðə ˈpʊə]   die Armen
single [ˈsɪŋgl]   ledig
expect a baby   ein Kind erwarten
   [ɪkˈspekt_ə ˈbeɪbɪ]
different from [ˈdɪfrənt frəm]   anders als

weekday [ˈwiːkdeɪ]   Werktag
•. . .changed out of our best   •. . . zogen unsere
   clothes   Sonntagskleider aus
   [tʃeɪndʒd_ˈaʊt_əv_ˌaʊə
   best ˈkləʊðz]
•. . . back into them   •. . . zogen sie wieder an
   [bæk_ˈɪntə ðəm]
•evening service   •Abendgottesdienst
   [ˈiːvnɪŋ ˈsɜːvɪs]
•in recent years   •in den letzten Jahren
   [ɪn ˈriːsnt ˈjɜːz]
lose* touch with one another   Kontakt zueinander ver-
   [luːz ˈtʌtʃ wɪθ wʌn_əˈnʌðə]   lieren
out of work [aʊt_əv ˈwɜːk]   arbeitslos
•as they go [əz ðeɪ ˈgəʊ]   •im Laufen
•can [kæn]   •Dose
restless [ˈrestlɪs]   rastlos
thick [θɪk]   dick
•bible [ˈbaɪbl]   •Bibel
walking-stick [ˈwɔːkɪŋstɪk]   Spazierstock
steep [stiːp]   steil
freezing [ˈfriːzɪŋ]   eiskalt
•by contrast [baɪ ˈkɒntrɑːst]   •im Gegensatz dazu
sense of . . . [sens_əv]   Gefühl/Sinn für . . .
•community [kəˈmjuːnətɪ]   •Gemeinschaft
•miner [ˈmaɪnə]   •Bergarbeiter
•nine years earlier   •vor neun Jahren
   [ˈnaɪn jɜːz_ˈɜːlɪə]
•comfort [ˈkʌmfət]   •Trost
once more [wʌns ˈmɔː]   noch einmal
•refer to [rɪˈfɜː tʊ]   •sich beziehen auf

👁👁👁

•Ironbridge Gorge   •Gebiet in Mittelengland
   [ˈaɪənbrɪdʒ ˈgɔːdʒ]
•remarkable breakthrough   •bemerkenswerter
   [rɪˈmɑːkəbl ˈbreɪkθruː]   Durchbruch
•workshop [ˈwɜːkʃɒp]   •Werkstatt
•retain [rɪˈteɪn]   •behalten, bewahren
•consist of [kənˈsɪst_əv]   •bestehen aus
•spread over [ˈspred_ˌəʊvə]   •verteilt über
•square mile [skweə ˈmaɪl]   •Quadratmeile
      (= 2,59 km²)
•the places illustrated   •die abgebildeten Orte
   [ðə ˈpleɪsɪz_ˈɪləstreɪtɪd]
•Blists Hill Open Air Museum   •Freilichtmuseum
   [ˈblɪsts ˈhɪl ˈəʊpən_ˈeə
   mjuːˈzɪəm]
•mine [maɪn]   •Bergwerk
•steelworks [ˈstiːlwɜːks]   •Stahlwerk
•blast furnace [ˈblɑːst ˈfɜːnɪs]   •Hochofen
•manufacture [ˌmænjʊˈfæktʃə]   •herstellen
•rebuild [ˌriːˈbɪld]   •wiederaufbauen
•Coalport China Works Museum   •Museum der
   [ˈkəʊlpɔːt ˈtʃaɪnə wɜːks   Porzellanherstellung
   mjuːˈzɪəm]

• fine bone china [faɪn bəʊn 'tʃaɪnə] — • Feinknochen-Porzellan

• works [wɜːks] — • Fabrik

• restore [rɪ'stɔː] — • restaurieren, wieder-herrichten

• span [spæn] — • überspannen, über-brücken

• tollhouse ['təʊlhaʊs] — • (Wege-)Zollstation

• exhibition [ˌeksɪ'bɪʃn] — • Ausstellung

• structure ['strʌktʃə] — • Bauwerk

• Severn Warehouse ['sevən 'weəhaʊs] — • ehemaliges Lagerhaus

• Coalbrookdale Company ['kəʊlbrʊkdeɪl 'kʌmpənɪ] — • Eisenwarenhersteller

• store [stɔː] — • lagern

• load [ləʊd] — • (be-)laden

• iron-founding collection ['aɪən.faʊndɪŋ kə'lekʃn] — • Sammlung von Produkten aus der Eisengießerei

as soon as possible [əz 'suːn_əz 'pɒsəbl] — so früh wie möglich

the sooner the better [ðə 'suːnə ðə 'betə] — je früher, desto besser

Lost Property Office [lɒst 'prɒpətɪ_'ɒfɪs] — Fundbüro

police officer [pə'liːs_'ɒfɪsə] — Polizeibeamter/-beamtin

the day before yesterday [ðə 'deɪ bɪ'fɔː 'jestədɪ] — vorgestern

a week ago yesterday [ə 'wiːk_ə'gəʊ 'jestədɪ] — gestern vor einer Woche, vor acht Tagen

stay with friends [steɪ wɪð 'frendz] — bei Freunden wohnen

handbag ['hændbæg] — Handtasche

I wanted to stay for another two weeks [aɪ 'wɒntɪd tə steɪ fər_ə'nʌðə 'tuː 'wiːks] — ich wollte noch zwei Wochen bleiben

in two days' time [ɪn 'tuː 'deɪz 'taɪm] — in zwei Tagen

just after breakfast ['dʒʌst_ˌɑːftə 'brekfəst] — gleich nach dem Früh-stück

surname ['sɜːneɪm] — Familienname

Christian name ['krɪstjən neɪm] — Vorname

• description [dɪ'skrɪpʃn] — • Beschreibung

• contents ['kɒntents] — • Inhalt

• remark [rɪ'mɑːk] — • Bemerkung

signature ['sɪgnətʃə] — Unterschrift

Unit 9

rate of exchange [reɪt_əv_ɪks'tʃeɪndʒ] — Wechselkurs

exchange [ɪks'tʃeɪndʒ] — (Um-/Aus-)Tausch

• loss [lɒs] — • Verlust

• theft [θeft] — • Diebstahl

available [ə'veɪləbl] — erhältlich, verfügbar

not fully accepted in all European countries ['nɒt 'fʊlɪ_ək'septɪd_ɪn_'ɔːl 'jʊərə'piːən 'kʌntrɪz] — werden nicht in allen europäischen Ländern problemlos ange-nommen

A 1

UK (= United Kingdom) [ˌjuː'keɪ (juː'naɪtɪd 'kɪŋdəm)] — Vereinigtes Königreich von Großbritannien und Nordirland

stay at [steɪ_ət] — (vorübergehend) wohnen bei/in

sometime this afternoon ['sʌmtaɪm ðɪs_ˌɑːftə'nuːn] — irgendwann heute nach-mittag

walk round [wɔːk raʊnd] — herumspazieren

notice ['nəʊtɪs] — bemerken, feststellen

note [nəʊt] — (Geld-)Schein, Note

small change [smɔːl 'tʃeɪndʒ] — Kleingeld

• identity card [aɪ'dentɪtɪ kɑːd] — • Personalausweis

in that case [ɪn 'ðæt keɪs] — in dem Fall

about this big [ə'baʊt 'ðɪs 'bɪg] — ungefähr so groß

without delay [wɪ'ðaʊt dɪ'leɪ] — unverzüglich

delay [dɪ'leɪ] — Verzögerung, Aufschub

A 2

worth £250 [wɜːθ] — im Werte von £250

• replace [rɪ'pleɪs] — • ersetzen

not on me [nɒt_'ɒn mɪ] — nicht bei mir

settle ['setl] — begleichen, bezahlen (Rechnung)

the only thing we could do [ðɪ:_'əʊnlɪ θɪŋ wɪ 'kʊd duː] — das Einzige, das wir tun können

• prove* your identity [pruːv jɔr_aɪ'dentətɪ] — • sich ausweisen

prove* [pruːv] — beweisen

they'll let you have new papers [ðeɪl let_jʊ hæv njuː 'peɪpəz] — sie werden Ihnen neue Papiere ausstellen

telegram ['telɪgræm] — Telegramm

by the time you get back [baɪ ðə 'taɪm jʊ get 'bæk] — bis Sie wieder zurück sind

branch [brɑːntʃ] — Zweigstelle, Filiale

we'll see to it at once [wiːl 'siː tʊ_ɪt_ət 'wʌns] — wir kümmern uns sofort darum

B 1

• attract [ə'trækt] — • anziehen, anlocken

pay back [peɪ bæk] — zurückzahlen

• High Street ['haɪ striːt] — • (in Großbritannien) wichtigste Einkaufs-straße einer Stadt

furniture ['fɜːnɪtʃə] — Möbel

• credit limit ['kredɪt 'lɪmɪt] — • Kreditrahmen

• currency ['kʌrənsɪ] — • Währung

agreed [əˈgriːd] — vereinbart
... carrying enough cash on you [ˈkærɪŋ ɪˈnʌf ˈkæʃ ɒn juː] — ... genügend Bargeld bei sich haben
statement [ˈsteɪtmənt] — •Kontoauszug
with full details [wɪθ ˈfʊl ˈdiːteɪlz] — ausführlich
18 years of age or over [ˈeɪtiːn ˈjɜːz ˈəv ˈeɪdʒ ɔː ˈəʊvə] — 18 Jahre alt oder älter
whichever [wɪtʃˈevə] — welche(r) auch immer
impression [ɪmˈpreʃn] — •Eindruck

judge [dʒʌdʒ] — Richter(in)
warn of [wɔːn əv] — warnen vor
prison sentence [ˈprɪzn ˌsentəns] — Freiheitsstrafe
sentence [ˈsentəns] — Strafe, Urteil; verurteilen
spending spree [ˈspendɪŋ spriː] — •Großeinkauf, Einkaufs-tour
... bought himself new clothes [bɔːt hɪmˈself njuː ˈkləʊðz] — ... kaufte sich neue Kleidung
West End [ˈwest ˈend] — •Einkaufs- und Amüsier-viertel in London

taxi [ˈtæksɪ] — Taxi
pay for in cash [ˈpeɪ fɔː ɪn ˈkæʃ] — bar bezahlen
I walked out with the goods [aɪ wɔːkt ˈaʊt wɪð ðə ˈgʊdz] — •ich spazierte mit der Ware hinaus
without even having the feeling ... [wɪˈðaʊt ˈiːvn ˈhævɪŋ ðə ˈfiːlɪŋ] — ohne das Gefühl zu haben, ...
fool [fuːl] — Narr
take* to court [teɪk tə ˈkɔːt] — vor Gericht bringen
fine [faɪn] — Geldstrafe
just as [ˈdʒʌst əz] — genauso
guilty [ˈgɪltɪ] — schuldig
stop them from ... [stɒp ðəm frəm] — sie hindern an ...
on condition [ɒn kənˈdɪʃn] — unter der Bedingung

moustache [məˈstɑːʃ] — •Schnurrbart
recognize [ˈrekəgnaɪz] — erkennen

A 3

... is back in films [ɪz ˈbæk ɪn ˈfɪlmz] — ... tritt wieder in Filmen auf
commercial [kəˈmɜːʃl] — •(Fernseh-)Werbespot
gun lobby [ˈgʌn ˈlɒbɪ] — •Interessengruppe für den privaten Besitz von Schußwaffen
gun [gʌn] — Schußwaffe
prevent [prɪˈvent] — (ver-)hindern
have* a 1 in 33 chance [hæv ə ˈwʌn ɪn ˈθɜːtɪˈθriː ˈtʃɑːns] — die Chancen stehen 1 zu 33
for reasons of ... [fɔː ˈriːznz əv] — aus Gründen des/der ...

safety [ˈseɪftɪ] — Sicherheit
defend [dɪˈfend] — verteidigen
weapon [ˈwepən] — Waffe

A 4

scientist [ˈsaɪəntɪst] — Wissenschaftler(in)
get* out of [get ˈaʊt əv] — aussteigen
case [keɪs] — Koffer
afterwards [ˈɑːftəwədz] — nachher, danach
drive* away [draɪv əˈweɪ] — wegfahren
shout [ʃaʊt] — rufen, schreien
fortunately [ˈfɔːtʃnətlɪ] — glücklicherweise
•bunch of keys [bʌntʃ əv ˈkiːz] — •Schlüsselbund
metal comb [ˈmetl ˈkəʊm] — Metallkamm
drop [drɒp] — fallen lassen; hier: verlieren
search [sɜːtʃ] — Suche
licence number [ˈlaɪsns ˈnʌmbə] — (Auto-)Kennzeichen
so far [səʊ ˈfɑː] — bisher

B 2

•capital punishment [ˈkæpɪtl ˈpʌnɪʃmənt] — •Todesstrafe
hang* [hæŋ] — aufhängen, henken
at that time [ət ˈðæt ˈtaɪm] — damals
•violence against the person [ˈvaɪələns əˈgenst ðə ˈpɜːsn] — •Gewalt gegen die Person
rise [raɪz] — Zunahme, Anstieg
•violent crime [ˈvaɪələnt ˈkraɪm] — •Gewaltverbrechen
crime [kraɪm] — Straftat, Verbrechen
sooner or later [ˈsuːnər ə ˈleɪtə] — früher oder später
•sure deterrent [ˈʃʊə dɪˈterənt] — •sicheres Abschreckungs-mittel
deserve [dɪˈzɜːv] — verdienen
•a recent radio programme [ə ˈriːsnt ˈreɪdɪəʊ ˈprəʊgræm] — •eine Rundfunksendung, die neulich ausge-strahlt wurde
lawyer [ˈlɔːjə] — (Rechts-)Anwalt/Anwältin
argue [ˈɑːgjuː] — streiten, ein Streit-gespräch führen
•Scotland Yard [ˈskɒtlənd ˈjɑːd] — •Hauptsitz der Londoner Kriminalpolizei
support [səˈpɔːt] — unterstützen

•humorous [ˈhjuːmərəs] — •humorvoll, lustig
•injustice [ɪnˈdʒʌstɪs] — •Ungerechtigkeit
•read* between the lines [ˌriːd bɪˈtwiːn ðə ˈlaɪnz] — •zwischen den Zeilen lesen
•verse [vɜːs] — •Strophe
•tell* a lie [tel ə ˈlaɪ] — •lügen
•justice [ˈdʒʌstɪs] — •Gerechtigkeit
•murderer [ˈmɜːdərə] — •Mörder
•elect [ɪˈlekt] — •wählen

Unit 10/Revision

R 1

point at [pɔɪnt‿ət]　　　　zeigen auf

R 2

... who is speaking to whom　　... wer mit wem spricht
['hu:z ˌspi:kɪŋ tə 'hu:m]

R 3

concerning [kən'sɜ:nɪŋ]　　betreffend
•responsible [rɪ'spɒnsəbl]　•verantwortungsvoll
•highly qualified　　　　　•hochqualifiziert
['haɪlɪ 'kwɒlɪfaɪd]
the remaining seven months　die übrigen sieben
[ðə rɪ'meɪnɪŋ 'sevn 'mʌnθs]　Monate
•bored [bɔ:d]　　　　　•gelangweilt
•frustrated [frʌ'streɪtɪd]　•frustriert
one another [wʌn‿ə'nʌðə]　einander
start [stɑ:t]　　　　　Beginn, Anfang
•job-sharing ['dʒɒb ʃeərɪŋ]　•Verfahren, bei dem sich
　　　　　　　　　　　zwei Arbeitnehmer
　　　　　　　　　　　einen Arbeitsplatz
　　　　　　　　　　　teilen
and so on [ən 'səʊ‿ɒn]　　und so weiter

R 4

•wheel of fortune　　　　•Glücksrad
[wi:l‿əv 'fɔ:tʃu:n]
wheel [wi:l]　　　　　Rad
nuclear power station　　Atomkraftwerk
['nju:klɪə 'paʊə 'steɪʃn]
stop smoking　　　　　mit dem Rauchen
[stɒp 'sməʊkɪŋ]　　　　aufhören
miss a turn [mɪs‿ə 'tɜ:n]　eine Runde aussetzen
warning ['wɔ:nɪŋ]　　　Warnung

•outer circle ['aʊtə 'sɜ:kl]　•äußerer Kreis
•inner circle ['ɪnə 'sɜ:kl]　•innerer Kreis
twice [twaɪs]　　　　　zweimal
... moves around the outer　... rückt im äußeren
circle　　　　　　　Kreis vor
[mu:vz‿ə'raʊnd ði:‿'aʊtə
'sɜ:kl]
it is the second player's turn　der zweite Spieler ist an
[ɪts ðə 'sekənd ˌpleɪəz 'tɜ:n]　der Reihe
as above [æz ə'bʌv]　　wie oben

R 5

•the odd word out game　•etwa: das „Ein-Wort-paßt-
[ðɪ‿'ɒd wɜ:d‿'aʊt geɪm]　nicht"-Spiel
•pyjamas [pə'dʒɑ:məz]　•Schlafanzug
sail [seɪl]　　　　　segeln

R 6

•recorded information service　•Fernsprechansagedienst
[rɪ'kɔ:dɪd ˌɪnfə'meɪʃn 'sɜ:vɪs]
record [rɪ'kɔ:d]　　　aufnehmen, aufzeichnen
　　　　　　　　　　(Tonband/Video)
•British Telecom　　　•Fernmeldewesen in Groß-
['brɪtɪʃ 'telɪkɒm]　　　britannien
•dial ['daɪəl]　　　　•wählen (Telefon)
•channel ['tʃænl]　　　•Kanal
•bedtime stories　　　•Gute-Nacht-Geschichten
['bedtaɪm 'stɔ:rɪz]
•motoring information　　•Verkehrshinweise
['məʊtərɪŋ ˌɪnfə'meɪʃn]
•recipe ['resɪpɪ]　　　•Kochrezept
•skiing information　　　•Wintersport(wetter)-
['ski:ɪŋ ˌɪnfə'meɪʃn]　　bericht
•weather forecast　　　•Wettervorhersage
['weðə 'fɔ:kɑ:st]
•recording [rɪ'kɔ:dɪŋ]　•Aufnahme, Aufzeichnung
　　　　　　　　　　(Tonband/Video)

R 7

forgive* [fə'gɪv]　　　verzeihen
since I last wrote　　　seit(dem) ich das letzte-
[sɪns‿aɪ lɑ:st rəʊt]　　mal geschrieben habe
trade was so bad　　　die Geschäfte gingen so
[treɪd wəz səʊ bæd]　　schlecht
close down [kləʊz daʊn]　schließen
look round [lʊk raʊnd]　sich umsehen
in sight [ɪn 'saɪt]　　　in (Aus-)Sicht
rather disappointing　　ziemlich enttäuschend
['rɑ:ðə ˌdɪsə'pɔɪntɪŋ]
I'm off [aɪm‿'ɒf]　　　ich gehe weg
a bit more luck [ə bɪt mɔ: 'lʌk]　ein bißchen mehr Glück
regards [rɪ'gɑ:dz]　　Gruß (Briefschluß)
•enclose [ɪn'kləʊz]　　•beilegen, beifügen
sales manager ['seɪlz ˌmænɪdʒə]　Verkaufsleiter
•mother tongue ['mʌðə 'tʌŋ]　•Muttersprache

Unit 11

•advertise ['ædvətaɪz]　　•werben
•advertiser ['ædvətaɪzə]　•Inserent(in)
influence ['ɪnflʊəns]　　beeinflussen
it is difficult to decide between　es ist schwer, sich für das
them [ɪts 'dɪfɪkəlt tə dɪ'saɪd　eine oder andere (Pro-
bɪ'twi:n ðəm]　　　　dukt) zu entscheiden
even though ['i:vn 'ðəʊ]　obwohl
nor do I like ... ['nɔ: dʊ‿aɪ laɪk]　noch mag ich ...
packet ['pækɪt]　　　Päckchen, Packung;
　　　　　　　　　　hier: Schachtel

particular [pəˈtɪkjʊlə] — besondere(r, s), bestimmt, speziell
•brand [brænd] — •Marke
twice as expensive [ˈtwaɪs_əz_ɪkˈspensɪv] — doppelt so teuer
the exact words [ðɪ_ɪgˈzækt ˈwɜːdz] — der genaue Wortlaut/Text
bring* this problem to people's notice [brɪŋ ðɪs ˈprɒbləm tə ˈpiːplz ˈnəʊtɪs] — die Leute auf dieses Problem aufmerksam machen

A 1

provide [prəˈvaɪd] — zur Verfügung stellen
working week [ˈwɜːkɪŋ ˈwiːk] — Wochenarbeitszeit
hurry up [ˈhʌriː_ˈʌp] — sich beeilen
make* a greater effort [meɪk_ə ˈgreɪtər_ˈefət] — sich mehr bemühen, mehr unternehmen für
effort [ˈefət] — Anstrengung, Bemühung
I don't altogether agree [aɪ dəʊnt_ɔːltəˈgeðər_əˈgriː] — ich stimme nicht völlig zu
social services [ˈsəʊʃl ˈsɜːvɪsɪz] — Sozialeinrichtungen
reduce [rɪˈdjuːs] — verringern, reduzieren
•retirement age [rɪˈtaɪəmənt_eɪdʒ] — •Rentenalter
put* up taxes [pʊt_ʌp ˈtæksɪz] — die Steuern erhöhen
the arts [ðɪ_ˈɑːts] — •Geisteswissenschaften
job-sharing [ˈdʒɒbˌʃeərɪŋ] — •Verfahren, bei dem sich zwei Arbeitnehmer einen Arbeitsplatz teilen

A 2

state of the country [steɪt_əv ðə ˈkʌntri] — Lage der Nation
•public opinion poll [ˈpʌblɪk_əˈpɪnjən pəʊl] — •Meinungsumfrage
elect [ɪˈlekt] — wählen
election [ɪˈlekʃn] — Wahl
carry out [ˈkæriː_ˈaʊt] — •durchführen
come* into power [kʌm_ˌɪntə ˈpaʊə] — an die Macht kommen
majority [məˈdʒɒrəti] — Mehrheit
voter [ˈvəʊtə] — Wähler(in)
the well-off [ðə ˌwelˈɒf] — die Wohlhabenden
the middle-class [ðə ˌmɪdlˈklɑːs] — die Mittelklasse
trade-unionist [ˌtreɪdˈjuːnjənɪst] — Gewerkschafter(in)
in power [ɪn ˈpaʊə] — an der Macht
that is to say [ðæt_ɪz tə seɪ] — das heißt, mit anderen Worten
defense (US für: defence) [dɪˈfens] — •Verteidigung
policy [ˈpɒləsi] — Politik, Programm
are you satisfied with/that ... ? [ɑː jʊ ˈsætɪsfaɪd wɪð/ðæt] — sind Sie zufrieden mit/daß ... ?
lead* [liːd] — führen, leiten
dissatisfied [ˌdɪsˈsætɪsfaɪd] — unzufrieden

•employment [ɪmˈplɔɪmənt] — •Beschäftigung
•housing [ˈhaʊzɪŋ] — •Wohnungsbau

B 1

•typical of ... [ˈtɪpɪkl_əv] — •typisch für ...
•House of Commons [haʊs_əv ˈkɒmənz] — •Unterhaus des britischen Parlaments
•constituency [kənˈstɪtjʊənsi] — •Wahlkreis
•educated [ˈedjuˈkeɪtɪd] — •hier: ausgebildet
•background [ˈbækgraʊnd] — •Hintergrund
•Labour (Party) [ˈleɪbə] — •Arbeiterpartei in Großbritannien
•Conservative (Party) [kənˈsɜːvətɪv] — •Partei der Konservativen in Großbritannien
•Liberal (Party) [ˈlɪbərəl] — •Partei der Liberalen in Großbritannien
officer [ˈɒfɪsə] — Offizier
•Royal Navy [ˈrɔɪəl ˈneɪvi] — •Königliche Marine
•trade union official [ˌtreɪd ˈjuːnjən_əˈfɪʃl] — •Gewerkschaftsfunktionär(in)
•well educated [ˌwel ˈedjuˈkeɪtɪd] — •gut ausgebildet, qualifiziert
talker [ˈtɔːkə] — Redner
•Tory [ˈtɔːri] — •Mitglied der konservativen Partei in Großbritannien

•lecturer [ˈlektʃərə] — •Dozent
get* out of touch with ... [get_aʊt_əv ˈtʌtʃ wɪð] — die Verbindung zu ... verlieren
general election [ˈdʒenərəl_ɪˈlekʃn] — Parlamentswahl
public school [ˈpʌblɪk ˈskuːl] — Privatschule in Großbritannien
•amazing [əˈmeɪzɪŋ] — •erstaunlich
neither of the two [ˈnaɪðər_əv ðə tuː] — keine(r) der beiden
share [ʃeə] — Anteil
•under-represented [ˈʌndəˌreprɪˈzentɪd] — •unterrepräsentiert
•manual worker [ˈmænjʊəl ˈwɜːkə] — •Arbeiter
occupy [ˈɒkjʊpaɪ] — besitzen, innehaben
•public relations [ˈpʌblɪk rɪˈleɪʃnz] — •Öffentlichkeitsarbeit
•ability [əˈbɪləti] — •Fähigkeit, Fertigkeit
•represent [ˌreprɪˈzent] — •vertreten, repräsentieren
•totally unrepresentative of ... [ˈtəʊtəliːˌʌnreprɪˈzentətɪv_əv] — •völlig unrepräsentativ für ...
population [ˌpɒpjʊˈleɪʃn] — Bevölkerung
the rich and the poor [ðə ˈrɪtʃ_ən ðə ˈpʊə] — die Reichen und die Armen
•the haves and the have-nots [ðə ˈhævz_ən ðə ˈhævˈnɒts] — •die Besitzenden und die Besitzlosen
examine [ɪgˈzæmɪn] — näher betrachten, untersuchen
democratic [ˌdeməˈkrætɪk] — demokratisch
•civil servant [ˈsɪvl ˈsɜːvənt] — •Beamte(r)

S 1

pay attention to [peɪ_əˈtenʃn tʊ]	(etwas) beachten
run* risks [rʌn rɪsks]	Risiken eingehen
practical [ˈpræktɪkl]	praktisch
•midday heat [ˈmɪdeɪ ˈhiːt]	•Mittagshitze
uncooked [ʌnˈkʊkt]	ungekocht, roh
take . . . along with you [teɪk əˈlɒŋ wɪð jʊ]	nehmen Sie . . . mit
•item [ˈaɪtəm]	•Gegenstand, Artikel
cough [kɒf]	Husten
•inquire about [ɪnˈkwaɪər_əˈbaʊt]	•fragen, sich erkundigen nach
in good time [ɪn ˈgʊd ˈtaɪm]	rechtzeitig
the small print [ðə smɔːl prɪnt]	das Kleingedruckte
make* sure [meɪk ˈʃʊə]	achten auf, sich vergewissern
•fully covered [ˈfʊlɪ ˈkʌvəd]	•etwa: voller Versicherungsschutz
•climate [ˈklaɪmɪt]	•Klima
thorough examination [ˈθʌrə_ɪgˌzæmɪˈneɪʃn]	gründliche Untersuchung
take it easy [teɪk_ɪt_ˈiːzɪ]	entspannen Sie sich
lie* down [laɪ ˈdaʊn]	sich hinlegen
•bottled water [ˈbɒtld ˈwɔːtə]	•Wasser in Flaschen
sweat [swet]	schwitzen
•injection [ɪnˈdʒekʃn]	•Spritze
special treatment [ˈspeʃl ˈtriːtmənt]	Spezialbehandlung
•first-aid kit [ˌfɜːstˈeɪd kɪt]	•Verbandskasten
•travel-sickness tablet [ˈtrævl ˌsɪknɪs ˈtæblɪt]	•Tablette gegen Reisekrankheit

S 2

icy [ˈaɪsɪ]	eisig
frequent [ˈfriːkwənt]	häufig
•period of frost [ˈpɪərɪəd_əv ˈfrɒst]	•Kälteeinbruch
bright [braɪt]	hell, strahlend
thunderstorm [ˈθʌndəstɔːm]	Gewitter
thunder [ˈθʌndə]	Donner
season [ˈsiːzn]	Jahreszeit
. . . seem more and more alike [siːm ˈmɔːr_n ˈmɔːr_əˈlaɪk]	. . . scheinen sich immer mehr zu gleichen
windy [ˈwɪndɪ]	windig
foggy [ˈfɒgɪ]	nebelig
rainy [ˈreɪnɪ]	regnerisch
all the year round [ˈɔːl ðə jɜː ˈraʊnd]	das ganze Jahr über
shower [ˈʃaʊə]	Schauer

S 3

dust [dʌst]	Staub
smoke [sməʊk]	Rauch
port [pɔːt]	(See-)Hafen
•I'm in a dither about . . . [aɪm_ɪn_ə ˈdɪðər_əˈbaʊt]	•ich bin ganz durcheinander wegen . . .
•memorize [ˈmeməraɪz]	•sich einprägen, auswendig lernen

🔴🔴🔴

•percentage [pəˈsentɪdʒ]	•Prozentsatz, Anteil
•House of Commons [haʊs_əv ˈkɒmənz]	•Unterhaus des britischen Parlaments
•actual result [ˈæktʃʊəl rɪˈzʌlt]	•tatsächliches Ergebnis
•period of office [ˈpɪərɪəd_əv_ˈɒfɪs]	•Amtszeit
•it proved to be . . . [ɪt pruːvd tə bɪ]	•es stellte sich heraus . . .
•previous [ˈpriːvjəs]	•vorhergehend, vorangegangen
•electoral system [ɪˈlektərəl ˈsɪstəm]	•Wahlsystem
•constituency [kənˈstɪtjʊənsɪ]	•Wahlkreis
•direct representation [ˈdaɪrekt ˌreprɪzenˈteɪʃn]	•Mehrheitswahlsystem
•as a consequence [æz_ə ˈkɒnsɪkwəns]	•folglich
•proportional representation [prəˈpɔːʃənl ˌreprɪzenˈteɪʃn]	•Verhältniswahlsystem
•gain [geɪn]	•gewinnen, erzielen
•movement [ˈmuːvmənt]	•Bewegung
•parliamentary system [ˌpɑːləˈmentərɪ ˈsɪstəm]	•parlamentarisches System

Unit 12

•Campaign for Nuclear Disarmament [kæmˈpeɪn fə ˈnjuːklɪə dɪsˈɑːməmənt]	•Friedensbewegung in Großbritannien
•please turn over [ˈpliːz tɜːn ˈəʊvə]	•bitte wenden (b.w.)
bed and breakfast [ˈbed_ən ˈbrekfəst]	Zimmer mit Frühstück (Fremdenzimmer)
•European Economic Community [jʊərəˈpiːən_ˌiːkəˈnɒmɪk kəˈmjuːnətɪ]	•Europäische Gemeinschaft (EG)
•British Broadcasting Corporation [ˈbrɪtɪʃ ˈbrɔːdkɑːstɪŋ ˌkɔːpəˈreɪʃn]	•staatliche Fernseh- und Rundfunkanstalt in Großbritannien
•Trades Union Congress [treɪdz ˈjuːnjən ˈkɒngres]	•Gewerkschaftsbund in Großbritannien
•Greenwich Mean Time [ˈgrɪnɪdʒ ˈmiːn taɪm]	•Westeuropäische Zeit (WEZ)
•Automobile Association [ˈɔːtəməbiːl_əˌsəʊsɪˈeɪʃn]	•britischer Automobilklub mit Pannenhilfsdienst
•National Health Service [ˈnæʃnl ˈhelθ ˌsɜːvɪs]	•gesetzliche Krankenkasse in Großbritannien

air mail [ˈeəmeɪl]	Luftpost
correct [kəˈrekt]	korrigieren
Norway [ˈnɔːweɪ]	• Norwegen
risk [rɪsk]	riskieren
catch* a cold [kætʃ_ə_ˈkəʊld]	sich erkälten
tinned food [tɪnd fuːd]	Nahrungsmittel in Dosen
by the sound of it, . . . [baɪ ðə ˈsaʊnd_əv_ɪt]	wie man hört, . . .
sound [saʊnd]	Geräusch, Klang, Laut
pretty [ˈprɪtɪ]	hübsch, nett
so I think I'll . . . [səʊ_aɪ ˈθɪŋk_aɪl]	also, ich glaube, . . .
is there any point in . . . ? [ɪz ðeər_ˈenɪ ˈpɔɪnt_ɪn]	hat es einen Sinn, wenn . . . ?
equipment [ɪˈkwɪpmənt]	• Ausrüstung; hier: Zubehör
weigh [weɪ]	wiegen

A 1

day of action [deɪ_əv_ˈækʃn]	• Aktionstag
disagreement [ˌdɪsəˈgriːmənt]	Meinungsverschiedenheit
pay rise [ˈpeɪ raɪz]	Gehaltserhöhung
economy [ɪˈkɒnəmɪ]	Wirtschaft
advise [ədˈvaɪz]	(be-)raten
the strike is over [ðə straɪk_ɪz_ˈəʊvə]	der Streik ist vorbei
who are afraid to strike [huː_ər_əˈfreɪd tə ˈstraɪk]	die Angst davor haben, zu streiken
you could try telling them . . . [jʊ ˈkʊd traɪ ˈtelɪŋ ðəm]	Sie könnten versuchen, Ihnen klarzumachen . . .
on strike [ɒn ˈstraɪk]	im Streik/Ausstand
which looks as if it might be . . . [wɪtʃ lʊks_əz_ɪf_ɪt maɪt bɪ]	was so aussieht, als ob es . . . sein könnte
take* early retirement [teɪk_ˈɜːlɪ rɪˈtaɪəmənt]	• vorzeitig in Rente gehen

A 2

industrial action [ɪnˈdʌstrɪəl_ˈækʃən]	• Streik, Ausstand
work unsocial hours [wɜːk_ʌnˌsəʊʃl_ˈaʊəz]	• außerhalb der normalen Arbeitszeiten arbeiten
hurt* [hɜːt]	schaden, verletzen
principles [ˈprɪnsəplz]	• Prinzipien
exploit [ɪkˈsplɔɪt]	• ausbeuten
if we don't fight for our rights [ɪf wɪ ˈdəʊnt ˌfaɪt fər_ˈaʊə_raɪts]	wenn wir nicht für unsere Rechte kämpfen
carry on [ˈkærɪ_ˈɒn]	fortsetzen, weitermachen
exception [ɪkˈsepʃn]	Ausnahme
trade union official [treɪd ˈjuːnjən_əˈfɪʃl]	• Gewerkschaftsfunktionär(in)
negotiate [nɪˈgəʊʃɪeɪt]	• verhandeln
management [ˈmænɪdʒmənt]	• Unternehmensleitung; hier: Arbeitgeber
voice [vɔɪs]	hier: Mitspracherecht
catastrophe [kəˈtæstrəfɪ]	• Katastrophe

if it hadn't been for the unions [ɪf_ɪt ˈhædnt bɪn fə ðə ˈjuːnjənz]	wenn die Gewerkschaften nicht gewesen wären
the fear of getting hurt [ðə fɪər_əv ˈgetɪŋ ˈhɜːt]	die Angst, verletzt zu werden
I pity the poor shiftworkers [aɪ ˈpɪtɪ ðə pʊə ˈʃɪft.wɜːkəz]	die armen Schichtarbeiter tun mir leid
good-looking [ˌgʊdˈlʊkɪŋ]	gutaussehend
bet* [bet]	wetten
sunrise [ˈsʌnraɪz]	Sonnenaufgang
sunset [ˈsʌnset]	Sonnenuntergang
and see your work undone [ənd siː jə_wɜːk_ʌnˈdʌn]	und zusehen, wie Ihre Arbeit umsonst war
hell [hel]	die Hölle

B 1

• call [kɔːl]	• hier: Aufruf
• ignore [ɪgˈnɔː]	• ignorieren
• staff [stɑːf]	• Personal
interrupt [ˌɪntəˈrʌpt]	unterbrechen
disturb [dɪˈstɜːb]	stören
• mine [maɪn]	• Bergwerk
• dock [dɒk]	• Ladeplatz im Hafen
• shipyard [ˈʃɪpjɑːd]	• (Schiffs-)Werft
• engineering industry [ˌendʒɪˈnɪərɪŋ_ˈɪndəstrɪ]	• Maschinenbau
• printing industry [ˈprɪntɪŋ_ˈɪndəstrɪ]	• Druckindustrie
public services [ˈpʌblɪk ˈsɜːvɪsɪz]	öffentlicher Dienst
• affect [əˈfekt]	• sich auswirken auf, beeinflussen
• sympathetic action [ˌsɪmpəˈθetɪk_ˈækʃn]	• Sympathiekundgebung/ -streik
capital [ˈkæpɪtl]	Hauptstadt
• march [mɑːtʃ]	• Marsch; marschieren
peaceful [ˈpiːsfʊl]	friedlich
• marcher [ˈmɑːtʃə]	• Demonstrant(in)
struggle [ˈstrʌgl]	Kampf
give* in [ˈgɪv_ˈɪn]	nachgeben
cheat [tʃiːt]	betrügen
think* over [ˈθɪŋk_ˈəʊvə]	sich (etwas) überlegen, nachdenken über
though [ðəʊ]	obwohl

S 1

tooth (Mehrzahl: teeth) [tuːθ (tiːθ)]	Zahn
star [stɑː]	Stern
shine* [ʃaɪn]	scheinen, leuchten
shake* hands [ʃeɪk ˈhændz]	sich die Hand geben
welcome [ˈwelkəm]	Willkommen
waterproof [ˈwɔːtəpruːf]	wasserdicht
-proof [pruːf]	-dicht, -fest, -sicher
sheet of glass [ʃiːt_əv ˈglɑːs]	Glasscheibe
. . . gave the police a rough time [geɪv ðə pəˈliːs_ə ˈrʌf ˈtaɪm]	. . . machte der Polizei schwer zu schaffen

instrument ['ɪnstrʊmənt]	Instrument
basement ['beɪsmənt]	Untergeschoß, Keller
guard [gɑːd]	Wache, Wächter
body ['bɒdɪ]	*hier:* Leiche
surface ['sɜːfɪs]	Oberfläche
disappear [ˌdɪsə'pɪə]	verschwinden
for ever [fər_'evə]	für immer
depth [depθ]	Tiefe
North Sea ['nɔːθ 'siː]	Nordsee

• pronunciation [prəˌnʌnsɪ'eɪʃn]	• Aussprache
• affect [ə'fekt]	• sich auswirken auf, beeinflussen
• syllable ['sɪləbl]	• Silbe
• stress [stres]	• betonen
• equivalent [ɪ'kwɪvələnt]	• Entsprechung

Unit 13

• height [haɪt]	• (Körper-)Größe
I enjoy myself [aɪ ɪn'dʒɔɪ maɪ'self]	ich amüsiere mich
once a week ['wʌns_ə 'wiːk]	einmal pro Woche
I prefer fresh fruit to sweets [aɪ prɪ'fɜː ˌfreʃ 'fruːt tə 'swiːts]	ich ziehe frisches Obst Süßigkeiten vor
• mark [mɑːk]	• Note

A 1

• survival [sə'vaɪvl]	• Überleben
• survive [sə'vaɪv]	• überleben
attack [ə'tæk]	Angriff
• Civil Aid [ˌsɪvl_'eɪd]	• Zivilschutz
or rather kept quiet [ɔː 'rɑːðə kept 'kwaɪət]	oder besser gesagt, verschwiegen
secret ['siːkrɪt]	geheim
• Home Office [ˌhəʊm_'ɒfɪs]	• Innenministerium
before the bomb drops [bɪ'fɔː ðə 'bɒm drɒps]	bevor die (Atom-)Bombe fällt
• preparation [ˌprepə'reɪʃn]	• Vorbereitung
keep* food [kiːp fuːd]	Lebensmittel haltbar machen/lagern
• vice-chairman [ˌvaɪs'tʃeəmən]	• stellvertretende(r) Vorsitzende(r)
when they run out of food [wen ðeɪ 'rʌn_aʊt_əv 'fuːd]	wenn ihnen die Lebensmittel ausgehen
save [seɪv]	aufheben, zurücklegen
• frog [frɒg]	• Frosch
though you would have to wash ... away [ðəʊ_jʊ_wʊd hæv tə 'wɒʃ_ə'weɪ]	obwohl Sie ... (zuerst) abwaschen müßten

• shelter ['ʃeltə]	• Bunker
• nuclear fall-out ['njuːklɪə 'fɔːlaʊt]	• radioaktive Niederschläge
match [mætʃ]	Streichholz
light* [laɪt]	anzünden
string [strɪŋ]	Schnur, Bindfaden
needle ['niːdl]	Nadel
cotton ['kɒtn]	*hier:* (Baumwoll-)Garn
• stove [stəʊv]	• Ofen
... have a word to say about [hæv ə wɜːd tə seɪ_ə'baʊt]	... verlieren ein Wort über
• pollute [pə'luːt]	• verschmutzen, verseuchen
• radiation [ˌreɪdɪ'eɪʃn]	• Strahlung
• give* the impression [gɪv ði:_ɪm'preʃn]	• den Eindruck vermitteln
• Gloucestershire ['glɒstəʃɪə]	• *Grafschaft in Westengland*
• misery ['mɪzərɪ]	• Elend
• radiation sickness [ˌreɪdɪ'eɪʃn 'sɪknɪs]	• Strahlenkrankheit
hit* ... over the head ['hɪt_ˌəʊvə ðə 'hed]	... auf den Kopf schlagen
joke [dʒəʊk]	scherzen, Witze machen
humour ['hjuːmə]	Humor
atomic attack [ə'tɒmɪk_ə'tæk]	Atomangriff
• contribution [ˌkɒntrɪ'bjuːʃn]	• Beitrag
in the event of nuclear attack [ɪn ði:_ɪ'vent_əv 'njuːklɪər_ə'tæk]	im Falle eines Atomangriffs
• place bag over head [pleɪs 'bæg_ˌəʊvə 'hed]	• *etwa:* die Tüte über den Kopf ziehen
• face the other way ['feɪs ði:_'ʌðə 'weɪ]	• *etwa:* sich abwenden, wegschauen *(von der Explosion)*

A 2

• Campaign for Nuclear Disarmament (CND) [kæm'peɪn fə 'njuklɪə dɪs'ɑːməmənt (ˌsiːen'diː)]	• *Friedensbewegung in Großbritannien*
half [hɑːf]	Hälfte
join two statements together [dʒɔɪn 'tuː 'steɪtmənts tə'geðə]	zwei Aussagen miteinander verbinden
• Stockholm Peace Appeal ['stɒkhəʊm 'piːs_ə'piːl]	• Stockholmer Friedensaufruf
• H-bomb ['eɪtʃbɒm]	• Wasserstoffbombe
• Pacific (Ocean) [pə'sɪfɪk ('əʊʃn)]	• Pazifik
spread* [spred]	(sich) aus-/verbreiten
powerful ['paʊəfʊl]	mächtig, gewaltig, stark
occupy ['ɒkjʊpaɪ]	besetzen
secret ['siːkrɪt]	Geheimnis
• crew [kruː]	• Besatzung
• march [mɑːtʃ]	• Marsch, Demonstration
• achieve [ə'tʃiːv]	• erreichen
fight [faɪt]	Kampf

last [lɑ:st] — (an-)dauern
peace camp ['pi:s kæmp] — Friedenslager
Greenham Common American base ['gri:nəm 'kɒmən_ əˈmerikən 'beis] — amerikanischer Militär- stützpunkt in der Nähe von London
submarine [ˌsʌbməˈri:n] — Unterseeboot
piece of paper [pi:s_əv 'peipə] — Blatt/Stück Papier

B 1

arms [ɑ:mz] — Waffen
military purposes ['militəri 'pɜ:pəsiz] — militärische Zwecke
comparison [kəmˈpærisn] — Vergleich
publisher ['pʌbliʃə] — Herausgeber(in)
British Council of Churches ['britiʃ 'kaunsl_əv 'tʃɜ:tʃiz] — Kirchensynode in Großbritannien
armed forces [ɑ:md 'fɔ:siz] — Streitkräfte
they are in firm control of the government [ðei_ɑr_in 'fɜ:m kənˈtrəul_əv ðə 'gʌvnmənt] — sie haben die Regierung fest unter Kontrolle
firm [fɜ:m] — fest, stabil
investment [inˈvestmənt] — Investitionen
the point is, . . . [ðə point_'iz] — es ist nämlich so, . . .
likely ['laikli] — wahrscheinlich
make* things worse [meik θiŋz 'wɜ:s] — alles nur verschlimmern
for sale [fə 'seil] — zum Verkauf
defence [diˈfens] — Verteidigung

S 1

approach [əˈprəutʃ] — (sich) nähern
receptionist [riˈsepʃənist] — Empfangschef, Empfangsdame
dining-car ['daiɲŋkɑ:] — Speisewagen

S 2

snake [sneik] — Schlange
paid employment ['peid_imˈplɔimənt] — etwa: Arbeit gegen Entgelt
equality [i:ˈkwɒləti] — Gleichheit; hier: Gleichberechtigung

S 3

proverb ['prɒvɜ:b] — Sprichwort
bush [buʃ] — Gebüsch
pencil ['pensl] — Bleistift
memorable ['memərəbl] — unvergeßlich
at check-out time [ət 'tʃekaut taim] — bei der Abreise (Hotel)
Lobby Credit Manager [ˌlɒbi 'kredit ˌmænidʒə] — Geschäftsführer des Hotels, der über Ge- währung und Höhe von Krediten entscheidet
assistance [əˈsistəns] — Hilfe

(the answer is) blowin' in the wind ['bləuin_in ðə 'wind] — etwa: die Antwort weiß ganz allein der Wind
movement ['mu:vmənt] — Bewegung
. . . was directed against . . . [wəz diˈrektid_əˈgenst] — . . . war gegen . . . gerichtet
nuclear armament ['nju:kliər_'ɑ:məmənt] — nukleare Aufrüstung
. . . has thus become . . . [həz 'θʌs biˈkʌm] — . . . wurde deswegen . . .
dove [dʌv] — Taube
cannon ball ['kænən bɔ:l] — Kanonenkugel
ban [bæn] — verbieten, verbannen
exist [igˈzist] — existieren
washed to the sea [wɒʃt tə ðə 'si:] — ins Meer gespült
pretend [priˈtend] — so tun, als ob
misery ['mizəri] — Elend

Unit 14

unidentified flying object [ˌʌnaiˈdentifaid 'flaiiŋ_'ɒbdʒikt] — unbekanntes Flugobjekt (UFO)
now then, . . . — nun/also, . . .
sleeping-car ['sli:piŋkɑ:] — Schlafwagen
turn out [tɜ:n_aut] — ausmachen (Licht)
cigar [siˈgɑ:] — Zigarre
unusual sight [ʌnˈju:ʒuəl 'sait] — ungewöhnlicher Anblick
British UFO Research Association ['britiʃ ju:eˈfəu riˈsɜ:tʃ_əˌsəusiˈeiʃn] — britische Gesellschaft zur Erforschung und Regi- strierung von UFOs
date of birth ['deit_əv 'bɜ:θ] — Geburtsdatum
observation [ˌɒbzəˈveiʃn] — Beobachtung
motor ['məutə] — Motor
print [print] — (Foto-)Abzug

A 1

apartheid [əˈpɑ:theit] — Apartheid, Rassen- trennung
be* in control of . . . [bi_in kənˈtrəul_əv] — . . . unter Kontrolle haben
rule [ru:l] — regieren
separate ['sepəreit] — trennen
coloured ['kʌləd] — Farbige(r); Mischling
determine [diˈtɜ:min] — bestimmen
basic civil rights ['beisik 'sivl 'raits] — Grundrechte
Soweto (= Southwestern Township) [sɔ:ˈweətəu] — Vorort von Johannesburg für Schwarze und Farbige
hostel ['hɒstl] — Wohnheim
hut [hʌt] — Hütte

rough [rʌf]	grob, roh	•wood-carving ['wʊd ˌkɑːvɪŋ]	•(Holz-)Schnitzen
•asbestos [æz'bestɒs]	•Asbest	•ritual war-paint	•rituelle (Kriegs-)Be-
•concentration camp	•Konzentrationslager	['rɪtʃʊəl 'wɔːpeɪnt]	malung
[ˌkɒnsən'treɪʃn kæmp]		spoil* [spɔɪl]	verwöhnen
sharp [ʃɑːp]	hier: empfindlich,		
	geschärft	**B 1**	
mixed smell of [mɪkst smel_əv]	gemischter Gestank von	•Maori ['maʊrɪ]	•Ureinwohner(in)
mix [mɪks]	mischen		Neuseelands
•rubbish ['rʌbɪʃ]	•Abfall	the native people	die Ureinwohner
•cowshed ['kaʊʃed]	•Kuhstall	[ðə 'neɪtɪv 'piːpl]	
cow [kaʊ]	Kuh	•New Zealand [ˌnjuː_'ziːlənd]	•Neuseeland
it made me sick and ashamed	etwa: es ist widerlich und	•community [kə'mjuːnətɪ]	•Gemeinschaft
[ɪt meɪd mɪ 'sɪk_ənd_ə'ʃeɪmd]	beschämend	•criticize ['krɪtɪsaɪz]	•kritisieren
be* ashamed [biː_ə'ʃeɪmd]	sich schämen	•peacefully integrated	•friedlich eingegliedert
human ['hjuːmən]	Mensch	['piːsfʊlɪ_'ɪntɪgreɪtɪd]	
wild [waɪld]	wild	•contribute [kən'trɪbjuːt]	•beitragen
•and yet [ənd_'jet]	•und doch/trotzdem		
sweat [swet]	Schweiß	**S 1**	
crowded together	zusammengepfercht	put* one's name down	sich eintragen (lassen)
['kraʊdɪd tə'geðə]		[pʊt wʌnz 'neɪm daʊn]	
in the narrowest of spaces	auf engstem Raum	practice ['præktɪs]	Übung
[ɪn ðə 'nærəʊɪst_əv 'speɪsɪz]		slang [slæŋ]	Slang, Jargon
centimetre ['sentɪmiːtə]	Zentimeter	•fee [fiː]	•Gebühr
touch [tʌtʃ]	(sich) berühren	•tuition [tjuː'ɪʃn]	•Unterricht
scene [siːn]	Schauplatz; Anblick	•accommodation [əˌkɒmə'deɪʃn]	•Unterbringung
		•deposit [dɪ'pɒzɪt]	•Anzahlung
A 2		envelope ['envələʊp]	(Brief-)Umschlag
•aborigine [ˌæbə'rɪdʒəniː]	•Ureinwohner(in)	timetable ['taɪmˌteɪbl]	Stundenplan (Schule)
	Australiens		
racial minority	rassische Minderheit	**S 2**	
['reɪʃl maɪ'nɒrətɪ]		great grandmother	Urgroßmutter
•exploit [ɪk'splɔɪt]	•ausbeuten	[ˌgreɪt 'grænˌmʌðə]	
who are least able to . . .	die am wenigsten in der	part [pɑːt]	sich trennen, auseinan-
[huː_ə_'liːst_'eɪbl tʊ]	Lage sind zu . . .		dergehen
•rob [rɒb]	•(aus-)rauben	both of them ['bəʊθ_əv ðəm]	beide
•inhabitant [ɪn'hæbɪtənt]	•Einwohner(in)	•widow ['wɪdəʊ]	•Witwe
race [reɪs]	Rasse	upstairs [ʌp'steəz]	nach oben, die Treppe
•. . . have suffered great harm	•. . . haben sehr gelitten		hoch
[həv ˌsʌfəd greɪt 'hɑːm]		•pile up [paɪl_ʌp]	•sich stapeln
deep [diːp]	tief	at the foot of her stairs	unten an der Treppe
•continually [kən'tɪnjʊəlɪ]	•(an-)dauernd, ständig	[ət ðə 'fʊt_əv hɜː 'steəz]	
. . . are being forced off	. . . werden von ihrem	•hip [hɪp]	•Hüfte
their land [ə ˌbiːɪŋ 'fɔːst_ɒf	Land vertrieben	drop [drɒp]	Tropfen
ðeə 'lænd]		•award [ə'wɔːd]	•Auszeichnung
•legal ['liːgl]	•juristisch, legal	get* up [get_'ʌp]	aufstehen
trick [trɪk]	Trick, List	shout [ʃaʊt]	Ruf, Schrei
0.35 (= nought point three five)	0,35 (= null Komma	bright [braɪt]	hell, intelligent
['nɔːt pɔɪnt 'θriː 'faɪv]	drei fünf)	•design [dɪ'zaɪn]	•konstruieren, entwerfen
34 times ['θɜːtɪ fɔː 'taɪmz]	34 mal	•inquiry [ɪn'kwaɪərɪ]	•Untersuchung
•leprosy ['leprəsɪ]	•Lepra, Aussatz	•contestant [kən'testənt]	•Kandidat(in)
•diabetes [ˌdaɪə'biːtiːz]	•Zuckerkrankheit		(Fernsehquiz)
•life expectancy	•Lebenserwartung	upper floor ['ʌpə 'flɔː]	obere Etage
[ˌlaɪf ɪk'spektənsɪ]			
•adapting to 'civilization'	•Anpassung an die	**S 3**	
[ə'dæptɪŋ tə ˌsɪvɪlaɪ'zeɪʃn]	'Zivilisation'	get* ready for [get 'redɪ fɔː]	sich vorbereiten auf
•corrugated iron huts	•Wellblechhütten	once in a while [wʌns ɪn_ə 'waɪl]	gelegentlich
['kɒrʊgeɪtɪd_'aɪən 'hʌts]		embarrassment [ɪm'bærəsmənt]	Verlegenheit

by accident [baɪ_'æksɪdənt]   aus Versehen; durch Zufall
• air-traffic controller   • Fluglotse
['eə,træfɪk kən'trəʊlə]
signal ['sɪgnəl]   Signal, Zeichen
take* off ['teɪk_'ɒf]   starten (Flugzeug)
• runway ['rʌnweɪ]   Startbahn
• confuse [kən'fju:z]   verwechseln
• defeat [dɪ'fi:t]   besiegen; hier: außer Gefecht setzen
smile [smaɪl]   lächeln
pick up ['pɪk_'ʌp]   mitnehmen

S 4
second-hand [,sekənd'hænd]   gebraucht, aus zweiter Hand
engine ['endʒɪn]   Maschine, Motor
cheerio [,tʃɪərɪ'əʊ]   tschüs, Wiedersehen
due to [dju:_tʊ]   aufgrund, wegen

• exist [ɪg'zɪst]   • existieren
• treaty ['tri:tɪ]   • Vertrag
• Indian tribe ['ɪndjən 'traɪb]   • Indianerstamm
• the principal chiefs   • die wichtigsten Häuptlinge
[ðə 'prɪnsəpl 'tʃi:fs]
• approve [ə'pru:v]   • billigen, gutheißen
• in a most horrible manner   • auf furchtbarste Weise
[ɪn_ə məʊst 'hɒrəbl 'mænə]
• spare [speə]   • entbehren
• stagecoach ['steɪdʒkəʊtʃ]   • Postkutsche
• announce [ə'naʊns]   • verkünden, bekanntgeben
• feast [fi:st]   • Fest
• gather ['gæðə]   • sich versammeln
• government official   • Regierungsvertreter
['gʌvnmənt_ə'fɪʃl]
• rifle ['raɪfl]   • Gewehr
• pile [paɪl]   • Haufen
• . . . everyone was in place   • . . . jeder seinen Platz eingenommen hatte
['evrɪwʌn wəz_ɪn pleɪs]
• who was accused of robbing . . .   • der beschuldigt wurde, . . . ausgeraubt zu haben
[hʊ wəz_ə'kju:zd_əv 'rɒbɪŋ]
• pot [pɒt]   • Kessel, Topf

Unit 15/Revision

R 1
• comparison [kəm'pærɪsn]   • Vergleich

R 2
• cab [kæb]   • Taxi
parcel ['pɑ:sl]   Paket

• gift [gɪft]   • Geschenk
• favourably ['feɪvərəblɪ]   • günstig, vorteilhaft
• demand [dɪ'mɑ:nd]   • Nachfrage, Bedarf

R 3
occupy ['ɒkjʊpaɪ]   bewohnen, beziehen (Haus)
at all costs [ət_'ɔ:l kɒsts]   um jeden Preis
• food supplies ['fu:d sə'plaɪz]   • Lebensmittelvorräte
tidy ['taɪdɪ]   aufgeräumt, ordentlich
• machinery [mə'ʃi:nərɪ]   • Geräte, Maschinen
• knit* [nɪt]   • stricken
• leisure activities   • Freizeitbeschäftigungen
['leʒər_æk'tɪvətɪz]

R 4
• board [bɔ:d]   • (Spiel-)Brett
• ring [rɪŋ]   • hier: Bahn
slip of paper [slɪp_əv 'peɪpə]   Zettel
• score [skɔ:]   • (Punkte-)Stand
• place [pleɪs]   • setzen, plazieren
forwards ['fɔ:wədz]   vorwärts
backwards ['bækwədz]   rückwärts

R 5
on foot [ɒn 'fʊt]   zu Fuß
• basic things ['beɪsɪk 'θɪŋz]   • hier: Grundausrüstung
• camping equipment   • Campingzubehör
['kæmpɪŋ_ɪ'kwɪpmənt]
• raft [rɑ:ft]   • Floß
extremely rough country   äußerst unwegsames Gelände
[ɪk'stri:mlɪ 'rʌf 'kʌntrɪ]
• desert ['dezət]   • Wüste
• ammunition [,æmjʊ'nɪʃn]   • Munition
• free [fri:]   • befreien, laufen lassen
• rabbit ['ræbɪt]   • Kaninchen
• escape [ɪ'skeɪp]   • flüchten; hier: entlaufen
• sheep station ['ʃi:p 'steɪʃn]   • Schafzuchtfarm
• aborigine [,æbə'rɪdʒəni:]   • Ureinwohner(in) Australiens
keep* a record of   Buch führen über, registrieren
[ki:p_ə 'rekɔ:d_əv]
make* up one's mind   sich entschließen
['meɪk_ʌp wʌnz 'maɪnd]
• edge [edʒ]   • Rand, Kante
here and there [hɪər_ənd ðeə]   hier und da

R 6
• level ['levl]   • Niveau
• maintain [meɪn'teɪn]   • aufrechterhalten, wahren
• possibility [,pɒsə'bɪlətɪ]   • Möglichkeit
that have proved to be useful   die sich als nützlich erwiesen haben
[ðət həv pru:vd tə bi:_'ju:sfʊl]
• attend [ə'tend]   • besuchen (Kurs)
• concentrate on   • sich konzentrieren auf
['kɒnsəntreɪt_ɒn]
• convince [kən'vɪns]   • überzeugen

Vocabulary: alphabetical word list   Wortschatz: alphabetisches Wortregister

Die Zahlen und Buchstaben geben die *Unit* und den A- oder B-Schritt (bzw. *Revision-* oder *Special*-Teil) an, in dem ein Wort oder Ausdruck in einer bestimmten Bedeutung zum erstenmal vorkommt. (① im *Review*-Teil = ♀1 im Wortregister)

Die mit einem • versehenen Wörter gehören nicht zum verbindlichen Lernwortschatz. Sie müssen nicht aktiv beherrscht werden.

(sb = somebody; sth = something)

A

- ability 11/B1
- about: bring about 7/B1
- above: as above 10/R4
  - the above 3/♀1
- accept 3/B1; 9/♀1
- accident: by accident 14/S3
- accommodation 6/A1
- according to 1/B2
- account: bank account 2/A3
- accurately 8/♀2
- achieve 13/A2
- act *(Theater spielen)* 3/A1
- action: day of action 12/A1
- actor 3/A1
- actress 3/A1
- actually 3/B1; 7/A1; 7/B1
- adapt 14/A2
- add up 8/B1
- admit 6/A4
  - no ... admitted 6/A1
- adventure 6/A1
- advertise 11/♀1
- advertiser 11/♀1
- advise 12/A1
- aerial 2/B2
- affect 12/B1
- afterwards 9/A4
- against: for and against 3/A2
  - fight against 4/B1
- age: ... years of age 6/A1
  - coming of age 7/A1
- ago: a week ago yesterday 9/A1
- agree: agreed 9/B1
  - agree on 1/♀3
- agreement 6/A4
- ahead: look ahead 4/A3
- air: by air 4/B1
  - air mail 12/♀2
- air-traffic controller 14/S3
- alike 11/S2
- alive 4/B1
- all: ... have all got ... 8/A3
  - all in favour of 8/A4
  - all over Britain 4/A1
  - all the time 8/A3
  - of all time 3/A1

- along: along the roads 8/A3
  - go/sing along 4/A5
  - take along 11/S1
- aloud: read aloud 3/A1
- altogether: I don't altogether agree 11/A1
  - cut out of ... altogether 3/A1
- amazing 11/B1
- ammunition 15/R5
- amount 3/B1
- anagram 5/R5
- anniversary 1/A4
- announce 7/A1
- another: for another 2 weeks 9/A1
  - one another 10/R3
- answer: in answer to 2/A3
- anybody 4/♀3
- apart: apart from 1/♀3
  - 20 inches apart 6/♀1
- apartheid 14/A1
- appliance 2/A5
- application 2/A2
- apply for 7/♀1
- approach 13/S1
- argue *(streiten)* 9/B2
- argument 3/B1; 7/♀1
- armed forces 13/B1
- arms 13/B1
- around: all around 8/A1
  - move around 10/R4
- arrange a day 2/A5
- arrangement 4/A4
- arrest 7/♀1
- art: the arts 11/A1
- as: as if 12/A1
  - as long as 3/A2
  - as the name says 1/♀3
  - as they go 8/B2
  - as to 7/B1
  - much as 8/A3
- asbestos 14/A1
- ashamed 14/A1
- assistance 13/S3
- assistant 6/A1
- assurance 6/A1
- at last 4/♀2

- atomic 13/A1
- attack: *(angreifen)* 3/B1
  - *(Angriff)* 13/A1
- attempt 8/A4
- attend 15/R6
- attention 11/S1
- attract 3/A2
- Australian 7/B2
- authorities 4/B1
- auto(mobile) 2/B1
- available 9/♀1
- average 7/A4
- avoid 6/A3
- award 14/S2
- aware 7/B1
- away: drive away 9/A4
  - throw away 4/A2

B

- back: be back 9/A3
  - get back 7/A2
  - go back 8/A3
  - have back 3/A4
  - move back 7/A2
  - pay back 9/B1
  - send back 3/A4
  - back into 8/B2
  - back yard 2/♀3
- background 11/B1
- backwards 15/R4
- balance 2/B1
- ball pen 3/A4
- band 5/R4
- bank account 2/A3
- barbecue 4/♀3
- base 7/B2; 13/A2
- basement 12/S1
- basic 14/A1; 15/R5
- bath: take a bath 8/♀4
- be: if ... is to be improved 7/B1
- beat 8/A2
- bed and breakfast 12/♀1
- bedtime 10/R6
- before: the day before yesterday 9/A1
- behind: the idea behind 8/A2
  - leave behind 7/A2

- believe in 8/B2
- below zero 4/B1
- bend 7/A2
- bet 12/A2
- beyond 6/A4
- bible 8/B2
- bicycle 2/A4
- bin 8/♀1
- birth: date of birth 14/♀1
- bitter 3/A3
- blind 1/B2
- block: blocked 2/B2
  - apartment block 7/A4
- bloody 8/A4
- board: full-board 6/A1
  - *(Spielbrett)* 15/R4
- body *(Leiche)* 12/S1
- bomber 5/R6
- border 4/B1
- bored 10/R3
- boring 3/♀1
- both of them 14/S2
- bottled water 11/S1
- bottom 4/♀2
- bowls 4/A4
- branch 9/A2
- brand 11/♀1
- brass 6/A5
- break: break a leg 7/♀1
  - break into 3/B1
  - break up 3/A1
- breakfast: bed and breakfast 12/♀1
- breathe 4/B1
- bright 11/S2; 14/S2
- bring about 7/B1
- broad 4/♀2
- broken 2/B2
- brutal 3/B1
- budget 2/B1
- build 2/A4
- bunch of keys 9/A4
- burnt 3/A3
- bush 13/S3
- business *(Handel)* 1/♀3
- button 3/A4
- by: by air/rail 4/B1
  - by themselves 8/A1
- by-law 8/A4

C

cab 15/R2
cake 3/A3
calculation 8/A2
calculator: pocket calculator
    2/A3
call: please call me … 1/A2
    • (Aufruf) 12/B1
camp fire 4/Q2
can (Dose) 4/A2
Canadian 4/A1
cancer 6/B2
cap 8/A3
capital 12/B1
    • capital punishment 9/B2
captain 4/A4
card: game of cards 4/A4
care 6/A4
    care for 8/Q3
    take care of 5/R6
career 3/A1
careless 6/A4
carriage 8/A3
carry 9/B1
    carry on 12/A2
    • carry out 11/A2
case: (Fall) 2/A3; 9/A1
    (Koffer) 9/A4
cash: in cash 9/B1
catastrophe 12/A2
catch: catch a cold 12/Q2
    • caught in a traffic-jam
      4/B1
cause: (verursachen) 3/B1
    cause and effect 3/B1
caution 6/A3
celebrate 1/Q3
celebration 1/B2
cellar 2/A4
centimetre 14/A1
certain: I'm not certain 7/Q2
change: change one's
      mind 6/Q2
    • change out of 8/B2
    change places 8/Q4
    small change 9/A1
chapel 8/B2
charge. (berechnen) 5/R4
    extra charge 6/A1
charming 5/R4
cheat 12/B1
check in 3/Q2
checkbook 2/B1
check-out time 13/S3
cheer 3/B1
cheerio 14/S4
chess 8/A2

chocolate 8/Q3
choice 6/B1
choose from 2/Q1
Christian name 9/A1
• cigar 14/Q1
• circle 10/R4
civil: civil aid 13/A1
    • civil rights 14/A1
    • civil servant 11/B1
class: first-class menu 5/R4
    the middle-class 11/A2
clean 3/A3
clear 7/B1
clever 3/A1
climate 11/S1
climb 6/Q2
    go climbing 7/Q2
clock: round the clock 6/A1
close: close one's eyes 6/Q1
    close down 10/R7
cloud 4/B1
coal 1/B2
• coffee-break 8/Q2
• coke: sniff coke 6/A5
cold: catch a cold 12/Q2
    die of cold 4/B1
• collapse 6/A5
collect 4/A2
• coloured 14/A1
comb 9/A4
come: come from 8/A3
    come in 1/A1
    come off 2/B2
    • come over 6/Q1
    come true 8/A2
    • coming of age 7/A1
• comfort 8/B2
• comment 1/B1
• commercial 9/A3
common: (üblich) 1/B2
    in common 1/A5
• community 8/B2
• comparison 13/B1
complain 3/A4
complaint 3/A4
    • letter of complaint 5/R4
• completely 4/A3
computer-controlled 0/A1
• concentrate on 15/R6
• concentration camp 14/A1
concerning 10/R3
condition: (Zustand) 2/B2
    on condition 9/B1
• condolence 7/A2
• confirm 3/Q2
• confuse 14/S3
• congregation 8/B2

connection 3/B1
• consider (meinen) 2/A3
• constituency 11/B1
• contents 9/A1
• contestant 14/S2
    Continent 2/Q1
• Continental (breakfast) 2/Q2
• continually 14/A2
• contrast: by contrast 8/B2
• contribute 1/B1
• contribution 13/A1
control: (kontrollieren)
      2/B1; 4/A3
    computer-controlled 8/A1
    beyond my control 6/A4
    in control of 14/A1
    get out of control 5/R1
    lose control 7/A2
• convince 15/R6
• cook (Koch) 3/A3
• cooker 2/A5
    copy (Kopie) 8/A2
    correct (korrigieren) 12/Q2
• corrugated iron huts 14/A2
cost: at all costs 15/R3
cotton 3/A4; 13/A1
cough 11/S1
• count 4/A1
    counter 5/R3
• course: four-course meal
      5/R4
    court 3/B2
    take to court 9/B1
• cover 7/B2; 11/S1
cow 14/A1
• cowshed 14/A1
cream: shoe-cream 8/Q3
• create 8/A1
    credit: credit card 2/A3
    • credit limit 9/B1
• crew 13/A2
crime 9/B2
criminal 3/B1
• criticize 14/B1
• crop 4/A3
cross (Kreuz) 7/B2
• crossword 7/Q1
crowd: crowded together
      14/A1
• cruel 6/A5
• currency 9/B1
custom: old customs 1/B2
cut: cut down 4/A1
    cut the grass 8/A4
    • cut out of 3/A1
    • cut short 1/A5
    get my hair cut 7/Q2

D

damage: cause damage
      4/A3
dark 2/B2
    dark-haired 1/B2
• darling 1/A2
darts 4/B2
date of birth 14/Q1
day: the day after tomorrow
      2/A4
    the day before yesterday
      9/A1
    • day of action 12/A1
deal with 6/A4
death: worried to death 6/A4
decide between 11/Q1
deep 14/A2
defeat 14/S3
• defence 13/B1
defend 9/A3
• defense 11/A2
• definite 7/Q2
degree 5/R6
• de-humanized 6/A5
delay: (verzögern) 7/B1
    without delay 9/A1
• demand 15/R2
democratic 11/B1
department: department
      store 3/A4
    • (Ministerium) 4/A1
• deposit 14/S1
depth 12/S1
• description 8/A2
• desert (Wüste) 15/R5
• deserve 9/B2
• design 14/S2
• destroy 3/A1
• determine 14/A1
• deterrent 9/B2
development 7/B2
• dial 10/R6
diary 1/Q3
dice 5/R3
die of cold 4/B1
difference: make no
      difference 8/A4
• different from 8/B2
• dining-car 13/S1
• diploma 2/A1
direction (Anweisung) 6/Q1
director 3/A1
    • managing director 1/A2
disadvantage 8/B1
disagree 4/A2
disagreement 12/A1
disappear 12/S1

• this point was made 7/B1
point of view 6/A4
poison: *(vergiften)* 4/A3
(Gift) 2/B1
policy 11/A2
political 1/A5
politician 5/R1
• pollute 7/A4
• pool 7/A4
• poor: the poor 8/B2
population 11/B1
pork 3/A3
port *(Hafen)* 11/S3
porter: night porter 3/Q2
possibility 15/R6
possibly 4/A4
• post: by separate post 3/A4
postage 6/A1
• pot *(Marihuana)* 6/A4
• pour 6/A5
power: greater powers 3/R1
in power 11/A2
come into power 11/A2
nuclear power 7/A4
• power line 4/B1
powerful 13/A2
practical 11/S1
practice *(Übung)* 14/S1
prefer ... to ... 13/Q1
• preparation 13/A1
prepare: prepare a meal 2/B1
prepare for 2/B1
be prepared to 3/Q2
• pressure-group 4/A2
pretty 12/Q2
• prevent 9/A3
• principle 12/A2
print: small print 11/S1
(Fotoabzug) 14/Q1
• printer 8/A2
• printing industry 12/B1
prison 9/B1
prisoner-of-war 5/R6
prize 7/Q1
• produce 0/A2
• product 3/A4
• profession 5/R1
• profit 8/B1
progress 6/A2; 8/A1
promise *(Versprechen)* 6/A1
promising 5/R6
property: Lost Property Office 9/A1
• protect 4/A2

protest: *(protestieren)* 4/A1
(Protest) 4/A1
prove 9/A2; 15/R6
• proverb 13/S3
provide 11/A1
public: public holiday 1/Q2
• public opinion poll 11/A2
• public relations 11/B1
public school 11/B1
public services 12/B1
publish 5/R2
• publisher 13/B1
pull 4/Q2
• punishment 9/B2
pure 3/A4
• purpose 8/A2
on purpose 5/R1
• pursue 5/R2
• pusher 6/A5
put: put your name down 14/S1
put off 7/B1
put on 4/A2
put one's arguments to 3/B1
put together 2/A5
put themselves to great trouble 5/R6
put up 3/Q2; 11/A1
• put their views 6/A5
• pyjamas 10/R5

Q

• qualified 10/R3
quality 8/A2
question: out of the question 2/A4
• questionnaire 2/A3
queue: *(Schlange stehen)* 7/A4
(Menschenschlange) 8/Q4
quickly 8/Q2

R

• rabbit 15/R5
race *(Rasse)* 14/A2
• racial 14/A2
• radiation 13/A1
• raft 15/R5
rail: by rail 4/B1
rainy 11/S2
• rape 3/B1
• rapidly 4/A3
• rat 4/A3
• rate 5/R6

rather: rather disappointing 10/R7
or rather kept quiet 13/A1
reach: *(erreichen)* 3/A1
(Reichweite) 6/A1; 6/Q3
ready: get ready for 14/S3
real: in real life 3/A1
realize 8/A3
reason: give reasons 4/Q2
for reasons of 9/A3
receipt 3/A4
• recent 8/B2; 9/B2
• receptionist 13/S1
• recipe 10/R6
recognize 3/A1; 9/Q2
record: *(aufzeichnen)* 10/R6
keep a record of 15/R5
• recording 10/R6
• recover 7/B1
• recycling 4/A2
• reduce 11/A1
• refer to 8/B2
• refresher 6/Q1
• refreshing effect 6/Q1
refuse 4/A2
regards *(Briefschluß)* 10/R7
regret 6/B1
• regulation 5/R6
• related: drug-related problems 6/A5
relationship 2/B1
relative 5/R2
religious 1/Q3
remaining 10/R3
• remark 9/A1
remind 8/A1
• replace 9/A2
• reply: in reply to 3/B1
• reporter 3/A2
• represent 11/B1
• reservation 3/Q2
• responsibility 3/B1
• responsible 3/B1
restless 8/B2
• retire 7/A4
• retirement 11/A1
return ticket 7/A3
re-usable 4/A2
re-use 4/A2
review 1/Q1
rich: the rich 11/B1
• riddle 8/Q2
ride: ride a bike 4/A2
go for a ride on the bike 7/Q2
• right: come right over 6/Q1

ring: *(Ring)* 1/B1
• *(Bahn)* 15/R4
rise: *(Zunahme)* 9/B2
pay rise 12/A1
• risk: risk catching a cold 12/Q2
run risks 11/S1
take risks 7/A2
no-risk form 6/B1
• ritual war-paint 14/A2
• rob 14/A2
robot 8/A1
rock 6/A3
• roll a joint 6/A5
room: there's enough room 7/A2
rose: grow roses 6/Q2
rough 14/A1
rough country 15/R5
a rough time 12/S1
round: round the clock 6/A1
all the year round 11/S2
look round 10/R7
walk round 9/A1
• roving reporter 3/A2
row *(Reihe)* 8/A1
• rubbish 14/A1
• ruin: *(zerstören)* 4/A3
in ruins 8/B2
rule *(regieren)* 14/A1
run: run into a lorry 7/A2
run out of food 13/A1
run risks 11/S1
go for a run 4/A4
• runway 14/S3

S

safe: *(ungefährlich)* 2/B1
• *(Tresor)* 3/Q2
safety 9/A3
sail 10/R5
sale: for sale 13/B1
ticket sales 3/B1
sales manager 10/R7
salesman: export sales-man 2/A2
salty 3/A3
satisfied 6/B1; 11/A2
sausage 2/Q1
save food 13/A1
say: is said to 8/A3
that is to say 11/A2
scene: *(Szene)* 3/B1
(Schauplatz) 14/A1
science 2/A3
• science fiction 3/Q1
scientist 9/A4